'OH, YE HAI

'OH, YE HAD TAE BE CAREFUL'

Personal recollections by
Roslin gunpowder mill
and bomb factory workers

Ian MacDougall

TUCKWELL PRESS
in association with
The European Ethnological Research Centre
The Scottish Working People's History Trust

First published in Great Britain in 2000 by
Tuckwell Press
The Mill House
Phantassie
East Linton
East Lothian EH40 3DG
Scotland

ISBN 1 86232 126 4

British Library Cataloguing in Publication Data
A Catalogue record for this book is available
on request from the British Library

Typeset by Hewer Text Ltd, Edinburgh
Printed and bound by Cromwell Press, Trowbridge, Wiltshire

CONTENTS

ILLUSTRATIONS

FOREWORD

Roslin village is perched above the North Esk River in Midlothian. There is little sign today of its considerable industrial past. The coalmine has closed, and where once the powdermill stood, with its waterwheels and beam engine, down in Roslin Glen, there are now the leafy woodlands of the Country Park. A few ruins and the mill race are the only reminders of the past. Across the river, the high railway track from Auchendinny, along which Lydia Neil remembers walking to the 'bomb factory', is today a bridle path for cyclists and horses. The 'tin tunnel' against sparks has been demolished, and of Roslin Castle Station only the platform remains. The wooden huts, where hand grenades, smoke flares and Verey lights were assembled during World War II, have long gone. Gone too is the carpet factory, which used to dye the river every colour of the rainbow.

The memories recounted in this collection are part of a submerged industrial history. Roslin can stand as a kind of metaphor of rise and decline. In little more than two hundred years, the 'old' industrial revolution has come and gone in this rural hinterland of Edinburgh, creating mines, factories and mills which once employed all the young people of the villages around. Of the former mills along this stretch of the Esk, only the papermill at Auchendinny is still working. Any new industries are clean, discreet and employ very few people, like the famous scientific research station.

We know more about some aspects of this local history than about others. Coalmining, because it was so extensive, so crucial to development and so hard on its workers, has been well recorded. The subject of this book, the manufacture of gunpowder and explosives, is less well known, and there is surprisingly little archive evidence. It was connected to mining: most of the explosives were used for blasting in pit and quarry, rather than for munitions. But the beginning and end of its history – the Napoleonic wars and World War II – made Roslin powdermill part of the national war effort. The last war connected the powdermill with another submerged aspect of Scottish history: women as industrial workers. We are beginning to know more about Scottish women's work, but it is still very under-recorded compared to men's.

This book contains the testimony of one man and ten women, painting a picture of a vanished past. James Paris's evidence provides a valuable context for the women's voices, since he worked at Roslin before and after them, and since his tasks allowed him to see most parts of the enterprise. Significantly, the women, Barbara Scott, Sheila MacPherson and the others, all worked in the 'bomb factory' – the assembly section, high above the mill itself – and then only for the short space of the wartime emergency. Their generation – born between 1918 and 1922 – was drafted into wartime service in its youth. Like many British women of their age, they have had interrupted working lives, being employed full-time mostly during their teens and twenties, sometimes returning to work at a later date.

Ian MacDougall, who has collected these testimonies for the Scottish Working People's History Trust, is a skilled and experienced gatherer of working people's memories. As he reminds us, oral history has both strengths and weaknesses: it provides quite unique evidence, although people may sometimes have imperfect recollections, or unintentionally contradict themselves. But what is impressive here, in this set of unusually connected lives, is the extent to which the witnesses' accounts do tally over a wealth of small details, bringing vividly to life the felt reality of work fifty years ago. We don't have the written regulations of the bomb factory, but even if we did, they would not tell us how it felt to remember to remove your wedding ring or kirby grips, or any other metal objects before going in; how everything went by the board during air raids; or how the audience shouted in fear and anger when an E.N.S.A. entertainer

Foreword

smuggled a cigarette into a hall where the workers had gun-powder ingrained in their clothes.

It is the purpose of the Scottish Working People's History Trust to discover and preserve unique memories like this, both in the form of written archives and records and in the form of tape-recorded interviews. The professional historian and the general reader can both enjoy them, in different ways and for different purposes. Putting together apparently unconnected pieces of information can help the historian build explanations of unsolved past mysteries. And reading the individual life-stories of ordinary people, whose names are not usually recorded in history books, can encourage us all to locate ourselves and our families in our own history.

Sian Reynolds,
Department of French,
University of Stirling.

INTRODUCTION

These recollections, presented in their own words, are by ten women and one man who worked at the now long closed and demolished gunpowder mill and bomb factory at Roslin in Midlothian.

The mill, which began production of gunpowder in 1801 and was by the middle of the nineteenth century the largest of its kind in Scotland, closed in 1954. Few of its former employees now survive. James Paris, the only man among the eleven workers who recall their experiences here, and who himself (apart from his wartime service in the army) worked at the powder mill from 1931 until its closure, knows of no other Roslin man still alive who worked there. Few documentary records of the powder mill and bomb factory appear to survive. It is therefore in such situations that oral recollections like these can make at least a useful, at best an indispensable, contribution toward preserving for present and future generations the industrial but also the housing, educational, recreational, and other experiences of working men and women, few of whom ever write down their experiences.

The experience that was common to all eleven veterans whose recollections, recorded in interviews in 1996–7, are presented here was their employment at the Roslin gunpowder mill and bomb factory. In the case of the ten women that employment was only during the Second World War. But all eleven also recall many other aspects of their lives, including other employments they had before and after they worked at the powder mill and bomb factory. Thus aspects of work are described in one or other of the then three paper mills at Penicuik, in Woolworth's, C. & A.'s, and the North British rubber works in Edinburgh, in Roslin carpet factory, in domestic service, in Auchendinny laundry, in civil service and commercial offices, in forestry on a private estate, in small local shops, and on farms.

In some of those other employments the working conditions recalled were burdensome, even oppressive. Thus Janet Peebles relates that when she left school aged fourteen in 1933 her first job was in a shop at Loanhead, where her wage was ten shillings (50 pence) a week. 'I started at half-past eight in the mornin' and finished at half-past seven at night – other than that it was nine o'clock at night. That wis Monday to Saturday. Saturday you worked till ten o'clock at night.' Ella Graham, who left school aged fifteen that same year, began work at once as a living-in domestic servant to an Episcopalian clergyman's widow at Roslin. 'Ah got up about six o'clock in the morning. We started work at half-past six and you were sort of on duty till ten o'clock at night. And you got two half-days off a week. You didn't get off till three o'clock in the afternoon really on the half-days.' For these approximately ninety hours of work per six-day week, during which, while serving the successive courses to the cler-gyman's widow, she had to eat her own main meals as best she could, Ella Graham's wages were £2 a month (the same in effect as Janet Peebles' 50 pence a week), plus of course provision of board and lodging.

Other aspects of their lives that these eleven working people recall include their housing conditions, and their educational and recreational or leisure experiences.

Some of their memories of housing conditions are of tied housing occupied by their parents as mill workers or miners. They tell us of their own or other families, sometimes large families – 'Ma father had eighteen brothers and sisters. Quite a few died in childhood, ye know,' recalls Sheila MacPherson – living in single ends or in a room and kitchen, where sometimes the water supply was outside at a tap or well shared with other families, with dry closets round the back of the house or up the garden, houses lit by paraffin lamps or gas, and of course no baths or showers. Marion Bryce tells us there never was a bath or shower in the houses she lived in until at the age of fifty-five she moved from Milton Bridge to a council house in Penicuik in 1975. And Catherine Smith recalls how her parents, her sister and herself, her four brothers, and three young men lodgers all lived in a two-bedroomed house in Roslin in the 1920s. Her father, three of her brothers, and the three lodgers were then all miners working in the local pit, the Moat. 'There were no pit baths then,' she points out. 'They all had tae come home and ma mum had the tub in the middle o' the floor wi' the hot water in the pot. She heated the water on the fire . . . it wis jist an open fire.' The constant toil, not to say heroism, of working class wives and mothers in those times emerges repeatedly in these recollections.

School is another aspect of their experience of which these eleven working people speak. Several of them passed the notorious 'Quali', the examination sat by all eleven or twelve year old pupils in Scotland and which qualified those who passed it for entry into senior secondary education at a high school. Of these eleven working people here only two – James Paris and Ella Graham – actually entered high school. For various reasons that they recount four others who passed the 'Quali' did not in fact go on to high school. 'Looking back now,' says Janet Peebles, who, like almost all of the eleven, left school at the minimum age of fourteen, 'ah wish ah'd had the chance to carry on at school. Oh, ah'd like to have went to Lasswade [High] School and learned languages.' These recollections are a reminder, if any is needed, of the waste of actual and potential young talents and the frustration of youthful ambitions. Sheila MacPherson, whose schooling ended in 1935 at the age of thirteen after the death of her mother, recollects: 'Ah wis keepin' house then for ma father and ma two brothers, looking after the family . . . Ah had no option . . . Ma ambition as a girl wis always nursing.' Her ambition, like those of several others of the eleven and countless others of their generation, was not realised. Some among the eleven seem scarcely to have dared to harbour any ambitions at all: 'Ah thought frae the very start,' says Marion Bryce, 'ah would go and work in the paper mill !' But self-pity is remarkably absent in these recollections.

Recreational interests and activities, including cinema-going, dancing (the latter of which was particularly popular with several of the eleven), cycling, and courting arrangements are also recalled, as are other aspects of their experiences, including their families, church-going, trade unionism, holidays, illness, local characters, marriage, lodgers, pocket money, social deference, and the impact of war.

But the heart of these recollections concerns employment at the Roslin gunpowder mill and bomb factory. These eleven working people inevitably recall some more clearly than other aspects of that employment. 'Ah've no idea what ah got paid there – none !' Mary Murray frankly admits – and she is not alone among the eleven in not being able to recall whether wages at the bomb factory were better, worse, or much the same as in previous employments. There is also considerable difference in their recollections about, for example, the number of workers employed at the powder mill and bomb factory in the war years. Partly, that difficulty understandably arose because there were generally either two or three shifts worked, and consequently there was little or no knowledge of how many were turning out on the other shift or shifts.

But each of the eleven has clear recollections of many other aspects of work at the powder mill and bomb factory. Each contributes particular memories of certain aspects, and these successive and distinctive recollections create collectively a fairly clear picture of the works, its management, its workforce (including estimates of the respective proportion of women and men workers), its working conditions, and its many other features, including where the workers themselves lived, how they got to work each day, how they coped with the strains of night shifts, wartime E.N.S.A concerts – 'Oh, ah think they jist picked them up off the street,' says Lydia Neil – and the actual tasks these eleven working people were employed upon in the powder mill or bomb factory.

Wartime air raids are recalled – a particularly frightening experience for workers employed, as these eleven were, in a gunpowder mill. James Paris vividly remembers being at the mill during one such raid, evidently in 1941: 'We said, "Here's the bastards comin' again." And we heard the bomb droppin' and the explosion and we dived for cover. We dived into a bloody big

4

pile o' nettles ! And oo were standin' cursin' and swearin' aboot thir nettles, and there were no damage tae us at a'. They never got near the powder mill.' Nights or hours spent in the air raid shelters by the workers were, however, lightened by spontaneous concerts or sing-songs. 'And there wis two on ma shift especially – Bernie Gallacher and Betsy McGeary – oh, they were beautiful singers !', Lydia Neil recalls. 'And they used tae sing *Ave Maria*. And then Betsy would sing it in Latin.'

Not least, the eleven recount what appear to have been the comprehensive and systematic safety precautions prescribed and practised at the works in Roslin Glen. These precautions were essential in preventing, or at least reducing to an irreducible minimum given the inherently dangerous nature of the work, any repetitions of the explosions or other accidents, sometimes costing lives or causing serious injuries, that had occurred from time to time throughout the history of the Roslin powder mill and bomb factory.

The precautions included body searches or frisking at the entrance gate – though here, too, the eleven have different and sometimes conflicting recollections of the extent or rigour of these searches – that were intended to preclude the taking in of matches, cigarettes or other items for smoking, as well as metal objects including jewellery, wedding rings, kirby grips and stays in corsets. The provision of special clothing and footwear, the exclusion of married women from the powder mill as distinct from the bomb factory, the systematic weekly scrubbing out of the huts or houses, as they were officially called, where the work was carried on, the employment of not more than two or three workers in each hut or house, the prohibition on sisters working in the same hut or house, the special phosphor-bronze shoes that had to be worn by the horses used for transporting gunpowder or other loads within the complex of huts and mills, the regular checks or inspections by supervisors: all these and many other aspects of the work are recalled and described.

There are several accounts given of accidents, some of them fatal, at the powder mills. 'Ah had two uncles killed in the powder mill,' Barbara Scott says. 'They were both . . . married to ma mother's sister Barbara, the same name as me. She wis widowed twice by explosions at the powder mill.' Ella Graham, who grew up in Roslin Glen, states: 'I never wanted to work in the powder mills, because when I was seven there used to be explosions, and the girl next door to me, Peg Lauder, she was killed there in 1925, along with Pim Arnott from Station Road in Roslin.'

As almost every one of the eleven working men and women who present these recollections emphasises: 'Oh, ye had tae be careful.'

These recollections are examples of oral history that illustrate some of its characteristic strengths and also, no doubt, some of its problems or shortcomings. Each of these eleven working people contributes his or her testimony as honestly and fully as memory permits of events that, after all, took place half a century or more ago at their place of work in the Roslin gunpowder mill and bomb factory. Only parts of their recollections can be checked against surviving documentary sources, such as contemporary newspaper reports or other materials. In the nature of oral history, many of the experiences or events or persons recalled were never the subject of any contemporary or later written account. But where possible, recollections have been checked against documentary sources, and notes are offered that confirm, clarify, amplify, or occasionally question or contradict the spoken recollection.

On the other hand, the strength and attraction of these recollections lie in the directness and often detailed recall and vivid speech of the eleven working people, as well as in the fact that they are often providing the only record of events. By these recollections they are preserving and making available for present and future generations their distinctive contribution to the vast mosaic that is the industrial, social, economic, political, cultural past of Scotland. The history of working people in Scotland, as perhaps elsewhere, cannot be exclusively based on documentary source materials because very few working people ever write down their experiences.

These recollections of Roslin gunpowder mill and bomb factory workers are the first publication undertaken by the

Introduction

Scottish Working People's History Trust. The Trust, a chari-
table body founded only a few years ago, is principally
concerned to do all it can to interview and record working
men and women throughout Scotland about their experiences
of work (and, alas, of unemployment), but also of their
housing, education, recreation, etc. Simultaneously, the Trust
has embarked on the equally huge and unending task of
searching for, cataloguing, and encouraging permanent preservation by deposit in public repositories throughout Scotland
of all surviving documentary sources of working people's
history north of the Border. The Trust is also committed to
editing and securing publication of such documentary sources,
and is preparing for publication by the Scottish History Society
the minutes from 1894 to 1918 of the Mid and East Lothian
Miners' Association.

Since 1996, when it began these tasks systematically by
employing a research worker to carry them out on its behalf
(though, because of lack of adequate funding, only on a part-
time two-days-a-week basis at present), the Trust has interviewed in depth and recorded the recollections of hundreds of
working men and women in Scotland. These recollections by
Roslin gunpowder and bomb factory workers are therefore
intended to be the first of a comprehensive series of published
recollections by similar representative groups of working men
and women, occupation by occupation. Groups already interviewed and recorded, or in the process of being so, and whose
recollections it is intended will be the subject of forthcoming
volumes include: miners, journalists, Borders farm workers,
Leith seamen, public librarians, Penicuik paper mill workers,
bondagers, Co-operative society employees, Leith dockers, veteran working men and women in the Outer Hebrides, railway
workers, Peeblesshire textile mill workers, and Leith shipyard
workers. Clearly, the number and variety of such occupational
groups is almost limitless. But if even part of such a huge and
vital chapter of Scotland's history is to be harvested and pre-
served for future generations, the task is urgent. The Scottish
Working People's History Trust will do all it can to continue this
vital and urgent work upon which it has embarked. But the

Trust can only succeed in that work if it can secure adequate funding.

The Trust is glad to acknowledge here the generous support it has received from these eleven Roslin gunpowder mill and bomb factory workers in allowing it to interview them in their own homes and to record their recollections. Apart from necessary transpositions and some deletions of repetitious or other matter, their recollections are presented here in their own words. Each of the eleven has approved this edited version of the original verbatim transcript of his or her interview. The order of presentation of the recollections follows more or less the order in which the eleven became successively employed at the gunpowder mill and bomb factory. The tapes and verbatim transcripts of the interviews will be deposited in due course for permanent preservation and public access in the archives of the School of Scottish Studies at the University of Edinburgh.

Thanks are also due to all those librarians, archivists, local residents, and others who have helped, in one way or another, the undertaking and publication of this project of the Scottish Working People's History Trust. In particular, thanks are due to Alan Reid, Chief Librarian of Midlothian Libraries, and his colleague Marion Richardson, Local Studies Librarian, as well as to George Campbell of Roslin, Elaine Donald, Janice Dagg, and Agnes Shaw, Bob Thomson and his colleagues at the UNISON office in Edinburgh, Fiona Myles and her colleagues in Edinburgh Public Libraries, Dr Diana Henderson, Director of The Scots at War Trust, Dorothy Kidd, archivist at the Scottish Life Archive, National Museums of Scotland, and to the Scottish United Services Museum and Imperial War Museum. Professor Sian Reynolds has been characteristically generous in agreeing to write the Foreword. As always, my wife Sandra has put up uncomplainingly with the demands of the work in progress and given much practical support. Dr John and Mrs Val Tuckwell have proved consistently patient, expert, and enthusiastic publishers. Above all, thanks are due to the Scottish Working People's History Trust for appointing and enabling me to undertake these projects on its behalf, and also to all those persons and organisations that have made donations to the Trust to enable it thus far to carry out its tasks.

Ian MacDougall,
Secretary and Research Worker,
The Scottish Working People's History Trust.

irkcaldy

Firth of Forth

EAST
LOTHIAN

eith

Portobello

Haddington

Trapain
Law

RGH

Traneant

River Tyne

Laswade

Bonnyrigg

Newtongrange

osewell

Gorebridge

Carrrington

HIAN

Gala Water

Leader Water

Stow

JAMES PARIS

When ah went tae Roslin at first ah used tae drive the taxi at the Royal Hotel – it's now the Roslin Glen Hotel – and it wis when ah got ma books off o' there ah wis on the dole for aboot six weeks and then ah started in the gunpowder mill.

Ah was born on the 4th of January 1912 in the Peacock Hotel in Newhaven. Ma mother was a servant at the Peacock Hotel. Her name was Rourke, an Irish name. Ah never had contact wi' ma mother when ah grew up, never saw her again. I was adopted when ah was about six weeks old. The family ah lived with their name was Paris and ah was given their name. Ah don't really know who ma father was. All ah remember ah grew up at Daisy Cottage, East Calder, as James Paris. But, as ah say, I surmise one or two things. There were nine o' the family at East Calder, you see, and the oldest o' the family wis a bit o' a bad rogue, ye know – well, ah'll no' say he wis bad but he knew what he was doin'. His first name was James. So ah always thought o' him would be the father. That's why ah always was known as Jim. He had a contractin' business in Broxburn and we never saw him. He wis the bad sheep o' the family Paris. Ah never made any enquiries but ah wis told wi' a lot o' ma so-called friends that I had been adopted and that. Anybody havin' an illegitimate kid was a right bad . . . But ah never had any trouble at all, no, no, it wis never brought up. No, no, ah wis jist one o' the boys. Ah wis jist known as Jimmy Paris.

Ma adopted mother, well, she was the local midwife. Grace Paris wis her name and she wis well known all round in different villages – Mid Calder, Kirknewton, and all round about. Ma adopted father Paris at first he was a shale miner, then he worked in Oakbank oil works on some retorts or something. He was strict, oh, yes, strict. He wis strict wi' the whole family. Ah wis treated equally wi' the others, oh, yes, ah wis one o' the family.

Well, countin' me there wis five sons and four daughters. And they're all dead except me. It wis a long lived family, they were all in their nineties. Ah was the youngest in the family. It was a happy family, ah felt quite secure – a happy childhood. They all had jobs. One o' ma brothers – Willie – wis postman at Mid Calder. Mid Calder wis a sort o' central post office. And then George, oh, he'd been in a few jobs, but he worked in Wylie's paper mill at Mid Calder. They jist made that brown paper packin' stuff. And he was a boilerman. And then Jessie, one o' ma sisters, worked in the West Calder Co-operative. And then another younger sister worked wi' Stark the draper in East Calder. And another sister wis a telephonist at this Mid Calder post office.

It wis East Calder ah grew up at. It was just a wee village, it wis jist a main street. Ah wouldnae like tae say how many lived there when ah was a laddie, say, maybe about 500.[1] There were a lot o' shale mines round about the district at West Calder, at Westwood and Addiewell and all round aboot. And there wis a big refinery at Pumpherston and a refinery at Oakbank and that's where they made the petrol out the shale. So most o' the men in East Calder were in the shale mining industry. Either that or they'd be agricultural workers, ye know – quite a lot o' decent sized farms round about.

At our house at East Calder there wis a room and kitchen downstairs and then there was a couple o' bedrooms up the stair. By that time there wis some o' them married and they were away from home when ah wis growing up. There wis three of us – George and Bill and I – slept upstairs in one o' the rooms, and, oh well, ah dinnae ken who, the actual sisters that slept in the other. Ma adopted parents they were in the room downstairs. So it wasn't too crowded then, och, no. Ye never thought anything about it at that time. It wis a dry toilet down the bottom o' the garden. But at the finish up, before ah went to live in Roslin, we had an inside toilet. And we had electric light put in, ye ken. We didnae have a bath – jist a bath in front o' the fire. And the girls had to leave the room while the boys were getting bathed. That was the usual arrangement in those days.

Ah went tae the school about five years o' age, tae the local school, East Calder primary school, and ah wis there tae, well, it wis the old Qualifyin'. And after ah passed the Qualifyin' ah went to West Calder High School till ah wis sixteen. Ah liked both schools. Ah wisnae a swot or anythin' but ah liked tae learn what wis goin' on. Languages interested me most – English, but especially when ah went to the High School I was keen on French. I got French and Latin at the High School but ah preferred French to Latin. Oh, some o' the teachers were sort o' taken up wi' ma name Paris, ken. Ah wis in the High School till ah wis sixteen but ah didnae go on for tae go tae the university and that. Ah don't know if ah would like tae have done that, ah widnae like tae say. But ah got a job wi' the Earl o' Buchan at Almondale House as a forester.[2]

Ah never had any particular ambitions about jobs when ah wis at the school. Ah never gave it a thought. Well, ah had five and a half miles tae cycle tae the High School and cycle five and a half miles home again. There were no buses. It wis a long day for a laddie but, och, ye never thought much about it. Ah wis quite fit and ah got a new bike ! Ach, it wis fine.

Before ah left the school ah used tae go wi' the Store vanman and ah used tae drive the Store van. That's how ah learned tae drive a car. It wisnae a Saturday job at all, ah just sat beside him in the van, ah wis jist goin'. Oh, ah knew him well – Pipsy Miller we used tae call him. He wis a well known character. But he used tae go away up round by Harper Rig and that, and ah used tae get tae drive on these quiet roads. Ah would be roond about thirteen, fourteen, fifteen. Ah never sat a test later on, no, no, you jist went intae a kind o' central post office and asked for a driver's licence and ye filled up the form and signed it. You had tae be seventeen then and that's how you got your licence.

But, as ah say, ah got a job wi' the Earl o' Buchan at Almondale House as a forester. Well, it was a case o' we knew the head forester. Ma adopted mother knew him. She had been the midwife all round there and that's how she got to know them. She spoke tae the heid forester and ah got the job. It wis a job. Ah wis pleased tae get workin', oh, yes. Ah left the school on the Friday and started work on the Monday. That would be

1928. There wis unemployment at that time but there were jobs. It wisnae a case of what you knew, it wis who you knew.

The Earl o' Buchan's place, Almondale, was a fair sized estate. It stretched frae East Calder and then it took in Broxburn. It is now a country park, Almondale Country Park. As ah say, och, it wis a' right when it was the meetin' o' the foxhounds. The Linlithgow and Stirlingshire foxhounds used tae meet there occasionally and, oh, at the big house gettin' their stirrup cup and ye were holdin' the horses and ye'd maybe get a tanner or a shillin' or somethin' for haudin' the horses. Well, ah didnae think very much of it, tae be perfectly truthful, because ah thought ah wis as good as some o' them that wis ridin' tae the hounds, because a lot o' them were farmers' daughters and that. It wis a kind o' rag-taggle affair.

Well, ma work on the estate wis mostly loppin' trees. It wis quite a big estate and anything that wis overhangin' fields and that we jist . . . And then they had a wee sort o' nursery where they grew young trees and they used tae plant them out. So there wis a kind o' variety o' work, chopping down a few trees, loppin' the branches, and plantin'. Ah think it wis jist from eight in the mornin' till five at night, and till midday on Saturdays. You never worked on Saturday afternoon or Sunday. Saturday it wis jist a case o' it wis a big entrance place and ye dutch hoed all roond in front and raked it a' on a Saturday mornin' tae make it look nice. And that wis aboot it. When ye met the lady or the earl, 'Good mornin', ma lady,' ye know. Ah didnae doff ma cap because ah didnae wear yin ! But, 'Good mornin', ma lady,' and 'Good mornin', ma lord' and that – och ! Ah felt very bad, ah didnae like it all. Ah thought, 'How the hell should ah speak like that ?' So far as ah could make out they were a damn sight poorer than me !

There wis nae overtime. Ma wage wis ten shillins a week, and they paid monthly ! £2 a month. Ah took it home and ah think it wis half-a-crown ah got for pocket money.

Ye didnae have very much contact wi' the domestic staff in the house. One o' the duties wis tae saw up wood for the fires and ah used tae barra it into what they called the servants' hall, and there were big bunkers and ah used tae empty it in. Och, ah occasionally spoke tae the cook and that. There were very few domestic servants there, you'd be lucky if there were about four, maybe five: the cook and then there were a laundry maid and then there wis a sort o' general maid – table maid. There wis no butler and no groom for the hounds and the horses. Oh, no, they come up from Linlithgow. Ken, they had a meet at a' the big places. But, oh, no, the stables and kennels were at Linlithgow. That's why they called it Linlithgow and Stirlingshire Hunt.

Lord Buchan didnae have a chauffeur. They had a pony and trap. Ye never saw him in it at all. It wis always Lady Buchan that yaised tae go up tae the village and go messages or somethin' and draw up at the grocer's and they would run oot tae see what she wanted. Ah had nothin' to do wi' her. That come under the gardener.

They had a couple o' gardeners, well, a gardener and boy like, three foresters, and there wis a gamekeeper. There were about a dozen employees altogether, about four or five in the house and five or six outside. So far as we were concerned our wages come from the office in Edinburgh. We never had anythin' tae do wi' Lord Buchan or that. There was a factor came out but, ye know, he never spoke tae kids like me !

At Almondale House ah got one week's holidays per annum and New Year's Day only – not Christmas Day. We used tae go tae the carnival at the Waverley Market in Edinburgh for New Year's day. Ah never went anywhere for my week's holiday – never had any money tae go anywhere. Ah wis in the Boy Scouts before ah left school and used tae go for a week-end camp or that. After ah started work ah forgot aboot that, ah wasn't in the Scouts after ah left school.

Ah wis a forester at Almondale maybe aboot a couple o' years. Och, it wis jist a glorified labourin' job. But ma brother George – Dod we ca'ed him, he worked in the paper mill, Wylie's – he used tae show the movin' pictures, ye know: one night at Mid Calder Hall and a night up at Kirknewton Hall and a night at East Calder, three nights a week. He had an old Ford-T van tae cart a' the equipment aboot and ah used tae be the driver. And, well, ah used tae help him and ah got back-handers. And he wis a bit o' a professional photographer, ye know.

Well, ah didnae care much for the forester job. There wis an awful lot of repetitive jobs – and, ach. But ma sister Jessie wis married and livin' in Roslin and her husband Willie Mitchell wis the chauffeur tae the manager o' the powder mills there. So Willie fixed me up wi' the job drivin' the taxi at the Royal Hotel at Roslin. Ah felt glad when ma sister and brother-in-law said, 'Come through and work at Roslin.' Ah lodged with them as well in Station Road. Ah had a wee room to myself. There wisnae any family at that time but once they got the family they got a bigger house.

It wis when ah got ma books off o' the Royal Hotel ah wis on the dole for aboot six weeks and then ah started in the gun-powder mill. Willie Mitchell wis the chauffeur to the manager, Mr William Ogilvy. And Mr Ogilvy wis a West Calder man tae, ye see. He wis related tae Pie Jock in West Calder – Jock Thomson. Jock had the bakery business and he had a garage. The Thomsons were well known in West Calder. That's what we used tae call him, Pie Jock, because when we were at the school we went tae his – well, it wisnae a dinin' room but it wis a big hall, ye know – and we got a penny for a cup o' tea and that. And Pie Jock used tae come round and we used tae say tae him, 'Have you got any damaged pies, Mr Thomson ?' 'Ah'll have a look.' And he went in and wid stick his finger in a pie or brek a bit o' the crust off. Ye got that for a penny insteed o' thruppence. So he damaged mair pies than what he . . . That's why we called him Pie Jock. He was a good man. Mr Ogilvy wis married on Pie Jock's sister. Well, there used tae be a powder mill at Camilty, above West Calder on the Harburn road. But it shut down and Mr Ogilvy came through to Roslin as manager.[3] So ma brother-in-law got me this job paintin' up in the bomb section in Roslin gunpowder mills. Ah think ah wid be roond aboot nineteen, so that wid be aboot 1931.

Well, as ah say, there wis the bomb section, which was really jist a series o' huts. They called it the bomb section but they made these flares and smoke bombs and things like that. They never made any sort o' high explosives, ye know. It wis nearly a' women that worked there. Ah got the job tae paint the outsides o' these wooden huts. And ah wis never allowed inside because ye had tae have special clothes on, ye know. After that wis finished ah jist went down tae the main mill and ah wis told jist tae carry on, oh, various types o' jobs.

Well, the first thing ah got when ah went down there, there wis an old spare lorry that wis used tae drive the raw materials from Roslin Castle station. Ah got put on it for a wee while. That caused another burst up wi' some o' the folk that thought they should have got the job, ye ken. But the foreman, Harry Dugan, he jist asked me to do it. So ah wis doin' that for a wee while, roughly a year, off and on. And then another time ah got a job drivin' a horse and cairt. Ah didnae even ken the front frae the back o' the bloody horse. But anyway some o' the other men yoked up the horse and that. And it wis jist a case o' takin' gunpowder from a magazine to whatever department was needin' it, the like o' up to where the girls made the pellets and that. But ah quite liked it. There wis a bit o' variety o' jobs for me.

And then for a long time ah wis in wi' the storeman in the powder mill, and then ah finished up as a magazine keeper. There were a big magazine jist inside the gates and this wis where all black powder wis kept. And then they had another magazine up at Oatslie. It wis licensed for 200 tons, and each box was stamped with sizes and dates when it wis packed. And the magazine keeper's job wis tae try, when there wis orders goin' out, to use the oldest – ye know, tae keep the dates in rotation. And that's what ah wis doin' when ah wis called up tae the army in 1942.

When ah started in the gunpowder mill at Roslin there were always around sixty-five, between sixty and sixty-five, workers employed. There were women, oh, they were in the minority. They'd be lucky if there wis a dozen women – roughly fifty men and a dozen women. There wis women, after the pellets were made and that, at the packin' them intae boxes, a hundred pound in each box; and then there wis women makin' the pellets – that wis further up the river North Esk. There were about six women, ah think, and it wis the machine that made the pellets. There wis a hopper at the top that they filled up wi' the powder and they worked this thing and filled up and another bit come down and made it intae a pellet. That wis another job ah had for a while.

We never made anything like ammunition or bullets at Roslin. It was purely commercial gunpowder, because we supplied a lot o' these shale mines, ye see, the likes o' Westwood at West Calder, and there was a place at Addiewell took a lot, and a' round about like that. And then a lot o' these quarries – they used tae run down as far as Traprain Law quarry in East Lothian. Ye see, they had sort o' regular customers. The lorry drivers, the delivery drivers, they wid say, maybe on Monday, 'We'll be goin' tae Castlecary' or 'We'll be goin' tae Traprain Law' or somewhere. They knew their journeys. They drove the gunpowder to customers in the south east o' Scotland really, not to the west o' Scotland or Fife. The west o' Scotland come from Ardeer, ye see. Ye see, we got a lot o' orders at Roslin when Camilty shut down and some o' their workers come through here. That would be round about the 1930s. Camilty wis near West Calder, up the Harburn road. Ye used tae get tae it, ye went tae Bell's Quarry and then ye went up the high road there up tae Harburn estate.

But, oh, no, there wis no ammunition or bullets made at Roslin. Even in the bomb section it wis jist smoke bombs and Verey cartridges and things like that – flares. The big smoke floats they made, oh, they must have been aboot three feet high. And they were for the navy. They must have been for flingin' overboard for smoke screens. And then they made Verey lights and other sort o' flares for the army, the navy or the air force. That wis goin' on all the time before the war. When the war came in 1939 it jist made the bomb section busier. It didnae affect the gunpowder – the mills – very much. They were still supplyin' the pits and quarries.

The gunpowder wis milled first. There wis a big mill, och, they were jist like big mill wheels, ye know. All the different ingredients were put in there. Ah wis tryin' tae mind what they were. Well, sulphur. There wis black lead but they called it plumbago, and the other main item wis nitrate or something. But anyway they were milled for about an hour, dependin' on what stuff they were makin'. Then it wis lifted out o' that and it wis taken tae a buildin' called the cornin' house. And it wis put through the process and it wis brought out in little flakes like corn, ye know – that's why it wis the cornin' house. And then frae there it wis taken tae different magazines for storage. Some customers took it loose and it wis packed in barrels, and there wis a hundred pound in each barrel. They worked on the 2,000 lb a ton, a short ton, 2,000 lb. And, well, that was that. And then other ones took these cartridges – they were different sizes, ah would say, about an inch and a half up to two inch, and different weights, it depends what they wanted – and they were packed in boxes. There wis another process across the river North Esk, where all the black powder was put in a big drum and more plumbago wis put in it and it wis revolvin' for ah don't know how long. But this was tae make the gunpowder more water-proof, because some o' the places were damp and watery and they wanted this polished stuff. And then it wis made intae cartridges or sold loose. That wis the main items.

But, as ah say, ah wis never actually a process worker. But ah finished up in magazines. I used tae go wi' the truck, wi' the lorries, up to the . . . They had a big magazine up in the bomb section where high explosive wis kept. But that come from Ardeer in Ayrshire – it wisnae made at Roslin – different types o' high explosive. And ah loaded lorries up there. There wis three delivery lorries at Roslin, and they went all round the country. Traprain Law in East Lothian wis the furthest away. They used tae like that. That wis a day's work, doon tae Traprain Law. Well, ah didnae get that, of course. Ah'd tae load the lorries !

And then ye had tae keep a stock like. Ye used stock sheets and ye put the stock sheets intae the lab every night and that wis it.

The Roslin gunpowder mills wis an old, old established business. They made gunpowder there for the troops when they were fightin' Napoleon, for the Napoleonic Wars. A lot o' the explosives used were made at Roslin. The heid yins used tae bring that up, ken, at meetins and that.[4]

When ah started first at Roslin gunpowder mills about 1931 it wis Curtis & Harvey, the explosives people, and then it wis ta'en over by I.C.I. The whole o' the Scottish factories wis taken over by I.C.I. That wis just before the war, somewhere about 1937 or 1938.[5]

The mills from one end tae the other it would be roughly about a mile. Oh, well, it's part o' Roslin Country Park now. Oh, it wisnae such a big area. There wis buildins on either side o' the Esk. And then the manager's house wis up above at Eskhill House, lookin' down on it, ye know. Mr Ogilvy lived there and when he retired after the war it wis a Mr Tyre that come and took over. And this Mr Tyre, och, we didnae fancy him sae much. He wis kindae . . . He wis always addressed as Mr Tyre. He wis there till the end o' the mill, he wis the last manager.

The safety precautions at Roslin were great, very strict. Of course, ye were searched every mornin' before ye started. Ah didnae smoke so it didnae maitter much tae me. Ye rung your ticket and then there wis a big thingmy wi' a wee bracket, holes in it, ye know, and ye put your cigarettes and matches in there and then the gateman jist run his hands down ye as much as tae say, 'Aye, right.' It wis the gateman always who did the searching. There wis three gatemen. They were on three different shifts. Bob Bolton, that wis ma father-in-law, he wis one o' them. And Joe Neil was another. And the other was an auld regimental man, ah forget his name – Robison, ah think it wis. But anyway that wis their job and when ye were finished at night they had tae go roond the factory as sort o' watchmen, ye know. Oh, no, they didnae live on the premises. Bob Bolton lived in the village and Joe Neil lived in the village, and Geordie Robison lived up Glenside way. The only person living on the premises wis the manager and he wis away up in the big house at Eskhill. And then Wullie Russell, the head foreman, he went round the mill every mornin' and inspected everything and, well, if ye got caught wi' the wrong things ye were up the shute. But most men took the responsibility . . .

But ah mean, when ye got a job – take the likes o' me – ye got supplied with boots which were sewn. There wis no nails on your boots. And ye got a boiler suit wi' no pockets, so that ye couldnae carry anythin' in in an explosives department. And then the likes o' these mill workers they got supplied with a sort o' fireproof suit. It wis a kind o' asbestos, awfy rough and ready, and no buttons on it. The jacket ye had tapes, ye know, tae tie it. And they got boots. But when they were workin' in an explosives buildin' they also had a pair of inside boots. So when they went tae their work in the mornin' they had tae sit on a bench outside it and change their boots before they went inside the buildin' Ye werenae allowed wi' boots – ye ken, ye had a clean pair o' boots and a workin' pair o' boots.

Ye see, when ye went in in the mornin' the sort o' place where ye changed clothes it wis in two sections. There wis the clean place, where ye took off your jaicket and that and ye walked through tae the dirty place, where the workin' boots and the overalls and that were kept. Then ye went through again tae where the washhand basins and the showers were. The men workin' wi' the powder and that, they had a shower every night before they went home. Ah mean, we stopped work at four o'clock but ye didnae check out till half-past four. That gave ye half an hour tae get changed and washed, and then ye had tae walk away out tae the front gate. But all the men who wore the clothes, ye know, protective clothin', they must have a shower. That wis compulsory. They all had a shower. The likes o' horsemen – there wis bogies through the place for transport – and these men had all tae have a shower as well.

The bogies were railway cairts on rails, a narrow gauge. And the horses all had brass shoes – well, we said brass shoes but they were actually phosphor-bronze – so that they wouldnae cause any sparks. They got a patterned shoe made at the village blacksmith's. Then they went through tae Ardeer and they got so many pairs made, ye know. The phosphor-bronze were all made at Ardeer. But when the horse needed shoein' the man had tae come up tae the village. But he had tae take the shoes up with him and he had tae bring back the old shoes because, well, they were valuable scrap. The horses had all the phosphor-bronze shoes so that there wouldnae be any sparks.

Most o' the workers were quite careful in obeying the rules, well, they were maistly older men, ye know. Well, they knew. Ye see, the likes o' the buildin' for the cornin' house it wis back in the bankin' and there wis solid walls built up, shieldin' the actual buildin'. And the explosives went in wi' the bogie and come oot again and that wis it. And the men that worked there were pretty responsible people. So far as I knew everything was bein' done to ensure safety. Ah mean, any time ah had tae go tae these buildins they made sure that ah changed ma boots and put on overshoes and things like that. They were leather boots, but they were sewn, the soles were sewn. There wis no tackets or anythin'. And they were repaired up in the village. It wis all sewn boots. And then, as ah say, the overalls had no pockets in them. Ye could jist put your hand through your trouser pockets tae get your handkie or anythin'. And you were searched every mornin' aboot the smokin' and that. But that wis aboot all.

There was one time there was some visitor come. Ah don't know who he was, but he wis goin' in through in his car and this man in the next bit in the buildin' saw him and he jumped oot and stopped him and hunted him back tae the gatehouse, and went doon wi' him and told the gateman that he wis smokin' and he had no bloody right tae smoke there. Oh, he got a long lecture aboot it, the driver. We got visitors from time tae time. Well, some o' them must have been comin' tae put in orders or that, and then there were people come from Ardeer or people from different places: West Quarter in Lanarkshire, where they made detonators – well, we kept detonators at Roslin – and they come. But that wis the visitors that come from these places. They must have been tae see the manager or somethin', ah don't know.

Och, ye never gave a thought tae the dangers. Ah don't suppose any o' the workers gave it a thought. Ye jist got accustomed tae it. As ah say, the men workin' in the buildings they had special clothin' and they had boots, and that made a big difference, ye see.

Well, there wisnae any accidents while I wis there. But before I went there in 1931 there was one at the girls' place and ah think it wis either four or six girls killed there. They were process workers. Ah cannae remember the dates but it wis long before ah went. Down in the village cemetery there's a big plaque up and all the names and that are put on it. Pim Arnott wis one. That's the only one ah can remember. And then jist before ah started the cornin' house went up and there wis two men killed there.

The cornin' house is a kind o' dangerous place – that wis the most dangerous. But so long as you obeyed the rules it seemed that everything wis a' right. [6]

Of course ye knew the dangers afore ye took the job. It never bothered me at a'. Of course, as ah say, ma brother-in-law wis the chauffeur, ma father-in-law wis a horseman and then a gateman.

During the war, well, there were jist fire watchers and that. In fact, ah wis on it when the Germans come near what they ca'ed the Cleuch. Well, it wis a sort o' rough field. There were one or two holiday caravans in it. But it wis away from the powder mills altogether. And this Jock Simpson and I were on fire watch this night. It wis the night that they bombed through at Greenock and the Clyde and ye heard them comin' back. We said, 'Here's the bastards comin' again.' And we heard the bomb droppin' and the explosion and we dived for cover. We dived into a bloody big pile o' nettles ! And oo were standin' cursin' and swearin' aboot thir nettles, and there were no' any damage tae us at a'. They never got near the gunpowder mill.

We went for a walk the next day and we saw where the explosion had been. It would be about 500 yards away or so. Ken, ye went up tae where the big magazine wis and then ye went doon towards the river, and it is jist a big field and they called it the Cleuch. But there wis jist a big hole in the ground, ye ken. Our opinion was that they were gettin' rid o' their load, because as soon as this dropped the engine speeded up and they were away. Ye knew it wis Germans because they had a sound like a diesel engine, ye know. But when they dropped that bomb at the Cleuch ye heard the engine wis speedin' up as soon as it dropped. That's what ah thought – they were unloadin' jist tae get away home.

Most of the workers at the gunpowder mill were from Roslin. One or two from Rosewell, but mostly from Roslin. It wis a lot o' family concern. Ah cannae mind anybody frae Penicuik. Most o' them belonged to Roslin and round about, because they knew the gunpowder mills.

Working conditions were good. Well, nearly everybody wis a union member like – Transport and General Workers. So far as ah knew there wis never any trouble wi' unions or that. Ah wis never in a union when ah wis a forester at Almondale. Ah wis never approached for that. It wis jist a typical private estate thing. Ah joined a union when ah wis in the powder mill, 'cause, well, one o' the men wis a sort o' union leader. Johnny McHale wis the union man. And ah don't know, ah wis made an auditor in the union and ah wisnae even at the meetin' ! And ah told him, ah says, 'Ye cannae make me an auditor. Ah wisnae at the bloody meeting' !' But he says there were only five at the meetin' ! So though most o' the workers there were in the union they weren't very active in it. Well, in my case it wis jist a case o' bein' in the union because everybody else wis in it. Ah wisnae much interested in it, ye know. Ah wis asked to join when ah went to the gunpowder mills. McHale asked us. Well, ah don't know what you would call him but he wis the head o' the union. He come from Rosewell. Och, aye, but there wis never any bother so far as ah know with unions.

There wisnae any social organised by the union. A' the union wis interested in wis payin' your subscription. As ah say, when they held a union meeting they were lucky if there wis half a dozen at it. The men werenae interested in it. They were like me, they joined the union because it wis the done thing. But ah wisnae in the least interested.

There were no strikes, oh, no. There wis never a strike that ah know of.

There was a round-the-clock shift system on certain things. The likes o' the mills, it wis three shifts. And it would depend what kind o' explosives they were makin'. Sometimes they milled for an hour, sometimes for two hours, it depended. You worked from eight in the mornin' till half-past four, wi' half an hour for your dinner – eight hours a day.

Ah had round about three shillins an hour roughly, 24 shillins a day. That was good money then. We thought we were quite well off, well, when ye heard what other people were gettin' for wages, likes o' agricultural workers and that. We got about twice as much as the agricultural workers. Well, as ah say, we had pretty fair wages. And where else could ah go in the village ?

We got the Edinburgh Trades week as holidays and jist New

Year's Day – no public holidays apart from that. When ah came back after the war it wis much the same. As ah say, when ah wis there before ah wis married New Year's Day used tae be spent in the Waverley Market in Edinburgh at the carnival. But ah don't remember gettin' the Edinburgh holiday or anythin' like that, because it wis a continuous process, ye see.

Political interests was a thing that never bothered me. Ah never took any interest. Ah wis never a member o' any political party or anything, never have been.

Ah got called up from the powder mill tae the army. Actually, ah don't know if this was true or not but there wis a clerk in the gunpowder mill office at Roslin and, well, him and I didnae get on. And he had tae do wi' this callin' up business. Ah wisnae on the process and ah got called up. Och, ah wis quite pleased tae go. From 1942 to '46 ah wis in the army. Ah did ma preliminary trainin' at Fort George up at Inverness, and then ah wis posted tae the Royal Electrical and Mechanical Engineers. Fort George was a typical old army style. It wis very strict up there. There wis nothin' tae be strict aboot but they were strict and they put ye through it a' right. We were in a big barrack room. Oh, there were a big squad, ye know. Of course, ah'd never seen anythin' like it before. Ah got put through a lot o' different courses, come out as a mechanic, and then ah wis sent tae the Middle East just the beginnin' o' '43. Ah wis there until '46. Well, ah never seen any fightin'. Ah got up as far as Sidi Barani and Tobruk but the fightin' was a' finished by that time. For a while ah wis in a Light Aid Detachment haulin' in tanks that had broken down and that, ye ken. The battlefields wis a' cleared up and any tank that was worth salvagin' was put aside and, well, an L.A.D. unit went up and brought it doon tae the main workshops. So we were repairin' tanks all the time. I was at Tel el Kebir in Egypt. I was in the same tent in the same bed in the corner for three years. Ah got demobbed from there. Ah came back tae the gunpowder mill in 1946.

Ah married while ah was in the services. Ah got married in 1942 before ah went overseas. Ma wife wis a Roslin girl. She wis a waitress at the tearooms in Roslin. She liked it a' right. Of course, it wis a job, and that wis it. And Margaret carried on until our daughter Marion was born, ah think it wis November '44. We lived in Roslin in Main Street. Ye see, that old lady Mrs Young my wife worked for as a waitress she had aboot, oh, four or five houses on the main street and, of course, Margaret got yin right away. Ye yaised tae pay six shillins a week rent and rates, oh, God ! In this house here ah'm payin' £23 a week ! Then we moved to Pentland View Terrace in Roslin and got a brand new council house there and were in it for aboot, oh, thirty-odd years.

As ah say, ah wis away for aboot four years roughly in the army and then ah come back there. Ah mean, after ah got demobbed ah took aboot a fortnight or three weeks' holidays afore ah started work, because ah thought ah wis well off. Ah wis a married man by that time, of course.

Well, as ah say, ah worked in the stores at the powder mill for quite a long time, ye know, jist issuin' stores and that, and then ah finished up as a magazine keeper. Ah liked the magazine job best because ye got outside occasionally, up tae the bomb section where the high explosives wis kept. Then when the lorries come from Ardeer with the high explosives you had tae be there tae check. Before ye signed for anything ye checked it goin' in. Jist the usual, ye put it out accordin' to the dates and that.

The big magazine up at Oatslie – it's now a dwellin' house – it had a licence for 200 tons. But it wis all enclosed, like a big high fence and that round about it. The walls were three feet thick and it wis a very light roof. If there had been an explosion it would have went wi' it, ye ken. The walls were made of stone, but a wooden roof wi' slates. To look at it wis a bit like a house – it is a house now, it'll be a good house, too, as ah say, the walls were three feet thick. There were no windows in the magazine, jist solid walls and a light roof. And a door and it had a porch, well, a double door, so that a lorry could back under the porch and it wouldnae be any water, ye know, the boxes would be kept dry. The front door wis a steel door, wi' keys aboot this bloody length, aboot nine or ten inches long, ye know. Then there wis an inside door as well. The inside doors were wood. And inside the door wis a pair o' overshoes, like rubber goloshes. Ah had tae put these on while ah wis workin' inside the magazine.

Inside the magazine it wis jist a big room. And the magazine keeper knew by the dates. You stacked everything in rotation, you know. Well, the head magazine keeper could lift the barrels aboot six high, but no' me. They were a hundred pound – a hundred pound o' gunpowder in it. Well, Jimmy Neil he wis a strong man, ye know, so he jist lifted them physically. But me, ah wis lucky if ah could put them three high. But there werenae a lot o' barrels. It wis mostly boxes, 50–lb boxes. And ye stacked them so that ye could see the dates. And when ye were puttin' anything out ye took the oldest one first. And ye kept everything in rotation. So from the door it went right round the buildin'. Ye jist worked round and as ye were puttin' stuff in ye jist filled up the gap, ye know.

The magazine wis an oblong shape, ah'd say maybe about 30 feet by 20 roughly. It wis licensed to hold up to 200 tons o' explosives. But, as I say, it wis well fenced in, a big high fence, and a big double gate wi' a big padlock and that. There wis barbed wire on the top o' the fence. But most o' the local people knew it wis a magazine and some people wouldnae go past it ! It wisnae on the main road, ye know. Ye go up what they called The Beeches – there were a big avenue o' beech trees – and at the far end is this magazine. There wis no night watchman there, well, ah suppose they would give it a call. Ye see, the night watchman at the powder mill had a big Airedale dog and, well, ye'd tae be very careful when ye went near this bloody kennel ! And he always took the dog with him and that wis protection.

That wis the magazine for black powder. The high explosives ones were up in the bomb sections. There wis two magazines up there and, well, it wis up tae the magazine keeper tae keep things tidy. They were the same sort o' idea. But they werenae sae big as Oatslie, because we got their supplies from Ardeer, the big place through at Stevenston in Ayrshire, and ye jist stacked it up so that ye could see the dates on it. It went out just the usual. When that opencast coal minin' started at first they went through a lot o' explosives. And they got it, it was in an awful big size – och, it must have been aboot six inches by aboot twelve inches – high explosives. And that's what they used at opencast. A driver used tae tell me he went tae an opencast place and they jist dumped it – there werenae magazines or onything ! Very risky !

Well, the two magazines for the high explosives werenae big – maybe hold about twenty, twenty-five ton each. Ye see, there wis quite a big turnover of high explosives and ye jist kept it in rotation. Well, ye see, as the shale minin' went down so the black powder went down. A lot o' the quarries used black powder: the Kaimes quarry at Kirknewton and then there wis Traprain Law and there wis other quarries they went tae. And the biggest place for the shale was at Westwood at West Calder, and there wis another big place at Addiewell. They didnae use high explosives, they used the black powder. Oh, ye used tae see the workers' goin' tae the shale mines when ah wis a boy at West Calder. Scottish Oils run a bus and ye'd see a' the miners. They always wore these white moleskins, and they were always white, they never got dirty – different frae coal minin'. Aye, ye'd see them comin' off their shift the next mornin'. They always wore white moleskins.

The big 200–ton store at Oatslie wis the only buildin' away from the mill in Roslin Glen. In the Glen itself, well, ye see, at the gatehouse there wis the big magazine where I worked. And there was a smaller magazine further up where the finished stuff was stored until the likes o' the packers needed it. Then there wis another place where they filled the barrels. Ah forget the name o' that buildin'. Then the next yin wis the cornin' house, and the press house. Then across the water – the North Esk river – was this place where they made it waterproof. And there would be at least two sets o' four mills, ye ken, there were four mills in a row. And some o' them were water-driven and some o' them steam-driven. But that wis aboot all. And then there wis Harry Dugan the foreman's office, and there wis a joiner's shop and an engineer's shop and an electric shop. And then there wis the packin' place. And then there wis two buildins where the girls made the pellets. There wis a staff canteen, it wis a separate buildin' in the bomb section, and the hot meals were brought down tae the powder mills.

And then there was a woman in the lab, of course, testin' the powders every day. Wullie Russell, the head foreman, was the head o' the lab as well. But there was one woman sort o' chemist – ah don't know if she had any qualifications or no'. It was just a case o' testin' the day's products and, ah don't know, she'd maybe write a report aboot it. The lab wis quite small. It wis attached tae the office, the main office. The manager had a private office then there wis the sort o' head clerk that looked after the general office, and there wis, ah think, three or four women in the office. So there were less than half a dozen office workers.

Wullie Russell, the head foreman, he wis an elder o' the church in Roslin, because he wis a good man. Ah liked Wullie Russell. And when ye were off sick or anythin' ye had tae report tae Wullie Russell. Ye ken, ye went intae his office and 'What wis wrong wi' ye ?' Ah mind yince ah telt him ah wis off wi' diarrhoea. 'Oh, aye, two days ?' 'Aye.' Then he says, 'Dia . . .' He couldnae spell the bloody word. 'Aw, tae hell,' he says, 'sick ! Ye were off sick.' He wis a good man, Russell. The next foreman – he looked after the sort o' oncost workers – Harry Dugan, he come from Auchendinny and he had a jazz band. He played one o' yon bloody dulcimer things. But he wis good, tae. Ken, Wullie Russell looked after the actual process workers, and Dugan looked after the transport workers and a' the boiler firemen and things like that. There were jist the two foremen.

The powder mill hadnae anything social. It wis jist the case in the wintertime they held one or two whist drives and dances in the Masonic Hall, and of course everybody wis there and everybody had a guid time. They held it in the Masonic Hall because it had a licence ! In Roslin itself there were two bowlin' clubs. Then there wis the British Legion. Well, of course ah joined that when ah wis demobbed in 1946. That's quite a thrivin' place now but at that time it wis jist an army hut, and the place belonged tae a Mrs Trotter, who had the Bush Estate. And she widnae allow the Legion tae have a licence. They had tae wait tae Mrs Trotter died afore they could get a licence ! Oh, she wis a right old aristocrat, ye know. But, ah mean, the Legion hut wis there rent free. Ye jist had tae do what Mrs Trotter said.

We a' walked tae work at the powder mill. Well, if ye cycled ye had tae leave your bike ootside. Ye werenae allowed tae take it in the factory. But, och, ah jist walked. Most o' us jist walked. It's jist along the top: ye went down the Powdermill Brae and the powder mill wis jist at the bottom, the gatehouse. But, as ah say, now it is part o' Roslin Country Park. The old huts have been demolished – they would have tae be. They couldnae allow anybody in afore the place wis cleaned up. And then there used tae be a carpet factory down there. It's demolished, too. And they had houses in the Glen. Well, ye see, that's all away now and it's all Roslin Country Park.[7]

As ah say, ah wis away for aboot four years roughly in the army and then ah come back there, and it wisnae long after that that the place was shut down. Ah cannae remember the exact date. After twenty-five years' service you got a silver watch, and for thirty years' service ye got a gold watch, and thirty-five years' service ye got a chimin' clock. Now ah never got any o' them. Ma father-in-law Bob Bolton wis retired before the powder mill closed and he got a chimin' clock for thirty-five years' service. It chimed every quarter o' an hour. And here he had a friend frae America and she couldn't sleep for this bloody chimin' clock, and she got up and stopped it and it never went again ! A braw clock it wis, ye ken ! He got a gold watch for thirty years' service in 1949, and the chimin' clock after thirty-five years, so ah think the powder mills must have closed soon after he retired in 1954.

After the powder mills wis shuttin' down there wis one or two men from Ardeer come and interviewed the workers. They offered a job at Powfoot in Dumfries, but ah wis married then and they couldnae guarantee ye would get a house. 'Oh, no,' ah said. Well, ah left the powder mill on the Friday and started at Esk Mills paper mill at Penicuik on the Monday.[8] As ah say, it wis who ye knew. Ah knew Jimmy Laing, the head joiner at Esk Mills – he come from East Calder, he wis the joiner in the oil factory – and ah jist went up and he took me tae see the manager and the manager says, 'Oh, jist start on Monday.' And that wis it. Ah got right away intae the engineers' shop as a fitter's mate. Ah wis never unemployed. All ma workin' life ah wis only on the dole for six weeks – when ah got ma books off o' the Royal Hotel at Roslin aboot 1931.

When ah went tae Esk Mills that wis a big change for me. Ah

32

wis lucky at Esk Mills, too, as ah got into the engineerin' shop, where ah made mates with Jimmy Martin, the engineer in charge o' the boilers. They made their own electricity, ye ken, and Jimmy Martin wis in charge o' that, well, if they had any breakdowns.

Ah think it wis around 200 people worked at Esk Mills when ah went there, oh, a bigger place than the powder mills. And it was different work altogether, ye ken. But ah got promoted a wee bit in the engineers' shop. There wis an old lathe there that had been made for grindin' tools, and of course down in the paper and that there wis machines for cuttin' the paper to exact sizes, and there wis circular knives. And ah got the job o' sharpening the knives. Ah worked this old lathe and there wis a stand beside it for the sharp knives and another one for the blunt knives and that wis ma main job.

At Esk Mills ye worked from eight till five, an hour for lunch. There were a canteen there, ye see. And workin' wi' the engineers you worked nearly every Sunday – about seven days a week – because when the machines were shut down that's when they got the maintenance done. Ye werenae allowed tae work wi' movin' machinery. So it wis only on a Sunday the maintenance wis done. I wis quite glad o' that because ma daughter Marion was goin' tae the university at that time and ah wis grabbin' all the overtime that wis goin'.

Ah wis paid over three shillins an hour in the gunpowder and ah went doon tae aboot 2/6d. an hour up there at Esk Mills. But, as ah say, we worked on Sundays at double time and that, and then we got quite a bit o' overtime, dependin' on what wis goin' on. It wis jist constant day shift, eight till five. Then ah had tae walk doon tae Penicuik tae get a bus home. That wis something ah wisnae accustomed tae, ah had bus fares tae pay. It wis quite a long day, och, well, ye had tae pit up wi' these things. At Esk Mills there wisnae anythin' like the dangers o' the powder mills. Ye jist went wi' your workin' clothes.

I was at Esk Mills aboot twelve or thirteen years. Ye see, Esk Mills got taken over by that Crown Wallpaper company. Well, they had paper mills, too. But, ye see, Esk Mills made paper for banknotes and they were after this big order. And when they made paper for banknotes the bank had representatives on the job. They looked after a' the cuttins and things and they saw that they were destroyed and all that. And that's what the Crown Wallpapers wis after – the orders for their English mills. Esk Mills and Valleyfield mill had tied houses for some o' their workers and Crown Wallpapers wisnae interested in that. They jist wanted orders. There wis a lot o' glamour girls havin' their photiegraphs taken at Esk Mills beside the bundles o' paper, ye know, and sittin' on barries and that. And the next thing we knew the place wis shuttin' doon ! It wis completely shut down. There were still aboot 200 workers at that time. We got our redundancy money and that. And then, och, ah wis lucky again. Esk Mills had a first class engineers' shop. The head engineer from Valleyfield paper mill, Mr Mackay ah think his name wis, he come tae buy machinery at the engineers' shop. And ah asked him if there wis any chance o' a job at Valleyfield. He asked me ma name, what ah worked at. 'Right,' he says, 'when this place shuts down come and see me.' And ah jist walked intae a job at Valleyfield. A lot o the Esk Mills workers come tae Valleyfield. But then there were a lot o' old men that didnae bother lookin' for a job, ye ken. Ah mean, men that had been at Esk Mills for donkey years got a lot o' money in redundancy. So a lot o' them didnae even bother.

When ah went tae Valleyfield in the later 1960s it wis the same number o' machines like, as at Esk Mills, four paper-makin' machines. Oh, there wis roughly 200 workers there as well. And then Valleyfield opened up a big new mill up at Pomathorn. It wis brand new and, oh, they made some special kind o' size o' paper and a lot o' them got jobs up there. There widnae be a hundred workers at Pomathorn, well, there wid be aboot eighty or so. So altogether there would be nearly 300 workers at Valleyfield.

Of course, the Valleyfield folk kind o' looked down on Esk Mills, ye ken. Oh, it wis sort o' rivalry, ah suppose. They said, 'Och, they cannae make paper at Esk Mills', ye ken. At Esk Mills they jist said the same thing aboot Valleyfield ! But ah liked both mills. Ah wis very lucky, as ah say, so far as work wis concerned. At Valleyfield ah hadnae tae walk sae far because the bus took ye down tae Valleyfield gate in the mornin' and round about five o'clock, when it wis lowsin', the bus wis up there instead o' bein' up at Penicuik Town Hall.

Well, ah worked at Valleyfield till ah wis 66. Ah wis over 66 when ah stopped work because Valleyfield was shuttin' down as well.[9] By that time ah wis the storeman in Valleyfield and ah wis kept on a bit longer than the rest because everythin' had tae be cleared up, ye know. Oh, it wis closed before ah retired because ah had tae stay there – ah mean, there were firms comin' tae break up machinery and ah had tae check oot the scrap and the brass and all that. Oh, ah cannae mind the dates but ah wis over 66 when ah finished.

Ah mind when Valleyfield shut down, there wis one man that ah knew very well. He wis a sort o' foreman where they made the paper-makin', and of course ah wis kiddin' him aboot redundancies. 'Redundancies ?' he says, 'The buggers wis £12,000 short.' He says, 'Ah made them short.' And he had aboot £5,000 or £6,000 redundancy. Of course, ah wisnae up there long enough tae get money like that ! But ah done a' right as well.

Well, lookin' back, oh, ah liked workin' in the powder mill. Ah don't know why. But it wis the first big job ah'd had. Ah, well, ah jist liked it. And then it wis near home. That wis one big consideration.

BARBARA SCOTT

Ma mother worked in the Roslin carpet factory for a little while and then she went into the powder mill, too. It must have been the First World War. She used to tell me that ah should never go into the gunpowder mill because ah wisnae very strong, ye see. But ah had tae end up there. And ah had two uncles killed in the powder mill.

I was born in Dryden Place, Roslin, the 4th of April 1920. Ma mother belonged Roslin, ma father belonged Fauldhouse. He wis a windin' engineman in the coal mines. Well, actually, ah think he wis in the Fauldhouse mine. And then I didnae keep well so we moved back into Roslin again.

Ah think ma mother and father met through the army really in the First World War. He wis in the Royal Army Medical Corps, ah think he would be stationed at Glencorse, and ma mother wis in the Roslin carpet factory – most o' the women were. They met possibly at dances or something like that they went to, and they got married during or just after the war. I'm the one and only child, ah wisnae blessed wi' brothers or sisters.

Ma father followed his father's footsteps – he wis also a windin' engineman. He drew the men up in the cages. I have jist a vague memory of ma father's mother. Ah think before she was married she would be in service, domestic service. Ma father had about three or four brothers and sisters. Ah think he wis the eldest.

Ma father was working in the Moat colliery at Roslin when I was born and then maybe after a year or two they moved back to Fauldhouse. Ah didnae go to school till ah wis about seven because ah had tuberculosis. Ah wis in East Fortune sanatorium in East Lothian for nine months. It must have been when ah wis four or five, I would think. And they had to travel in the train from Fauldhouse to there. And that's the reason why they came back through to Roslin because seemingly the weather in Fauldhouse didnae suit me, ye see.

Ah remember having T.B. and being in hospital, very much so, because as far as ah can remember about ma father ah think he wis the instigator o' gettin' a school built there at East Fortune. Ah'm sure ah heard him talkin' about it, that he thought it better if they could build a sort o' school there. Ah think it had jist sort o' been built by the time ah wis due tae leave. Ah think ah wis about five, you see, when ah took T.B., ah'm no' awfy sure. Ah jist remember feeling no' very well and ah wis taken to the hospital through there. There were quite a lot of children there at that time.

Ah think ah wis in bed all the time ah wis there, more or less. The only thing ah can mind sometimes when we used to stand in the cots, and that type o' thing. It wis a high-sided cot. Ah don't think we were in the open air, ah think we were a' closed in. Ah wis in hospital nine month. Ma parents come by train from Fauldhouse to visit me. If ah mind ah think they jist came at the week-ends.

When ah came back to Roslin we stayed wi' ma granny Neil. Ah'm called Barbara after her. Ma grandfather wis killed in the Moat pit, but as far as ah know that wis before ah wis born. Ah didn't know him at all.

Ah remember ma granny's house in Dryden Place, Roslin. It wis jist a room and a kitchen. Ma granny had about seven o' a family. Some o' them wis married, of course. But two o' ma mother's brothers were still living in ma granny's house. Ah had an uncle lost a leg in the First War, you see, so he wis there. He had the kilt and ah think it wis the Seaforths he wis in. Aye, it was a Highland regiment because he showed us the kilt and everything. And then he had a younger brother there but he never wis in the war. He wis much younger than him. He wis the youngest in the family. So there was ma granny, ma mother, myself, and ma mother's two brothers. See, they had double beds in the room. Ah think the two brothers would stay in that bed and maybe ma granny wis in that one and me and ma mother wid be in the back room. Either that or maybe the men got the back room, and then the women wis a' in the front. Ah think it's more liker it, aye, because, ye see, ye had the fire and that sort o' thing. Aye, ah think the men wis through the back.

Ma granny's house didn't even have a toilet. Ye'd tae go outside for the toilet. Ye had tae come out the front door and round the side. We bade on the ground floor. Well, there were two houses upstairs, one on either side o' the stair, ye see. There wis a long landing and ye had two houses, one on top o' that house, and one on top o' this house. And the people up the stair they had tae come away down and go away up past the garden. And that wis their toilet. But ours wis under the stair outside. It was a flush toilet. The neighbours upstairs were flush, too, but they were away beside the . . . It wis built, ah think, at the end o' most o' the coal places. Ma granny's neighbour on the ground floor shared our toilet.

And then another thing was for a wee while ma father was still in Fauldhouse. So actually he didnae stay much in Dryden Place. He visited us. Ah think he wis away all week till about the week-ends. It maybe jist depended on his shifts, and he cycled over then. He cycled from Fauldhouse to Roslin, 'cause ah can remember ma mother and I used tae go with him, up to – ah think he went the Balerno wey somewhere – so we went maybe part o' it wi' him, Damhead and through that way. Ah remember him coming and leaving. It wis a long way, ah dinnae ken how many miles – twenty or twenty-five ? Oh, it must have been further than that.

Ah started school when ah wis seven at Roslin. But ah think by that time ma father got the offer o' a house which belonged tae the pit, and then he came tae stay in Roslin. It wis a tied house, in Springfield Place. Ah remember that house. We had a sittin' room and a middle bedroom and then the livin' room and a toilet. It had no bath. It wis much better than ma granny Neil's house. The under-manager and ah think it wis the head engineer, they lived in Springfield Place. They were at the far end, nearer where we ca'ed the station, ye see. There wis one down the stair and one up the stair. But they had better houses than ma father's. Ah think they had an extra room there. They had a bathroom combined.

And, ye see, in Springfield Place we had a front and a back door. And when the children that came away from Rosslynlee, well, they walked from there right down to Roslin School, up the Powdermill Brae, and on a frosty day they couldn't stay outside – ah mean, if the toilets at the school wis frozen – we took some o' them in to our toilet. And they also had their piece and they jist had something from us. And they had tae eat their lunch there, ye see. Ma mother looked after them on wintry days, jist when we were there. Quite a lot o' the people at Roslin had tae do that, ye see, because there were quite a lot o' children frae the farms round about – Gourlaw and round that way. Gourlaw's towards Rosewell. Ye went up through Roslin Castle station and then Rosslynlee station and the farms wis jist roond aboot that. So these children had tae walk at least two or three miles and back again at night. Well, the people in Roslin took the children in and made sure they were all right on wintry days. Oh, they were quite pleased, ye see, because, well, they couldnae get the toilets or anything like that. Ah think maybe the teachers would jist ask if we could take them home. Most mothers would agree to do that. And then they were gettin' the heat when they had their lunch. And of course if it happened to snow before the school got out they sent them home right away before it got too dark, ye see.

The headmaster at Roslin village school wis Mr John Watson. There were eight teachers, ah think. Oh, there must have been maybe three or four hundred children. That wis the only school in Roslin. And if ye passed what we called the Qualifyin' ye either went tae Lasswade or Watson's. Ye ken, he had a class above the Qualifyin', Mr Watson. Ye maybe got bakin' and sewin, and the boys got joinery and that type o' thing. But if ye passed your Qualifyin' you went to Lasswade, that's a High School. Ah never went there, no, ah never went there. Ah sat the Qualifyin' but ah didn't get a place at the High School. Ah would have liked to have gone. Ah was quite keen on the school, up tae a point. Ah wis quite interested in history and geography, funny enough, ye ken. Ah wisnae bad at the spelling either. Ah'm a grand reader but ah never wrote essays !

Ah would like to have been a nurse. But then ah discovered

that ah wid never have been able to stay the pace with bein' this, ye see, asthmatic, well, no' asthmatic – bronchial – until that sort o' cleared. Well, ah'd like tae have had the education that wid have taken iz on tae something like that. But ma parents jist said, 'Well, ye're fourteen – to work.' And that wis it. They were more or less keen that ah should leave the school then. Well, ah jist think money wise, because ah wis jist there for a wee while and they started tae build a house so they would need the money.

Ma parents had moved again, from Springfield Place to Wallace Crescent. But that again wis the pit, ye see. That wis a better house, that wis two bedrooms and a livin' room, and a full bathroom. Oh, ah had a bedroom tae maself, oh, aye, and there wis a bath. We had electric light there – and ah think we had electric light in Springfield Place. Ma granny Neil, well, of course she had the gas by that time. But she wid be the one wi' the oil lamps. They had tae go on a Saturday tae clean them. She wis bedridden after that, ye see. Uncle Sam that had the missin' leg, he used tae leave it ready. Ah had tae polish his shoe that wis on that artificial leg and the other shoe. Oh, ah had some fun ! Then, of course, ma father had built a bungalow. Well, he got a builder frae Roslin, well, one o' the joiners frae Roslin got them that. Quite a few houses wis built along the Manse Road then, ye see.

Well, in thae days, if ye were aboot fourteen, ready tae leave the school, they jist sort o' released ye and ye went tae your work, if there wis work about. Ah went after a job in Edinburgh, in Blair's, next to the Empire Theatre, for tae be a seamstress. My mother had an old aunt, she wis head o' the seamstresses in there. And when we applied for the job she didn't think it would suit me because of the bronchitis. I had developed bronchitis, too, ye see. And she says she didn't think it would be good enough for me always bending most of the day, plus the fact if ma parents had to pay your bus fare. Ah think that stood in the way. Ah haven't a clue how much it was to get into Edinburgh, ah can only mind when ah wis able tae go in the bus it wis a shillin' return. So it wis a lot o' money for ma parents tae find.

Ah wasn't really disappointed at not getting a start as a seamstress, because ah had two cousins. A brother o' ma mother's he had twin girls and of course ah used tae pal wi' them. And they went to the carpet factory in Roslin Glen. So ah went, too. We sort o' all went together because we were a' aboot the same age. Ah left school on the Friday and more or less started in the carpet factory the next week. Ye didnae get much time.[10]

Ah think the factory started frae about eight o'clock till about five in the afternoon, if ah mind right. Ye couldnae go home for your lunch, no' for the short period – ah think maybe jist half an hour. Morning and afternoon there wis a break, it must have been in about ten minutes. We had a wee canteen, because ah aye mind o' havin' a wee green teapot, ye see. Ah cannae remember if we worked on Saturday mornings. Maybe somebody else can mind.

We trained at what they termed boxers, that wis actually changin' the colour in the boxes for what they termed drums. The thread for the carpets wis rolled round the drums, ye see. Then there wis a little sort o' machine and you popped the boxes in there and another woman she just worked handles and that, and that drove the thing underneath. Then when she had that colour done she would ask for a number which was on the boxes and you changed the one box to the other. So that drum wis jist about four feet wide, that size.

But then ah went from there tae what they termed the fifty-four size. That wis much bigger, but narrower. That's 54 inches in height. Then for a wee while ah worked on the seventy-twos. Ah think there were jist two drums belongin' that. So it took four o' us tae carry the full length. Most o' them were sort o' peacock designs and that, for churches maybe and something like that.

And where they got the colour to fill the boxes we had to have large jugs, ye see, and we went to another big place, called the colour shop, and we filled these jugs. Maybe we could manage two at a time. Of course, the number wis on the jugs o' the colour ye wanted, too. It wis dye we filled intae the jugs for the carpets, to fill this wee box, ye see, which run underneath. Well, it wid run dry if it hadnae been filled up. Once the box wis dry we jist went and filled the jugs when we had a spare minute tae go. It depended on the amount o' colour they used, ye see. Like maybe for a border it maybe wis jist used once on one or two o' the drums. But then if it wis, say, a red, ye maybe had tae keep fillin' it every so often. It wis tirin' work, oh, ah wis quite tired at the end o' the day. But it didnae affect ma health, not as far as ah know. It wis quite a clean job, well, except for the dye on your hands.

Well, that's what ah started on at the carpet factory in 1934, '35. Some other young girls might start on the yarn. Well, there wis a yarn place an' a', ye see. Some o' them put them round and made them intae things so that they could bring them into bobbins and put them on the drums and that. The drums went round and filled from the bobbin, ye see.

Ah think the wages were jist about £2 a fortnight. Ah wis paid fortnightly. Maybe some o' them wis paid weekly, maybe dependin' on the jobs.

Oh, it wis a noisy factory. The machinery went good. It wis difficult tae talk.

Widnell & Stewart owned the factory, the same as the Bonnyrigg one. Ah couldnae tell ye how many workers in the Roslin factory, oh, it must have been about a hundred or two hundred, because there were different sections, ye see. Oh, there wis more men than women, something like two-thirds men and one third women, aye, something like that. I knew quite a lot o' the workers. And when I went there wis a family called Handley. Well, the father wis the sort o' supervisor o' where I worked, ye see. Well, his son took over by the time I went there. So they used tae call them Young John and Old John. But the Handleys wis there for quite a wee while. They stayed in Roslin, too. Ah knew them before ah went to the factory.

There wis a lot frae Rosewell. They walked from Rosewell down to the carpet factory, ah think that's nearly three miles, easy. We walked too from Roslin but we werenae sae bad. We come down what they termed the Jacob's Ladder, or more so rather down by the Castle: there were steps down that way, too. Oh, it didnae take that long to walk, ten minutes or so.

Ah don't mind a trade union, not there, no. Ah wasn't a

member of a trade union there, not that ah remember. It sort o' wouldnae interest me so much about that.

Ah liked the work in the carpet factory. Ah think ah wis about three years there and then ah moved from there up tae the paper mills – Valleyfield. Ah wis seventeen when ah left the carpet factory – 1937, as far as ah can mind. It wis jist before the war started. Ah think it wis goin' sort o'slack, ye know, they werenae gettin' the same work and that type o' thing. The two cousins that ah had they had moved up there tae the paper mill, ye see. And ah think, too, they got a better thingmy wi' the money. Ah suppose they spoke for me at the paper mill.

Ah think it wid be before ah went tae the paper mill ah remember one time goin' to the Penicuik Store, the Co-operative, for a job there. Well, ah would have more or less preferred then tae be an office worker. Ah think ah passed the test, but ah had a relative workin' in the Penicuik Store at the same time: ma cousin Jim, he wis the butcher in the Store. And in thae days they were very strict. Therefore they widnae take two relatives at the one time. So ah heard anyway. But then it wis a girl o' eighteen that got the job: it wis only supposed tae be frae sixteen and seventeen. But how ah couldnae understand wis, if there wis a relative in the Store by rights they werenae supposed tae serve ye, so the Store must have had tae trust them an awfy lot that they werenae servin' anybody belongin' them. It wis a funny rule, I thought, oh, aye, it was queer. It wis the Store office that ah wid have liked tae have been intae when ah started work.

Ma first job at Valleyfield wis parcelling paper and it had tae be exact – that lady that taught us what to do. Well, ye got like writin' paper or something, say, two bundles o' writin' paper, and put them intae brown paper, and a certain length, and then ye folded them over and then made sure that the ends of the brown paper wis properly done before it wis parcelled up. It wis jist sort o' packin', ah wis known as a packer.

Ah cannae mind what ma wages were at the start. But they were more than ah'd got in the carpet mill. Ah think it wis three pounds odds. Ah think maybe it was a fortnight, aye, that would be right. Ah jist used tae hand mines all over tae ma mother more or less, except, well, a sweetie or somethin' like that. She gave me ma bus fare and that. Ah cannae remember what ma pocket money was – a sixpence, a shillin'. We didnae pay so much attention then, oh, well, ah didnae anyway. And of course if ye went tae the pictures or that, maybe on the Saturday, ye could get more then. Ah wis then a girl o' seventeen.

But ah went frae the packin' up tae the salle, as they talked aboot, for overhauling. Well, ah jist sort o' turned the paper over tae see that there wis no knots or anything like that in it, jist checkin' the paper.

The hours at Valleyfield wis about eight o'clock tae five, because we used tae catch the half-past seven bus up from Roslin. The women only worked one shift in the paper mill, as far as ah remember. The men they could maybe have worked different shifts. Then we managed tae get the five o'clock bus there from Penicuik, depends on what time we got up, ye see, because we had tae go right away down and round Bridge Street tae get intae the mill. It wis on the far side o' Penicuik from Roslin. It wis quite a long journey for me. And we had tae pay our fares. The mill didnae pay our fares. But we got wir dinner free if ye were three miles outwith the limit. There's a place that looks like a church – somebody said it wis a school – well, that's where we got wir dinner at Valleyfield.[11] Ye had to be outwith three miles, and we got it free. That wis quite a boon then. Some o' them that wisnae beyond, they paid so much. But all the workers could go there if they wanted tae go. The food wis very good – about two courses, ah think there wid be, soup and meat or pudding.

Ah cannae mind about a trade union at Valleyfield, ah cannae mind joinin'. Ah wisnae active at a'.

The people ah worked beside at Valleyfield were mainly women, in both the packin' and the overhauling. The only man that was there wis tae take away any big reams and reams o' paper, ye see, and he drove it in this wee trolley thing and took it downstairs once we had packed it, wherever it wis goin' tae. In the overhaulin' it wis a woman foreman, ah cannae mind her name. And there wis a woman foreman at the packin', although there wis men – they used the guillotines tae cut the paper for what we were packin', ye see. They put them intae sort o' heaps.

That wis a man's job. There wis three at that machine. And then through the other place there wis other things where mostly men worked, because they sent me for a left-handed screw driver ! Ah never found one ! That wis the usual trick, of course, when ye started – either that or a long stand. And when ah wis in the carpet factory ah wis tae go for a brush tae sweep the steam out the pipes. Ah didnae go – and ah never had a long stand either !

Oh, the paper mill wis a much cleaner job than the carpet factory. Ah enjoyed it more. They were friendly workers in both places. Oh, I thoroughly enjoyed that.

Ah cannae remember how many other girls came from Roslin to Valleyfield. It wisnae a full bus in the mornin'. It wis a double decker bus most o' the time. But there wis quite a few o' them, right enough, there must have been twenty or thirty women. They were in different departments, ye see. It's a possibility some would go tae Esk Mills. Of course, there would be maybe other workers for different places, ye see. They weren't all necessarily for the paper mill.

Ah didn't feel an outsider in the paper mill, they didn't shun ye because ye came from Roslin, no, no. We joined their tennis club and that, too, ye see, at Valleyfield. The mill had its own tennis courts, where the water tank used tae be, half-way up Kirkhill. We played mostly in the evenings. We came home and got a bus at night time.

And then the work wis slackened off there an' a' in the paper mill. It wis only three days a week it wis goin' tae be. It would be in aboot '38, '39, a few months before the outbreak o' the war. Ah think it wis tae do wi' orders more than anything. They were losin' the orders to what they normally got. But what caused it ah don't know. So we got the offer to work in what they called the rag house. The rags were a' clean, of course, we jist took the buttons off them. And ah worked in there a wee while. That wis jist tae sort o' have the week's work instead o' going on three days a week for the paper.

Then, of course, we were drafted frae there intae the powder mill. Ye see, they started gettin' us registered for the Forces. Well, ah must ha' been at Valleyfield tae what – '39 would it be ? It wis jist after the war broke out because we were sent down tae

Loanhead tae go on the register. The Ministry o' Labour had an office down there, down towards the Polton Mill brae. Then ah got a letter sayin' ah would have tae go tae the powder mill. A crowd o' us must have a' went from the paper mill tae the powder mill. Oh, ah knew quite a lot o' the other girls who went as well. That's when we met Mrs Neil and her crowd. Ah think it wis the end o' '39 ah went tae the powder mill. Oh, it wisnae half a bad winter in '39. That wis when we went down the Jacob's Ladder then, more so than goin' to the carpet factory. Ah remember Dunkirk very much, ah wis in the powder mill then. Ah wid be aboot nineteen or twenty when ah went.

When ah first went tae the powder mill ah think ah went tae what they called the smoke floats, which wis supposed tae be tae do wi' the navy, see. And everything wis brass. We had brass rods and brass – now what would ye ca' it, where they put the powder in ? It wis like a milk churn, a sort o' churn idea. And we pressed the gunpowder in wi' this big brass pole and we had tae use masks. It wis white gunpowder, if ah mind right. Ah suppose the smoke floats would cause a smoke screen. Nobody ever explained tae us what we were doing. It wis jist something that we heard o', aye ! But ah had tae ask off o' there because it affected ma chest. Ah had tae get a doctor's line.

Then ah wis moved there tae do wi' celluloid discs, pasted them with – it wis sort o' like a varnish. And we laid them out on a board until they dried wi' this . . . and then we dipped them in the powder and that wis tae do wi' the Air Force. But what they were used for, ah mean, ah never enquired but they were jist somethin' tae dae wi' the engines for the Air Force. There wis quite a lot o' them. But naebody said a word tae me what it was for, ah think that was because o' wartime secrecy, ah think so, more or less, aye. Maybe we werenae interested enough tae ask either, ye see. Maybe some o' the rest o' them could explain tae ye.

Ah did that job most o' the time, most o' the time. There was once ah wis sort o' short o' a job and they put me on tae wee bullet things. Ah filled them wi' black powder, ye see. That would be for something like Verey pistols. And then somebody else would put the top on them and lay them. Ah didnae work in that very often, jist when ah wis a bit slack in the disc things.

And then they took two o' us jist tae work two shifts, and we were sent doon to what they termed the bottom mill, where they had a powder house jist – no' actually a powder house, but a workin' house – half way down, ye see. But we mainly went back up to the top mill. Then ah wis moved right down to the bottom mill and worked down the bottom mill till ah left in '44.

Ah think there were more men than women workers at the powder mill, owin' tae the type o' work it wis, ye see. Ah wisnae the youngest woman there, oh, no, there would be younger than me ah would think. There wis one, well, she wis maybe a couple o' year younger than me. But when she married she went away tae Rosewell.

There wis men and women actually came frae Rosewell tae work at the powder mill. There wis quite a few from Rosewell, and one or two frae Loanhead. There wis a Mr Fairley that used tae stay at Kirkhill in Penicuik. There wis a crowd frae Auchendinny, Mrs Neil's crowd. They started frae Auchendinny, walked on the railway and got the railway along to the powder mill. Well, ye had tae be there for six o'clock – that wis the day shift like – so there werenae many trains before that, ye see. Ah don't think there wis much danger. As long as they werenae caught in the tin tunnel they were a' right. But the majority o' the workers more or less, ah think, wis Roslin. Ye went away down Jacob's Ladder in Roslin Glen, and right up and away up the hill again and on to Roslin Castle station. It wis a mile and a half anyway, it wis quite tiring.

And there were workers came from Camilty, near West Calder. There wis quite a lot o' them came there in the morning, on the day shift jist. They worked jist a day shift, like they must have started about half-seven or something till maybe four or that in the afternoon. They didnae come in a special bus, they come more or less either in taxis or cars. They must have been laid on by the powder mill, ah think, although one or two did stay in Roslin. They had digs in Roslin.

We were on three shifts. Well, it wis six till two day shift, two till ten back shift, and ten till six in the mornin'. Ye worked one week at each shift – six till two for a week and then ten till six the next week. But ah cannae mind o' workin' in the afternoon there. But ah did when ah went down to what they termed the bottom mill. Ah'm sure we worked on a Saturday, tae. But if it wis the night shift, ye see, we finished at six in the mornin', because ah mind o' bein' there when somebody wis gettin' married. We could see her at the church frae where we were workin'. Ah don't think she worked in the powder mill. She used tae work in the carpet factory, ah knew her in the carpet factory. She stayed in the Glen actually.

Ah cannae mind now if the wages wis more or about the same as the paper mill. Ah wis on piece work at the powder mill. Ah think we did get more money than in the paper mill, when ah think o' it. Ah gave ma wages to ma mother. Ah still lived at home.

The powder mill wis separate huts. They had a gatehouse right at the gate – ye see where the big gate is at the bottom o' the brae ? The gatehouse wis right in front o' ye. There wis a wee bend further up, it wis jist at the top o' Jacob's Ladder, jist before the hairpen bend. Ye didnae go round that hairpin bend – that wis leadin' back tae the carpet factory again. The powder mill wis away up towards Rosslynlee way. There were woods all around it. If ah can mind: through the big gatehouse and then there wis the big place where this uncle o' mine wis killed. And ah think there wis another house then – they ca'ed them houses, not huts – and then there wis a big openin' where the canteen wis and where they went for the store room and that, ye see. Then ye turned away tae the left, ye see, it wis covered wi' the wee railway. Then ye went right round and away towards the left. Now I know there is a house there but I never worked in it. Then there wis wee different places and sometimes on a Sunday if we werenae busy we went for walks and tried tae find out where other places were. The joiners' shop was miles – quite a long, long walk in. Oh, the huts were very dispersed. Then there wis a sort o' engine idea, away towards – well, ye see, we talked about the Cleuch. But that wis jist the road down, but most o' the houses lay jist quite near that. Ah think they've built houses, or they had caravans – it's a' changed now. And that's where Mr Paris worked. Oh, the whole thing covered quite a large area but they were smallish houses.

The number o' workers in each house, well, it depended on the size o' the house, ye see. When ah wis down in the bottom powder mill ah think it held about four. Ah mean, there were plenty space but ye had tae have, because we had tae lay all thir trays out – jist like a piece of cardboard and ye had tae lay all these discs on them, ye see. And what we were supposed tae do wis tae paint them wi' this stuff and then pop them into the powder and lay them out to dry. Well, ah know we shouldnae have did it, but ah've seen us jist thingmyin' like that and throwin' them intae a big bundle and then layin' them all out, jist tae get so many done within the time.

Oh, there were very, very strict regulations. They had a gatehouse right at the gate. And everybody wis searched for matches or cigarettes, well, the women were no' physically searched, sort o' jist asked, ah think, if ah mind right. Ah cannae mind aboot a woman searchin' the women. Ye were asked, 'Have you got any . . . ?' Ye jist said ye didnae smoke, ye see. Ah never smoked myself. There wouldnae be so many women maybe smoked then so much. Anywey, the men, ah think, were searched. And then, later on, if the men needed a smoke, or anybody needed a smoke, they had tae come back out tae the gatehouse before they lit up. Oh, the mill people were strict, very, very much so.

We hadnae tae wear rings nor nothing, no kirby grips nor nothing. No metal. No earrings nor nothing like that, no jewellery at all. No stays or anythin' like that. Oh, if the women goin' tae work had stays on they wid have tae take them off in the changing room. Maybe they jist didnae wear them, ye see, it wid be easier. Because thae things that were in the stays, ye see, they were sort o' metal stuff.

Of course, we had tae use the uniforms supplied. We had heavy overalls and hats made o' strong quilt sort o' stuff, sort o' heavy material anyway. Oh, it wis fireproof, very, very heavy material. Ye had jist wir big thick overalls and the hat wis the same material. Well, we had boots, we were a' supplied wi' boots, leather boots. And then for anybody that had jist tae come and visit ye, like the overseer or that, there wis big rubber boots. Ye slipped your feet intae them and ye walked round. But ye had always tae leave them inside the door, ken, before ye came oot.

So ye went through the gatehouse – and we walked straight in wi' ordinary shoes. Then we went to a sort o' canteen place and if ah mind right we put wir coats there and put on wir uniform things. And we walked from there up to our huts, wherever we were sent to. And then we had tae always change our shoes, take our shoes off at the door and change intae boots in wir building. Ye weren't allowed in any buildin' without changing your feet first.

Ah think the workers they more or less took care. They werenae accidents at the powder mill very often, not that I can remember. The only accident while ah wis there was for Uncle Dave.

Ah had two uncles killed in the powder mill. They were both ma mother's brother-in-laws. And they were both married on the one person – both married to ma mother's sister, Barbara, the same name as me. She wis widowed twice by explosions at the powder mill. She wis Manson for her first husband. Ah think he belonged the north, the Highlands, aye. And then this wis David Malcolm that she met and married and stayed in Loanhead after that. She wis a sad woman tae lose two husbands, oh, aye. But she did no' so bad. She had two o' a family, two boys to her first husband, ye see. David Malcolm's in Loanhead Cemetery. He belonged Loanhead. But the other one, Alex Manson – ah think it wis jist bits and pieces. So ah heard the story. They never ever said. Manson's buried in Roslin. But David Malcolm, he was in the first big powder house. Actually just what he did there ah never found out. They've never really found out as far as ah know what happened, whether he hadnae changed his boots or somethin', maybe somethin' ignited. One mornin' he had another fellow with him and he had gone away, but there wis a big wall between the two. And he went away to take down the black-outs – this was durin' the Second World War. Now this must have been about half-seven in the morning. And his neighbour had gone to lift the black-outs, ye see, and there'd been a slight explosion and he found David Malcolm on the floor. And he lived tae about eleven o'clock. The first husband

Manson wis killed it would jist be after the First World War. There were twenty years between the two.[12]

Ah wis quite surprised that ma aunt Barbara let David Malcolm go there tae the powder mill, because he worked in the brick work up at the Moat pit before that. And when ah heard that he had got the job in the powder mill, ye know what ye feel like after having one husband . . . He went there durin' the war. He wis killed in the March and ah wis married in '43, and his wee lassie wis eight years old when her daddy wis killed. Ah mind that mornin' we were sittin' at our breakfast and ma husband wis goin' oot, and ah cannae mind if ah wis goin out – no, maybe ah wis left the mill by that time. Ah didnae stay long there after ah got married in '43, a few months. Ah think ma Uncle Dave was killed jist after ah left. Ah remember, too, ma husband comin' in and sayin' they had been told tae go and work in the same place as ma uncle had worked in. He got a job beside the other man.

Ah met ma husband in the powder mill. He stayed in Rosewell actually. But he belonged the Borders. At the powder mill ma husband worked what they termed a bogie. He had a horse-drawn bogie and he ferried the powder, he went all over the powder mill deliverin' this powder, ye see, black powder, as far as ah can mind. Where the canteen wis and where they went for the store room and that, ye turned away tae the left and it wis covered wi' the wee railway for ma husband tae use the horse. Ah never thought tae ask ma husband about the horse's shoes. They wouldnae have been ordinary metal horse shoes, oh, they would have caused sparks. Because, ah mean, he went quite quickly through. Then there wis through tunnels, oh, it wis a very old works.

Ah didnae join a union at the powder mill, although we paid a pound, we did pay a pound for something. I can remember that. Ah think it wis more or less a sort o' savings thing. Ah cannae ever mind o' paying the union at all. Possibly there wis a union but they had never come tae ask, as far as ah can mind.

The manager o' the powder mill wis Mr Cattle. He stayed in Edinburgh, in yonder at Fairmilehead. The only time ah came in contact wi' him – actually, the work wis slackenin' off and to give us work, if we liked we could go up and work in the big house, which wis his offices, ye see. We went up and made his tea and cleaned the offices.

I used tae laugh, because if we worked on a Saturday, ye see, day shift or that, or sometimes even through the week, we jist got home and got somethin' tae eat, and dressed and went away to the dancin' and that. We went to Edinburgh, the Cavendish at Tollcross. Of course, ye'd sometimes have the pictures in Penicuik and the pictures in Loanhead. Then the dancin' at the Cowan Institute in Penicuik. Oh, ah liked dancing, and then there wis a Scout dance, too, on a Saturday night sometimes. But that wis in the paper mill more or less, ye see. I went to the dancin' jist whenever I was able to go. I didnae feel too tired to go. Ma husband he wisnae a dancer, he wisnae a dancer. Oh, ah enjoyed the dancin'.

Well, as ah say, ah wis married in '43. Ah wis at the powder mill for a wee while after that, till in aboot 1944. Ah think it wis mainly jist sort o' men that wis left latterly. Well, it wis gettin' slacker and slacker, ye see. We had jist tae give up after that. And also there was an explosion at Ardeer, in the Ayrshire mill. Ah can remember an explosion at Ardeer before ah worked at the Roslin powder mill. Now that must have been about '37, '38, because ah aye mind we were expectin' Prince Edward tae be the king, sort o' style. We had two brothers from Ardeer that worked there and we kept them, two brothers, one frae Stevenston and the other one wis a wee place jist near hand. They lodged wi' ma mother in Roslin. Ardeer had blown up then and, ye see, quite a lot o' people in Roslin put them up till they could go back tae Ardeer after it started again. It wis jist tae keep them in a job, ye see. They were at Roslin and then they went away home at the week-ends.[13]

Ah didn't have a job after ah left the powder mill about the end o' 1944. Ah jist helped ma mother and that type o' thing, helpin' in the house and lookin' after ma husband because he wis still on the three shifts, ye see. Ah wis stayin' wi' ma parents because we couldnae get a house, ye see. Then ah had a son. Ah remained a housewife. And then ma husband gave up the powder mill tae work wi' ma Uncle Sam Neil that lost his leg in the First World War. Uncle Sam wis a coal merchant. As far as ah know, when he came back from the war, ye see, the villagers at Roslin had started him off wi' sort o' sellin' dishes and that type o' thing. They must ha' put up the money for him. Well, he must have made something oot o' it, because he gave that up and started up a business with the coal and sort o' sticks. Ma husband started to work to him but he wisnae gettin' very far money wise. So he got the offer o' bein' the chauffeur at Beeslack House and we moved up there.[14] Ah started tae work again after ah lost ma son. He was ten year old. Ma mother died and ma son died the same year. Ah never had any more children. Well, ah didnae ken what tae dae and ah decided ah'd be a home help. Well, it wis something to do, ye see, because ma husband wis down at the House. Ah wis seventeen years a home help, mostly in Penicuik. And that's when ah started payin' a thing for the unions efter that.

Oh, workin' in the powder mill, ah think that wis the job ah enjoyed most. Aye, the company wis good.

ELIZABETH MCCORRY

Well, ma dad worked in the powder mills. I think he went to the powder mill about 1920. But, ye see, ah didnae want to really go to the powder mills because ma dad wis a foreman there. However, ah went away on ma own and ah got the things from the other foreman, Mr Russell. I think I was in the powder mills about three and a half years, something like that.

I was born at Bilston, jist as you go in to Roslin off the road from Edinburgh to Penicuik, on the 20th of August 1922. Well, ma grandfather, Tom Richardson, had the smallholdin' there and that's where we were all brought up. Ma mum and dad lived there and ma granny and grandpa. I have one brother and one sister, Richard and Chrissie, and a cousin Margaret that wis there before I wis born. Margaret's jist a year older than me. Her mother – ma mother's brother's wife – died when Margaret was jist six weeks old and, of course, ma granny bein' there Margaret was brought to us, ye see. Well, Margaret and I were brought up just like two sisters.

See where Bilston Glen pit was at Loanhead? Well, down there there was a small farm, Pathhead Farm. It was a dairy and that was ma grandfather's, and that's where ma mother was born. I think nearly all ma mother's family were born there. Oh, ma mum never had an outside paid job all her life. She worked wi' her father and that. When she wis young she went to Roslin wi' the eggs every week, because there wis hens, ye see. Ma mum didn't move very far in all her 96 years. She was at Pathhead farm and from there they came up to Bilston, where I was born, and then when the lease was out for the Bilston place we went to Auchendinny. Then when they built the new houses back at Bilston, ma mother came back to Bilston again. She hadn't really travelled five miles in all her years, you know. But she knew all

Roslin. All her old uncles were elders in the kirks, the different kirks: some went to one, and some went to the other.

Ma mum must have been born in 1897, because she was three years older than ma dad, and ma dad was born in 1900. Ma dad, Harry Dugan, belonged Stoneyburn in West Lothian and he worked in the pits through there, and then he came to Bilston and he went to work in the powder mills at Roslin. The pit he worked in at Stoneyburn wisnae worked out. I think he'd had an accident in the pit. He had a wee scar on his face and I think that finished him in the pits and then he came through here. My uncle, my mother's brother, married a Stoneyburn lady and my dad got friendly with him and that's how he met my mother.

Ma old Grandpa Dugan was a miner of course in West Lothian. Oh, I remember him perfectly: ginger hair and a ginger moustache. And he played the dulcimer as well and he sang.

Ah started the school at Roslin. Oh, I liked the school. I mean, I was just ordinary but I liked the school. Well, I had a lot o' friends at Roslin and I liked the teacher, Miss Murdoch. My cousin Margaret and I had to walk to school then from Bilston. It was a mile. Then I'd be seven or eight when ma mum and dad moved to Auchendinny, and then we went to Glencorse School. It wis a bigger school than Roslin, and at Glencorse School there were children from the barracks. And ye thought that they were great people. A lot of them had been abroad, oh, more excitin'. And ah can mind o' seein' the airship that wis in Edinburgh came over when we were at Glencorse School: what wis it – the R 101 ? And, oh, ah thought this wis the Germans ! That always stuck in ma mind about seein' that. [15]

And of course as you were gettin' older, well, you're gettin' cookery at the school. And ah liked drawin' and things like that. And, oh, the English and that wis a' right. Well, ah could have gone to Lasswade, like ah had passed the Qualifyin' exam tae go tae Lasswade. Ah'm all for children bein' educated, but it wis different when it was me. Well, ye see, when ah wis young it wis always the sort o' higher up folk's children that went tae Lasswade. Well, it wis usually the gaffer o' the mills, ye know, their families. Well, they were a wee bit – you know. The ordinary working class children tended not to go. Then you had to pay your own bus fares and all these things. Well, ma mother, as I say, had these other ones tae bring up and that. It wisnae like how they all go now. There were some that went to Lasswade from Glencorse School, but none out o' ma class. My age group they all left and went tae work. Well, everybody else wis gettin' jobs. So of course ah wis wantin' a job as well. Ah wis wantin' tae leave school tae work, tae get money. Ah left the school when ah was fourteen and ah went to work in the Auchendinny laundry.

Ma mum and dad didnae want me to go to the laundry. Well, ah wis determined tae go because ah wanted tae work and get money like the rest o' them ! Ah left school on the Friday and started in the laundry on the Monday, oh, somethin' like that. Other girls in Auchendinny had went to the laundry and they said, ye know, and ah went up and got started there. There were three o' ma friends, ye know, ah went tae school wi' them and we all started together more or less.

Auchendinny laundry wis up the road from the village as ye go to Leadburn and Peebles, up towards Maybank and you turn to go to Penicuik. Down in there – it's dog kennels now. It wis Cowan that had the laundry there, his wife was our old head-master Mr Ferguson's daughter. It wis different Cowans from the papermakers – maybe related but different Cowans.

It wisnae an awfy big laundry. Oh, I would say there would be sixty worked there maybe. The girls and women that worked there were from Penicuik and Auchendinny, Harper's Brae – round about, not from far away. Some o' them went tae the laundry and wis in the laundry all their life till they got married. There were men there as well, for the vans and different things, and an engineer in charge o' the machines. There werenae half a dozen vans, three or four. The van drivers were men. It was a small laundry. I think it wis a woman that wis in charge o' us. But, as ah say, ah wisnae that long there, jist months. Ah think ah wis only there about four months.

The job ah wis doin' in the laundry wis markin' the clothes that came in, ye know, puttin' these wee markins on. Ye'd tae write them on wi' a pen, ye know, in those days. Ye jist wrote it on the end, numbers, just like McCorry and a number sort o' thing. And then ye got up a bit. Ah liked when ah got up amongst the clean clothes.

Ah think it wis only seven shillins or somethin' a week at the laundry. Ah couldnae tell ye when ah started in the mornin', it's a long time ago. Oh, ye didnae get home for your dinner. There wouldnae be a canteen in those days, ye jist had tae sit and take your piece. No, there were no canteen then. There were no trade union, not that I remember, not at the laundry.

And then after that, of course, the Dalmore paper mill at Auchendinny was payin' more money.[16] Oh, well, ah went and asked. They put your name down then they sent for ye when they needed girls. That wis a common procedure. Of course if they asked, you know, if ye knew the families and that, well, we didnae have anybody in the paper mill. But, ah mean, all the local girls went there or, as ah say, the laundry. Ah went tae the paper mill a few months after ah had started in the laundry. And it was nearer hand. Ah got home for ma dinner and a' that sort o' thing.

At Dalmore we started at eight o'clock and we finished at five. We definitely finished at five and we had, ah think it was, an hour for dinnertime because we could come home and run back again. Well, ye got a break in the mornin', because some o' them came from Roslin, ye see, that worked in the paper mills, and ye got a break. They used tae carry a flask, ye see, and that. And on a Saturday mornin' – this was a highlight – the Roslin girls brought rolls from the bakery in Roslin. And we used tae have a bag o' crisps and we took our own bit butter. That wis only a Saturday we got that ! The Roslin girls brought rolls up and then we paid them. Oh, that wis a great thing, gettin' this. Well, there were the Store in Auchendinny but there were no' a baker's, gettin' fresh rolls like that. And it wis only a Saturday, 'cause they had tae come up wi' the bus, ye see. And some o' them walked as well from Roslin up tae the paper mill, that's about two and a half mile anyway. And this wis oor Saturday mornin'. Of course, we worked on Saturday.

There were quite a lot o' girls came from Roslin to work in Dalmore mill. I cannae think o' any men. There were a man came from Loanhead. He was the head joiner. And of course they cycled. And of course the head engineer and a' these people they had houses at Auchendinny station, ye know, the important people and that. It wis their children, some o' them, that tended to go to Lasswade High School then. There were whole families worked at Dalmore, whole families. Ah can remember the Hall family, and the father and the brothers were all in there.

There would be between a hundred and two hundred workers at the Dalmore mill when ah wis there, over a hundred anyway, because there were quite a lot o' women and there were women did men's work. Ye know, there were two women and they did men's work. They worked on the waggons for the ashes, the cinders and things. They worked there – Liz Mackay and Sis Hall, they were right worthies. Sis Hall came from Roslin. There were quite a lot o' women for they were on the overhaulin'. Maybe ah'd say about half and half men and women.

The work ah did, well, ah can still see maself sittin'. We worked at the cutters, we worked at the cutters. The paper came down off where they made the paper. They put the big rolls in, off the machine, and it came down and there were maybe four o' us sat along. Of course, there were men there, and we were the girls at the cutters. Well, there wis a long roll o' paper on the far side, and then it went through, and then it came up over, and then there were these knives that cut it, ye see. They were mechanical knives, it wis men that worked that. And we jist sat at the end o' . . . it wis like a big mill felt thing, and this paper came down the felt, and we took it off. There wis maybe three or four o' us sat. And then ye put this into these reams. We didn't count it, we put it into bundles, ye see, and then that went up the stair tae the overhaulin'. The thing went underneath and they lifted it up, it wis a hand thing, it wis jist like a barrow. Then they eventually took them on to the lift and took them upstairs. They checked the quality o' paper at the overhaulin', and then if there were any damaged bits they took it out. But ah wis never on the overhaulin', ah wis never up that stair.

The wages were 8/6d. a week at the paper mill – more than the laundry. Ah can always mind it wis 8/6d. ma first pay at Dalmore. We were jist paid a wage – 8/6d. Ah think you had to be about seventeen or eighteen before you got up the stair because, you see, they made their own pays and everything. They worked piecework – hard piecework it was called – whereas we were paid by the hour, a wage. Of course, it was an improvement on the laundry pay. Ah gave all ma wages to ma mum. I got half-a-crown pocket money in return.

The Dalmore wis Somerville's mill, and the manager was Mr Wallace. He didn't come round the mill often but we knew him. And of course he was on the council and everything then. He was a Conservative. He was the managing director and really the owner of the mill. He was in the big house and that, right beside the mill. Ah can remember under him some o' the gaffers wis . . . Davie Anderson he wis a gaffer. Ah can picture the assistant manager, a gentle old man he wis, but ah cannae remember about the name. Quite elderly but, ye know, a man that wouldnae say a wrong word. Ah can remember Thorburn wis the head engineer, and Jack Pratt wis the head electrician. It wis always men then that were foremen. It wis Mr Gowans wis in charge o' us at the cutters, oh, no women foremen, no, no, it wis a' men. Elder o' the kirk – Mr Gowans. I would say Dalmore was quite a friendly place. Ah wouldn't say you were driven by the management.

Ah think there was a union at Dalmore, but it wis jist coppers we paid. Ah wasn't active in the paperworkers' union. We paid the money. Ah never had any problems that took me to the union representative, no' really. Ah wisnae there long enough to do anything.

We got a week's holidays in July but then you didn't get paid. Ah went tae Burntisland each time wi' ma mum – ma mother ! We didnae get away wi' our friends when we were young, no' like the young ones now ! Ah did that from leavin' school until ah wis seventeen.

Ah didn't really enjoy working in Dalmore paper mill. It wis jist a job tae get money. Ah wis always wantin' tae be a nurse. Yes, I used to think I'd like to go away tae be a nurse. Well, sometimes the paper mill could be borin', 'cause, ah mean, you were continually doin' the same thing. But what job isnae boring ?! Ah wisnae old enough tae go up tae the overhaulin'. Well, you had to be a certain age, and then when people left, and things like that. You had to wait on somebody leaving. Ye see, people were at the jobs all their lives. You came to a certain age and of course you got up the stair when you were older. Ah think you would have to be eighteen. Ma cousin Margaret that wis brought up wi' me, she went tae the overhaulin'. I don't think there would be any overhaulers under eighteen. You had to be about seventeen or eighteen before you got up the stair, because they made their own pays and everything. Ah was in the paper mill at Dalmore for about three and a half years, till just after the outbreak of the war in 1939.

Some o' the houses in Auchendinny village belonged to the mill – up at Evelyn Terrace and Fountainhead. Fountainhead was on the other side o' the street. Well, of course the only ones that werenae mill houses wis the ones that belonged Dundas. That was Dundas of up at old Woodhouselee then – Winifred Dundas. They owned the house that we lived in. And they were related to the Dundases of Arniston. As ah say, it wis really Forbes' Buildins and then when Maule Ramsay – he wis the M.P. . . . that's how they're called Ramsay Gardens.[17] And that's where we stayed, this Ramsay Gardens. I can remember our house well. It wis a wooden outside stair at the back. We were upstairs, the Watsons were downstairs. Actually, there were three storeys. There were a cellar, because at one time that buildin' had been a hotel or something, because on the bedroom doors embossed you could see numbers. And in this cellar there were hundreds of bottles that were cleared out when the war came, because that wis our air-raid shelter. But, oh, the stair, ah can picture it. It wis a wooden stair, quite wobbly and up. And there were a cran, as we says, the tap for the water, out there. It wis at the stair there. Now there were no toilet, it wis a dry toilet. It wis downstairs, kind o' in the garden, but we could see if it was empty. It wis shared between the Watsons and us up above. That wis there. And we went up the stair. And we had a front door as well as a back door. It wis a long lobby out to the front and there were the passage and a big iron gate. And as years went on that wis taken away. When the houses were modernised that wis taken away, and what wis this lobby o' ours was givin' a room to the woman on the other side. And that's when we got the stair at the back and no front stair.

Now we went up the stair and first was a bedroom, and then there was the kitchen. Of course, long ago there had to be a bed in the kitchen. And there were a sink at the window. And we had gas lighting and I think we had one o' yon wee gas rings for cooking, and there was the open fire. But when Mrs Dundas did the alterations to the house and we got the back kitchen put on we had a gas cooker then and a gas boiler. And there were the larder. Ah wis at the school when that happened. It wis the Jubilee and they gave them a free rent.[18] But, well, we got the back kitchen built on. And it wis a toilet, of course, the flush toilet. That wis the first flush toilet we'd had. It wis outside when we were at Bilston, but that wis a' to oursel' at Bilston. But it wis lovely to have this flush toilet at Ramsay Gardens ! And we got the two sinks, a deep sink and the other sink. But no electric light, it wis gas. Ma mother didn't have electric light till she came back to Bilston. I can tell you when that was because ma daughter had her first birthday there: '49–'50. That wis the first time ma mother had lived in a house with electric light. But at Ramsay Gardens in Auchendinny it wis gas – we had the gas iron and a' these things. And they had the open fire, the range – that's where a' the cookin wis done. And a' the cleanin', oh, aye, and the oven, where the baking and everything was done. And then at the fireside there was a boiler, quite a small boiler, ye filled it and that there.

And then we had a big room. It wis called the parlour. That wis where the good furniture wis, and the piano wis there, oh, and an organ as well. And ma dad had a dulcimer and he had a piano accordion. Ye see, he wis musical. He had a band and that, you see. He played at dances, at barn dances and a' these things. We were brought up wi' music. But later on my husband used tae get his kill at the room we called the parlour. He says, 'Ye could put a golf ball there,' he says. The floor was sloped ! And not only that, they had great big floor boards. And when we first went to the house there had been rats in it !

And then we had another bedroom off o' this parlour, there were another bedroom through there. They had two double beds. Oh, it was quite a sizeable house, bigger than the houses in Evelyn Terrace. I think they had two bedrooms, the ones further down from us.

There were eight or nine of us at ma mum and dad's at Ramsay Gardens. There was ma grandmother Richardson, ma brother and sister and me, ma cousin Margaret. And then I must have been about seventeen, my aunt died. And, ye know, as she was dyin' she said to my mother would she take her two ? Well, one wis fourteen and one wis eleven. And they came tae live wi' ma mother. My mother – I don't know how she lived to be the age she was. She wis a hard working woman. She brought up six children – three of her own and ma three cousins. And she made no difference between us and my cousins: one didn't get any more than anybody else. So there were two boys and four girls in our house at Ramsay Gardens.

But in the back bedroom, of course, ma granny wis there then. And then there were ma sister Chrissie and ma first cousin Margaret and maself, we were there. And ma brother he had a bed in the room at the top o' the stair, as we talk about. And then when the other cousins came, of course the back kitchen had been built on and then there were a bed settee, ye see, and that wis put up in what wis the kitchen, the livin' room. The bed that used tae be there wis taken down and a bed settee was put up there. And ma brother and ma cousin used tae sometimes sleep there, because, ah mean, there were jist boys then, ye see. Ma granny Richardson died when ah was fourteen. Then an uncle came to live wi' us. He wis jist there a wee while till he got married. But ma mum had a lot o' work, ye know, washin' and cookin'.

And everybody that came got fed. Ah've seen sixteen and seventeen on a Sunday gettin' fed at ma mother's It wis a big mahogany table wi' big leaves, ye know, wide. Well, the table that wis in the parlour wis a round table tae begin with, and then she got the chance o' this one that wis kept in the kitchen. Well, we called it the kitchen and there were the scullery as we called the other bit. And it held a' that sittin' round it. Well, the other seven or eight visitors, when ma grandmother wis alive, that wis ma aunt, ma mother's sister, and she would come and bring some o' her family with her – children but, ah mean, some o' them were grown up. They were on a farm, it wis Gogar Mains farm at Turnhouse aerodrome, and they were allowed tae go round the perimeter o' the airfield and get out at Turnhouse, and they would visit granny on a Sunday. And the bus came into Auchendinny at eleven o'clock but it wis usually the two o'clock bus they came. And then the bus went at quarter to seven at night and quarter to ten, or else they had tae walk up to Glencorse. That's what everybody says: 'How your mother lived tae be that age !' She never grumbled, she jist had tae get on wi' it. Ah mean, when we got older and that, of course, we did the ironin'. And, of course, the menfolk's shirts, it was a' the hard collars then, ye know, the starch. Ma cousin Margaret says, 'Ah'm not touchin' the collars,' she would say, 'because if they're not right,' she says, 'we'll get the blame.' She used tae leave the collars for ma mother. The girls did the ironin' for the menfolk. Ma brother never did anything, and then the things that he did after he got married – ma mother says, 'Oh, he would never . . .' And ah says, 'No, because we did everything for him.' And ma granny didn't think that a man should do anything. The man's meal had tae be on the table and that. Oh, granny was a right old . . .

Oh, ah went tae the church. We went to Glencorse Church. We went to the Sunday School and then when we came of age we joined the church, and ah went to the church. And ah'll tell you when we were young, before we were left the school or anything, you were at the Sunday School. And then we came home and had a meal and then we were taken for a walk on a Sunday afternoon with ma mother and father, and sometimes away up round by Rosslynlee and down by Kirkettle and along the railway line back to Auchendinny – maybe about four or five miles anyway. But that wis jist the done thing. Ah mean, there wisnae the things then, ye see. Ah can remember when we got our first wireless. Ah wis still at school, Granny wis alive then. Of course, it wis the accumulators, and granny wisnae on for this thing at all. She didnae know what it wis. And here it wis Scottish dance music the first programme. When granny heard the Scottish dance music it wis quite all right !

'Oh, Ye Had Tae Be Careful'

I was never interested or active in politics. It wis a' the Unionist thing at Auchendinny, well, more or less, ye know, across at Mrs Dalmahoy at Auchendinny House. Her father wis – wis he a Q.C. or something in Edinburgh ? But, ye know, there were the Unionist things across there, and Mrs Dalmahoy she wis an Inglis o' Glencorse, she wis a daughter. But Mrs Dalmahoy, durin' the war her car wis in the garage and she went about on a push bike. She used tae come up tae ma mother's. Oh, she wis a proper lady. Mum would be washin' away on a Tuesday and this big table used tae sit there, and the door wis through, and Mrs Dalmahoy would sit on the end o' the table wi' the chenille cover on it, ye know. She would sit there and talk through to ma mother. Ah can always remember that woman, very nice.

There wis a sense of division between the ordinary folk in the village and the other ones. Of course, there always is in wee places like that. But havin' said that, as ah say, Mrs Dalmahoy, ah mean, she went into houses. There were no dividin' line wi' her at all, no. The Wallaces o' Dalmore mill were more . . . The daughter of the Wallaces she wis more snooty, ye know. She had the Guides.

Glencorse School had an annual gala. Oh, we had a school queen. I wasnae a queen, I was a maid. And it wis held – see where the North Camp is in Glencorse ? That wis the park then and that's where the gala day was held. Now after the queen wis crowned they came down there and went up tae Milton Cottages and down through Auchendinny and up Graham's Road and then for the sports. That and the Sunday School trip. They were your annual things. The trip wis tae, oh, Burntisland or Kirkcaldy or Kinghorn, some o' these places, more or less always Fife. Well, ye had tae go on the train from Glencorse and Auchendinny. Well, we had the two stations, you see. Of course, we used to talk about the three lines. There used to be the Pomathorn line. That went tae Peebles.

As ah say, when ah worked at Dalmore paper mill ah got half-a-crown a week for ma pocket money off ma wages. Well, you got your half crown and if you spent a shillin' at the week-end, the 1/6d. went into the Store bank on the Monday. Now that wis the Co-operative, there wis jist the Co-operative then. And it wis a Jessie Hogg that took the money. And that wis their savins bank. But if ye spent the 1/6d. it wis jist a shillin' that went in.

Well, we went to the pictures at Penicuik, jist at the week-end, on a Saturday night. See, we couldnae get out or else ma father came to get us up at the main road from Penicuik to Edinburgh, up at the barracks, because it wis dark the main road. Then the barracks wis there, ye see. There were never anybody gettin' attacked then, but ma father had tae come up, ye know, and get us. Parents kept an eye, especially on their daughters, if there were soldiers about. There were never any incidents, but it wis always, ye know . . .

And then we could go up to Milton Cottages. Milton Cottages wis the row o' houses on the main road. There are still two wee houses there up above Milton Bridge, there's houses sits back, jist on the bend. That was another road we could take, like if we were comin' from Loanhead or Roslin and ma dad had tae come tae meet us. But it used to be, if he wis comin', mainly the Graham's Road down the side o' Glencorse barracks, because he could shelter at the wall there, ye know. But we had tae come off that bus that ye were told to come off ! Well, ye would jist get told you werenae gettin' out again. But we usually went in twos and threes, in wee groups really. Of course, there were no lights in that Graham's Road from Glencorse School down to Auchendinny. Ah mean, there are buses go there now but we had no buses. The only bus we ever had through Auchendinny wis the Peebles bus, and that went tae Peebles and tae Edinburgh. But we had no buses. You had to walk up to Graham's Road or Milton Cottages tae get the bus.

And then of course ah liked the dancin', ah wis very fond o' the dancin'. Well, occasionally we went to Edinburgh but you had to sort o' save up if you were going tae go tae Edinburgh, because you had to pay the bus fare to get in. But then we had the dancing at the Tryst Hall at Milton Bridge. The pub is still there and behind that wis this hall. It's a nursery thing now. But that's where the dancin' was. That's where ah met ma husband ! That's where ah started goin' wi' him, from that dancin'. Ah wis jist seventeen when ah actually met him ! Of course, he thought ah wis older 'cause ah wis tall and that. But then ah knew his brother Charlie,[19] and then their father came to work at the powder mills, ye see, as a gateman. Oh, the dancin' there wis a popular attraction for the young people o' Auchendinny. And they came from Penicuik, Loanhead – Dick, ma husband, came from there – Roslin, oh, all over.

We went to the Masonic Hall in Roslin, and we used to go to the things in the church hall. And then we went to the Town Hall, which wisnae very often, in Loanhead, and the Cowan Institute in Penicuik. I was a long while afore I was ever allowed to go down the stairs in the Cowan Institute, ye know. That wis the big hall. We were allowed tae go and sit up in the gallery and watch them. Well, ma parents were strict. Well, we got a lot o' freedom but, ah mean, ah wouldnae have liked to have gone down below in the Cowan Institute to the dancing without asking, ye know. So we went to spectate there but then of course ah eventually got tae go downstairs once ah wis older, when ah wis eighteen. Oh, ah wis dancin' long before ah wis eighteen. Well, we got to go to the Tryst dancin' and all that, ye see. But the Cowan Institute was all older ones and then – oh, well, ah shouldnae maybe say this – but ah mean, some o' them, of course it's jist like now, they used tae go and take a drink and that, some o' the men and some o' the women as well. Well, they werenae rough but, ye see, ma mum and dad knew the ones that did that. But, oh, I used to love goin', sittin' watchin' them. And of course then they wore the long dresses. Ah think it was a sixpence or something tae get in to watch. Oh, ye'd to pay more to get in dancing – 1/6d. But we gradually got down the stairs at the Cowan Institute ! But, oh, ah loved the dancin'. That wis ma favourite thing, ballroom dancing, oh it was proper dancin'. Oh, that was ma favourite.

I remember that Sunday morning the war wis declared. And ye thought that that wis goin' tae be the end o' the world. Ma auntie had the sweetie shop at the Tryst at Milton Bridge, where the dancin' wis. Of course when ah went to the dancin' at the Tryst ah stayed wi' ma auntie on the Saturday nights, ye see. Well, when the war wis declared ah remember ma mother goin' away across to ma auntie: 'Oh, ah have tae go and see about

Maggie.' Oh, ah can remember that Sunday mornin', 3rd o' September 1939. The siren goin' off made it as if ye thought the war had started.

Ah wisnae called up but, you see, ah knew that we would have tae go out the paper mills, because you would have tae go to something. And then ma dad was in the Home Guard. Oh, he was an officer wi' the pips. We used tae laugh aboot him. And that's when ah decided tae go to the powder mills. Ah decided maself, well, it wis either that or to go away to the W.A.A.F.s, and it wis this leavin' home sort o' thing.[20] Well, of course, ah mean, ah wis never wantin' tae go away and leave ma parents, ye see ! That's why I went to the powder mills, because ah said to ma mother, ah says, 'Well,' ah said, 'ah'll have to leave the paper mill because,' ah says, 'ah'll be called up.' Ah says, 'Ah think ah'll go away tae the R.A.F. Ah think ah'll go and try for the R.A.F,' ye see. And then ah must have thought better of it. But, ye see, ah didnae want to really go to the powder mills because ma dad wis a foreman there, ye see, and things like that. However, ah went away on ma own and ah got the things from the other foreman, Mr Russell. Well, ma mother wisnae keen for us to go away anyway, but ah wisnae very keen tae go. Ah had never really left home before. Now when I see all the young ones gettin' away from home, ah mean, when ma daughter went away tae the university ah cried ma eyes out. Ah mean, her jist leavin' home ! But it's a different life. Ah mean, I'd never been to England before the war or the Highlands. Kirkcaldy and Burntisland and once on holiday wi' a friend to her aunt at Nitshill in Glasgow – oh, that wis quite a thing, goin' away tae Glasgow – that wis the furthest I'd been. Och, that would be true of most of the girls in Auchendinny. People didnae travel far then, ah mean, they jist went tae their aunts and that. And then people didnae have money tae go to hotels and things then.

It would be 1940, I think, ah went to the powder mill. Ah wis eighteen. Of course, you'd to be eighteen to get into the powder mill. You had to be a certain age to get in. Well, of course ma father said it wis up to maself. But of course he'd nothin' really to do wi' me goin', it wis jist because he wis there. When he started first at the powder mill in 1920 he drove the horse and that, and then he wis the storekeeper for years, and then he became a foreman. He didnae speak much about the powder mill, no' really, because, ah mean, there had been accidents and people killed and that. But he didnae speak much about it.

So ah went and got a form and filled it in. Then you had to have a medical – and it was a medical jist like what you get when you go into the army. It was a medical, done wi' an independent doctor, not your own doctor. It wis done in Roslin. But ye had tae go to an independent doctor, not your own doctor. And you were given a careful examination, oh, yes, before you were taken in, jist in case anything happened to you. Ah got through the medical examination and ah started in the powder mill.

Well, ah made the pellets for the mines and that then. Ah cannae mind the other thing. Ah think it wis something tae do wi' ships. The pellets were jist like a reel and they had a hole in them. Now there were this machine wi' the hopper. Well, ah mean, ah'm tall. And ah wis tryin' tae think today the quantity – but anyway the barrels were about a foot long. Ah jist can't remember how many pounds. And we had to lift them and put this black powder in there, and then it went round in this thing, and it pressed these pellets. And you got in a terrible mess wi' the black powder, well, the wee dusty bits came out. And that's how we had special clothing and everything. Of course, we had showers when we came down.

The skirts were tweed skirts, grey and white check, like birds I think. And it wis blue jumpers ye had with collars – wool. And then these overalls and the hats, they were thick – ah jist can't remember the name o' the material. But they were very, very thick stuff and the buttons were all wooden that wis on. Of course, there were no metal: there were no kirby grips in your hair, ye tied your hair up with a scarf, and then you had your hat on. And you could put a scarf in at the neck to keep . . . And then, like your underclothin', you hadn't to have anything that would cause sparks or anything – no metal, no metal. If women wore corsets they had to take them off: we definitely had no metal, no metal. And then you had your own stockins, thick stockins, and then your boots. The stockins were Lilles thread ones. And then you had your other boots for changin' into when ye went into the buildin'.

There was a search at the gate. Everybody was searched, the women and the girls, as well as the men. The women were searched by jist one o' the workers. And of course there were a gateman there, apart from the woman that wis there. It wis Jan Smith, ah can remember Jan did that. She jist ran her hands over you. Well, she had tae do that jist to safeguard herself, jist checked. Because, ah mean, there were very few – well, there were some girls smoked and that then, but, ah mean, they knew the ones that a' smoked. And the cigarettes had tae be put up in the wee pigeon holes, and their matches and things. Ah never did smoke maself.

But havin' said all that, walkin' up to our buildin' we used tae smell this tobacco or cigarette. Of course, I'd say, 'Oh, it's the men in the fields,' because Oatslie farm wis away across. But we smelt this for ages but I never ever like said to ma father, like, because, ah mean, we jist took it it came from the farm. Well, we were low down, you see, well, the farm wis jist above that, ye see. We used tae walk, for instance, at lunch time and we said, 'Oh, there's that smell the day again' sort o' thing. But then of course ye jist dismissed it. But one day there wis a person caught. And it wis a man in our place. And ah felt terrible about the whole thing because, ah mean, well, ah had nothing to do wi' catchin' the man. Ah don't think they caught him smokin' but they caught the matches and the tobacco hidden. Ah didn't know him personally but ah knew the man's name. He stayed at Damhead at the time. But, ah mean, it wis terrible, ye know. Of course he got dismissed. Well, ah mean, he wis doing something wrong. If there had been an explosion up where that man had been havin' this . . . Well, of course, he couldnae been havin' a smoke right at the buildin'. He must have been goin' up intae the wood. But jist the same, ah mean, it did happen, it did happen.

And did you know that the horses were shod wi' phosphorus bronze ? They werenae shod wi' the ordinary iron shoes, they would create sparks. It was phosphor bronze. And the bogie lines were made of oak, they were oak runners, a wee gauge thing and they were oak. The horses was for takin' the powder up to the houses, you see. They brought the bogies up and that. And then they had horses with carts as well on these wee bogie lines. They werenae Clydesdales but they were big horses. Ah'm no' sure if they were Shires or Percherons – one or the other: beautiful, beautiful horses, beautiful horses. There wis a stables there and, oh, they were well looked after and everything. There was a book o' ma father's – ah don't know if ah put it out or not when ma mum was movin' back up to Bilston – and it was when ma dad took the horses to be shod, and when they went in, and what it wis costin'. It wis a thick book. Well, ma dad wrote wi' his left hand but he wis a beautiful writer, ma father, he wis a beautiful writer. And ah read it one day, and a' the men's names, and the different horses' names and everything. It wis quite interestin' tae read this book.

Nobody wis injured when I was there. But it was when ma father was there first there was a big explosion when there were women killed in the powder mills. And there were a Mrs Hughes in Roslin, she had been a victim. Ah can always mind o' her eyes, ye know, bein' a' red and everything. But there were a Pim Arnott, she wis killed. They're in Roslin cemetery, the ones that wis killed. That wis before ma time but ma father wis there, when he was younger like. But when ah wis there there were a man killed. It was an unusual thing. This man that wis killed – the widow, that wis her second husband that had been killed in the gunpowder mills. She wis a Mrs Manson the first time, and a Mrs Malcolm the second time. Both husbands were killed in the gunpowder works. She lived in Roslin, she wis a Roslin wo-man.[21]

Oh, ye had tae be careful, oh, everybody. You were safety towards yourself and toward the person you were workin' with. Well, ah worked wi' Cathy Downie. Ah mean, we werenae takin' any dirt into that buildin'. That wis the idea o' shoes and that. I mean, if any foreign object had got in amongst the gun powder, well, it wisnae us that had done the thing. But there wisnae an atmosphere of fear, not really, no. Because there were no point in you workin' there if you were goin' tae be frightened, ye know.

To get to the powder works, well, we used tae go from

Auchendinny to Milton Cottages, get the bus, and if we missed the bus we walked down the back road. And there used tae be a big magazine at the bottom as you go up tae Oatslie, and we used tae walk down the back way, and then down the powder mill brae and then into where the gate is now. Well, the gate-house wis to the left o' that, and that's where ye went and got searched. Ye left your things there, your bag and things. The smokers left their tobacco and matches there. The things that ye could take in you took in like. Ah cannae mind what buildin' you came to first as you went from the gatehouse. Where that man Malcolm was killed was, I think, the second one in from the gate. See, it's a long time since that wis a' taken down. But there were a number o' buildins and they were spread over a fair area. And then they had a square bit inside, and that's where the offices were, and the clock and the first-aid room, and the showers and the canteen – really, in the middle. You came in from the gate and there were quite a lot o' buildins on the road in and then there there were this square bit where there were the foremen's offices and the first-aid. Oh, there were quite some distances between some o' the buildins at the powder mills. Some of us were quite a bit away. Well, ye see, when ye were that distance away ye got time for your walkin'. You went right along and then the water wis on the other side, the river Esk. And they had a big beam engine there.

There were quite a lot o' the powder mill workers travelled there. There was a Mr Leadbetter and Mr Nicol from Loanhead, the other Leadbetter was Penicuik. Mr Higginson he came from Lasswade. The Fairleys – Johnny Fairley and Alex Fairley – were Penicuik. Johnny Reid came from Parduvine – that's away across by Rosewell. And there were men came in the mornin' from West Quarter through in the west. It was through by West Calder way, that direction. That was the old Camilty mill and that had closed and they came from there tae Roslin. Willie Nimmo he came from there, and Andrew Barclay. Some tra-velled, some o' them had lodgins in Roslin and some o' them married local women, you see.

The powder mills had vans. They had vans for takin' stuff to the magazines, you know. They were covered, all covered in vans, special vans. I think there would be six. I'm tryin' tae think o' the men's names that drove the motors. Ma Uncle John wis one. Well, ah knew the men because they'd been there a' their lives, ye know.

And then there were office workers, oh, I'd say there would be six office workers when I wis there anyway, and then sometimes there were more. They were mainly girls and, oh, aye, there were men. And they moved up to that big house at one time, Eskhill House.

I think there would be a hundred workers altogether at the powder mills when ah wis there, or up tae it. Ma number, ah know, wis 104. Ah don't think there would be as many as 150. But, ye see, ah'm only talkin' about the black powder section. There wis the bomb section as well. They jist had a few women before the war. The old ones when we went had been there, you know. There were a Miss Frame, Jenny Frame. Now ah can remember she used tae tell us a piece o' poetry about never tae be ashamed o' a patch, that it wis a strip o' honour. Jenny could recite this, ye know, about a patch ! Oh, she wis very good. And, oh, she wis very proud, Miss Frame. She belonged Loanhead. She wis an ordinary production worker. Ah didnae always work wi' her. Ma cousin' Margaret worked wi' them. But sometimes if we werenae needin' all the machines on ye'd go tae this other bit. But, oh, Jenny Frame, she wis always so proud. She had worked there all her working life. Oh, she was an intelligent, well read woman. And another lady was Joanne Smith. She was a Roslin lady. They were older.

They had shifts at the powder mills. Ah wis never on shifts, well, ah wis never on shifts in the black powder section. Ah wis there till ah got married in October 1943. And after ah got married ah had tae go up to the bomb section, 'cause they didnae have married women workin' at the gunpowder. The married women that worked in the black powder section were either in the canteen, or they were widows or something. But there were no married women actually worked at the machines. Ah think that wis in case o' an explosion, ah think so. But after ah wis married ah had tae go up tae the bomb section. It was a safer thing, oh, aye, it wis. Ah jist knew that there were no married

72

women workin' on the actual gunpowder things. They were a' single people.

As ah say, I was not on shifts in the black powder section but up in the bomb section they had night shift as well. But ah wis jist day shift and back shift there. Ah wis never on night shift. Well, it would jist be because o' where I wis in whatever department. But ah know ah wis day shift and back shift, 'cause on the day shift ah wis leavin' Roslin about half-past five in the mornin' to walk up there to the top. Because when I got married I went to live in Roslin. Then we used to walk down between the two cemeteries. Ma mother used to say, 'Oh, you . . . !' Ah says, 'Mum, there are about six o' us and who's goin' tae be gettin' us ?' But it wis a tree that always creaked. But we used tae laugh about it. That wis the quickest way tae go, of course. I would never have gone alone to work, never, no, oh, no.

We started on day shift at half-past seven, half-past seven tae four. Well, we got the bus home at half-past four. We must have left the buildins about quarter to four or that. By the time, ye know, ye got yourself washed and checked out at half-past four – the bus left the Roslin hotel at half-past four. But we had a great bus driver and the old conductor. And the men of course were up from the powder mill before Margaret ma cousin and I, because it wis a steep hill tae get up. But they used tae keep the bus for us. They were wonderful. Oh, we would have had to walk home. But, oh, no, they were good at keepin' the bus waitin' for us.

There wis a canteen, oh, they had a nice canteen. We used tae stop work and come down. I think you did get cooked things. You could take sandwiches. And in the mornin – 'cause, ye see, some o' them frae Rosewell had tae walk and that – when we used to have the break in the mornin' some o' them would have a boiled egg or something. But you had to leave your work to take food and you had to change. You changed your boots, you'd always to change your boots, and then come down and get your hands washed and your face washed. Of course, you had tae come down to go to the toilet anyway. We got a break in the mornin' and your lunch break, but no break in the afternoon, because by the time we went back to work it wis usually two o'clock, ye see.

I can't remember what the wages was but I know it was good money.

There wis a union at the powder mill. I think it wis Transport and General Workers, and it wis the man Arthur Hetherington that took the money. He was the union man. He was English. He lived at Roslin, he was married to Lavinia Penicuik from Roslin. Ah wisnae active in the union. Ye jist paid your money, it wis the men sort o' thing, but most o' the girls were in it as well. But really in those days people werenae sae . . . about unions, well, ah wasnae. And ah'm sure that the one at the powder mill the management werenae very keen on it either.

Relations with management were quite friendly. The manager was Mr Cattle, who was English. He was quite a nice man. He lived up there at Fairmilehead in Edinburgh. He came to the door o' the hut this day where Cathy Downie and I were workin'. And 'Good afternoon,' ye see, and 'Good afternoon.' And Cathy Downie wis nearest tae the door and ah wis on the far side. And Cathy had a duster wrapped round this hopper because there were a lot o' dust comin' intae her face. And Mr Cattle he said, 'Miss Downie, what is that theah for ?' And Cathy says, 'The stowah is coming out theah.' Well, the man put his head down and started tae laugh and he walked away. And Cathy says, 'What is he laughin' at ?' Ah says, 'Cathy, do you know what you said to the man ?' 'Aye,' she says, 'ah telt him the stoor wis comin' oot there.' 'No, you didn't,' ah says, ' you said the stowah was coming out theah' !

Well, as ah say, I was married in October 1943. Ma husband worked in the pits, at the Ramsay at Loanhead. The mine rescue he was in and the first-aid. Later on he was at Knockshinnoch ma husband.[22] We'd tae get married when ma brother-in-law Charlie McCorry came on leave from the Forces, oh, we couldnae get married without him ! He was the best man. That determined the date. As ah say, ah had tae go up to the top, to the bomb section, as soon as ah got married. Ah worked at the bomb section till they started closin' the place. Ah finished workin' there before the end o' the war – they were payin' them off, ye know. There was a falling off in production, the war wis finishin'. Ah think it wis a few months before the war ended they started payin' us all off, ah think it wis before V.E. Day.

Ah wis jist at home then ! Ah didnae have another job. Ma daughter wisnae born till 1949. Ah went and helped an old lady, doin' her housework, two days a week. But ah didnae go back tae work till ma daughter wis eleven year old. Ah went to work then in C. & A.s in Edinburgh – oh, a complete change. Ah went and worked on a Saturday there for a while. Then they said, 'Would you like to work Monday to Friday ?' And ah said, 'Oh, well, ah don't know about that.' You see, ma daughter was eleven when ah went to work, even for that one Saturday, because her daddy was in the house, you see. Ah would never . . . It jist wasnae done. I'd have got shot wi' ma mother if ah'd even suggested it like that ! But ah went, as ah say, on a Saturday, and then as the years went on ah went this Monday to Friday for four hours, from twelve o'clock tae four, and it suited the family fine.

Ma daughter went to Lasswade High School. She was quite a good scholar. She wis always wantin' tae be a librarian. She could read before she went to the school. Of course, her daddy wis keen on readin' as well. And then it wis them at Lasswade: 'Oh, surely you're not going to give up your art ?' Well, she went away tae Duncan o' Jordanstone art college in Dundee and graduated in art there. And then she was teachin', but she was never keen on the teaching. But she gave everything up. Now she's a Buddhist monk.

I was there in C. & A.'s jist part-time for fourteen and a half years. Ah really did enjoy workin' at C. & A.'s. Oh, it wis entirely different from ma earlier jobs! It wis that you were workin' wi' the public. Ma ambition as a girl to become a nurse never materialised.

ANN TURNER

Ah went tae the bomb factory in Roslin Glen. Well, we a' had tae go because we were the age we were tae go. Either that or in tae the Forces. It wis jist efter the war broke oot.

Ah wis born on the 4th o' January 1918 in Roslin, Station Road. Ma father belonged tae Roslin, as far as we know anyway, because they lived in Station Road. He wis a miner, coal miner, a checkweighman at Roslin pit, the Moat. As far as ah know it wis the only place he worked. He finished up bein' the checkweighman. Oh, he wis active in the union, very.

Ma mother she come frae aboot Penicuik, Kirkhill, ah think. And ah mind ma grandfather Kemp, ma mother's father, but no' ma father's father. Oh, he must have been away before ah wis born. Ah remember ma faither's mother, Granny Munro. They lived doon the stair frae us in Roslin.

Ah went tae Roslin School, oh, ah liked the school, ah liked it all. Ah wisnae very bright. Ah don't think ah wis a scholar ! Ah sat the Qaulifyin' exam. It wisnae long efter that ah left the school. Oh, ah didnae want tae go to Lasswade High School, oh, no, oh, no. Ah never was interested. Ah left Roslin school as soon as ah wis fourteen.

Ah remember fine the 1926 General Strike. Ah'd only be eight. Oh, ah have clear memories o' that. We used tae go to the school for lunch or dinner. That wis the soup kitchen at the school. It wis a long strike. There wisnae much activity in Roslin durin' the strike that ah can mind o'.

In ma family there wis six o' us. Ma sister – she's Mrs Catherine Smith – and four brothers: three older brothers, one younger. Davie was oldest, eight years older than me, Peter six years older, then Jim, and then there wis four years – the 1914–18 War years – and then me, then Catherine and ma younger brother, George. Well, ah think all ma brothers they started off as miners. But they didn't stay in the pits – except the youngest, George. He worked at the Moat pit. He finished up bein' an oversman. Then he moved doon tae Stoke-on-Trent.

Ah lived as a girl wi' ma family in Wallace Crescent, Roslin – No.27. That wis one up, one doon houses. They were miners' houses. They were owned by the Shotts Iron Company. Ma father paid the rent to them. It wis tied housing. If he had lost his job he would have lost his house as well.

At home we always had books and comics and different things. Ah cannae mind now which comics we had. When ah wis at the school ah didnae have any ambitions. Ah wis wantin' tae leave and find work. Ah wouldnae like to have stayed on at the school if ah'd had the chance. It wisnae that ma parents needed the money, no, no, it wisnae money wise. Ma father wis quite well paid. So ah left the school as soon as ah wis fourteen. Well, there were plenty jobs then. That wis in 1932.

Ma first job wis doon at the carpet factory in Roslin Glen, on the numbers. Ah wis jist on the numbers, givin' them oot the numbers for the patterns. If somebody came to you and said 'Number 9' you gave them their numbers for the pattern. The numbers were in a rack. It wis the printers that came for the numbers.

Ah can tell ye about the wages ! 16/5d. a fortnight ! That wis eight and tuppence ha'penny a week. There used tae be insurance off o' that.

Ye started at eight o'clock till five. You had half an hour for your dinner. You didnae come home for your dinner, you carried a piece with you and jist ate it in the factory. There were nae canteens. There wis a place where ye could go and sit and have your piece, away frae the machinery, that's a'. In the mornin', well, ye made yersel' a tea break. Ah think ye did work on a Saturday morning – yes, yes – from eight till twelve. That's aboot 48 hours a week ye worked.

But ah only worked at the carpet factory there for eight months because ma mother died then. So ah had tae leave then. That wis it. Ma sister Catherine and ma brother George were still quite young then. So ah worked in the house. That wis me for aboot three years, till ah wis aboot seventeen or eighteen. Ah made the meals for ma father and ma three brothers that wis workin' and ah looked after the younger yins. Oh, it wis quite a responsibility for a girl o' fourteen or fifteen. It wis a' right. Oh, oo'd been better in the factory ! Ah would have preferred that but, well, ah jist had tae dae it. Ma faither and ma brothers wouldnae be in a position tae make their meals and look after the house. So ah learned tae cook then. Ma faither wis good though, oh, yes, he wis good, cleanin' and, well, ah mean, we had never been allowed tae dae any jobs or anythin' when ma mother wis alive. So we jist had tae change our way o' life. Oh, ye jist had tae get on wi' it, didn't ye ? Nothing else for it. Ah missed the company o' the girls in the factory.

Ma father got married again and ma stepmother came to live in the house at Wallace Crescent. Ah didnae go back tae the carpet factory. Ah got a job at Valleyfield paper mills. Ah went tae see them and ah got a job right away – straight tae over-haulin'. The job wis a' right. That wis aboot 1936, when ah wis aboot seventeen or eighteen.

Valleyfield wis a good place tae work. They were good there. You'd get a meal frae them every day. And wi' livin' in Roslin we got our season ticket for the buses. It wis the ordinary S.M.T. service bus we travelled on.[23] If ye'd been payin' the fare ah think it wis sevenpence ha'penny return, somethin' like that. So it wis quite a savin'.

The hours at Valleyfield wis eight o'clock tae five and ye worked Saturday mornin'. Oh, you got your hour for your dinner. And you got a tea break in the afternoon. And you got a little one in the mornin', ten minutes.

They had a canteen there. The food wis good. The food wis free, wi' us livin' in Roslin – them that travelled got a meal, but not the people livin' in Penicuik.

Ah can remember the best wage I ever had wis 25 shillins a week – and that wis a good wage for a girl then, jist before the war.

Oh, ah liked the work at Valleyfield. They were friendly, oh, ah had plenty o' friends there. There wis quite a lot o' other women and girls. It wis a big mill, Cowan's. It wis the biggest in

78

Penicuik. There wis two salles.[24] I wis in the plain salle, and there were the enamel salle. Oh, easy a hundred women and girls worked in the plain salle, and quite a lot in the enamel salle. Och, they were a' friendly.

The management were very strict aboot your work – everything had tae be jist so. Ye were closely supervised. They had tae be very careful aboot the quality o' the paper ye were overhaulin'.

Ah remember the outbreak o' the war in 1939. Ah wis still at Valleyfield then. Ah left and came tae the bomb factory at Roslin Glen. Well, we a' had tae go because we were the age we were tae go. Either that or in tae the Forces. Ah went tae the bomb factory.[25] Ah preferred that, ah don't know why. Ah didnae want tae go away frae home. We never went intae Edinburgh to register. Well, ye knew yourself, so ye applied for the job. We went and seen aboot it before we were actually called up. Well, they were lookin' for women for the bomb factory. Ah knew about it through ma friends and so on. Ah had a friend who already worked in the bomb factory – Nan Jenkinson. That wis when the bomb factory opened. She started before me. There were two or three in, they put ye right. So ah wis quite willin' tae go tae the bomb factory.

Eight hours we worked at the bomb factory, eight hour shifts. There were three shifts: six in the mornin' to two, two tae ten, ten tae six. Ye did a different shift each week: day shift, back shift, and night shift. Then ye started it again. But the job ah wis on ah only worked two shifts. Ah wis day shift and back shift, six till two and two tae ten. Oh, ah did work night shifts as well, different jobs. But more usually ah wis on two shifts, because ah wis on the smoke floats.

Ah think we had quite a good wage there, aye, ah think we got quite a good wage there. It would be more than the paper mill. And then we got rises, ye know, each year or so.

The work ah did in the bomb factory wis smoke floats mostly, mostly smoke floats. They were used by the navy. It wis sort o' smoke screen things for the navy. Oh – dirty work ! Ah wis on puttin' a' the stuff through, a' the different mixes for makin' smoke floats. Ye werenae told exactly what ye were doin'. Men mixed it, men did a' the mixin'. We jist put in the fillers, filled them up, put them through the machine, the mixers. Oh, ah enjoyed that work.

Oh, ah knew a' the people that worked in the factory, frae Rosewell and Roslin. There wis a lot frae Rosewell, a lot frae Rosewell. They walked. We a' walked. There wis no transport. We had tae walk up tae the Lee – up tae Rosslynlee – because there were nae buses. That's where the work wis, Roslin Castle – right up ower the Roslin Castle railway station.

They were a' separate buildins in the bomb factory. Oh, there would be mair than twenty. Ah cannae mind. There wis quite a lot. Oh, they were small buildins, huts. Of course, they'd got tae be. No' many workers in each hut. The huts wis small – two or three workers in each hut, maybe three and an inspector.

Ye had tae be very careful. And ye'd tae change your boots. Well, when ah worked in the bottom mill there were Dave Malcolm got blown up. The hut went up. He wis killed. He wis the only yin killed. The other man had jist stepped ootside the door when it happened. That wis Mrs Malcolm's second husband, tae, that wis killed in the powder mill. She wis a Roslin woman. Manson wis her first husband. There wisnae a lot o' children: two boys and a girl. Yin belonged tae Dave Malcolm. That wis the only one accident that ah knew. Ah wis never injured maself. Well, ye had tae be very careful, 'cause they made ye be careful.

Oh, we had a canteen. They made your meals, well, ye had tae buy them. But ye could get a cooked meal. You got your dinner there every day if you wanted, because we had wir dinners when we come home. Ah took a piece wi' me. But we usually bought something in the canteen. Oh, we aye got breaks – about three quarters o' an hoor, ah cannae mind. Ye got a tea break in the mornin', half way through your shift.

Oh, the workin' conditions were good. Oh, aye, they looked after ye. It wis friendly. Most workers were a' right. Oh, we all knew each other. There wis quite a number o' other women and girls from the paper mills in the bomb factory. They all come doon there for jobs, quite a lot o' them. Oh, there were more women than men durin' the war in the bomb factory. There wis some men an' a', but no' that many. The men did the heavier jobs – runners, well, they went and got the stuff for ye. They fetched it to the huts. Down the bottom there wis a railway, doon the bottom. But we were up the top in the bomb section. There wis a railway, ponies doon there. Ah did work on the bottom as well.

We got some laughs at the bomb factory. We used tae have a dance once a year in Roslin. But we used tae get E.N.S.A concerts on the Saturday night in the factory. Well, we worked Saturday night – we were back shift. Them that wis on the shift gathered up in the canteen. It wis jist them that wis on that shift, ye see, that went tae the E.N.S.A. concert. There'd be about fifty.[26]

Ah worked in the bomb factory right frae the war started in 1939, jist efter the war broke oot. Ah finished jit before ah got merried – 1945. Ma sister Catherine and me we both finished then. Ah went right through to the end o' the war. Ah got married on the 14th o' May 1945, when the war finished, on the Monday efter the war finished. Ma husband wis away in the Royal Engineers durin' the war. He wis in Germany, right up tae Germany. He wis on leave when we got married. Ah left the bomb factory jist aboot the same time ah got married. We a' finished at the end o' the war, we a' finished.

After ah got married ah went back to Roslin Glen carpet factory for a wee while, months. Oh, it wis different a'thegither. The wages were much the same as before the war. We hadnae an awfy good wage. But then we had our pension, ye know, the soldier's wife's pension. That wisnae much either – 29 shillins a week ah think it wis, somethin' like that !

The carpet factory wis a' a bit mixed up. They werenae makin' nothin' durin' the war, they had jist stopped production. When ah went back they were jist tryin' tae start up again. The hours were much the same as when ah'd been there before the war. Ah wis there for a few months, that's a'. And then ah left. Ah wis expectin' a baby. Ma son Leonard wis born in April 1946. Ah didnae go back tae work efter that, ah remained a housewife. Ah never worked in factories again. Ah've lived in Stoke-on-Trent for thirty year.

Well, ah don't know, but ah liked the paper mill best. Oh, ye were well looked after up there. The paper mill was the job ah enjoyed most.

CATHERINE SMITH

Well, actually what happened wis aboot a month before we were married in 1940 the boss at the Dalmore paper mill came and said, 'Cathy, they're peying off a' the married women. So are ye goin' tae cancel the weddin' ?' Ah said, 'No way.' So ah says, 'Ah'll jist look for somethin' else.' So a friend and I went in and got a job in the rubber mills in Edinburgh. Ah worked a fortnight and that wis the end o' that and then ah went to the bomb factory at Roslin after that.

Ma father worked in the pits all his days, always in the Moat pit at Roslin. Ah wis born at Roslin on the 15th o' March 1920. Mrs Ann Turner is ma older sister.

Ma father wis a right union man. He wid fight for anybody that wis hurt, or anything like that. He used tae go and collect the union fees. He used tae collect them at the pit when they got their pay on a Friday. And then there wis some he used tae go round the doors collectin', ah think a Friday night was his night for collectin'. Ah remember him goin' out and comin' back wi' the money. He wis jist a collector but very active. He wis never unemployed as a miner.

The only time he was out o' work that ah can remember wis durin' the 1926 strike. Ah wis only six then but ah remember it, very much. Well, ma dad used tae sit up there at the Cross at Roslin, him and another old miner – well, they werenae old then – a Mr Liddell. And they used tae have oval toffee tins and they had one o' thae sealed up and a hole in the top o' it and they used tae collect for the strikers. The people passin' by at the Cross put money in. And ah remember goin' then to the soup kitchen at Roslin school. Oh, well, ah wis the youngest at the school then and, as ah say, ah had a bad stomach and ah don't think ah could eat. So when we went up to that soup kitchen ye got porridge in the morning. Well, ah couldn't take porridge. It jist made me sick. They were very good at the kitchen. They gave me hot milk – which made me violently sick ! And then it wis jist a case o' leavin' me to see what ah could eat then. Before ah went to the school in the mornin' ma mother used tae give me a half a slice o' toast and ah used tae eat that, a scrapin' o' butter on it, jist a scrapin', and a half cup o' tea. Funnily enough ah could eat what the soup kitchen gave at dinner times. Saturday was mince and potatoes and ye got a pie or something to take home and Oxo cubes. Durin' the week it wis sometimes soup. Ah can't remember exactly, I wis only tiny at the time. Ye jist got breakfast and dinner at the soup kitchen. It wis difficult for me as a girl because o' ma stomach complaint.

Ma mother belonged to Kirkhill at Penicuik. She was in domestic service as a girl. She worked in a big house at Easter Howgate, just before ye come tae Flotterstone. I would be about eleven, nearly twelve when ma mother died. That wis heartbreakin' really. She died of a stroke. Well, they done nothin' for them in those days. She wis jist left there, never even got an aspirin. She wis forty-five when she died. Ma younger brother George would only be nine. Ma sister Ann left her job to look after the house and us. She was only fourteen, a big responsibility for her. She wis all right, she definitely was a kind of second mother for us. She cooked and ma father cooked as well and kept the house clean and tidy and all that. Ma oldest brother eventually got married after ma mother died and they came to stay. And his wife looked after the house for a while before ma dad got married again. Ah got on fine with ma sister-in-law, she looked after us well. But ma father got married again and ah think it wis jist for the sake o' – ye know, it wis a big responsibility havin' that family tae bring up. There were six o' us. Ma three older brothers all worked in the pits when ma mother died.

Ma mother died a few years after we had moved to Wallace Crescent in Roslin from Rae's Buildins in Station Road. That's where most o' us were born, Rae's Buildins. The buildins belonged to a private landlord. Our house there, well, we were round the back upstairs. It wis gas lightin'. Ah can mind when it wis a dry toilet right down the bottom of the garden, in the back greens. Then we got a water closet built on the landin' upstairs, so that gave us a water tank. The house had a big bedroom and a little bedroom off it – there wis only room for a bed in it – a livin' room, and that wis it. There were two beds in the livin' room. Ma mum and dad slept in one, and there wis Ann and ma younger brother George and I slept in the other. George was two or three years younger than me. Ma three older brothers slept in the wee bedroom. Through in the big bedroom – it wis a huge bedroom – ma mum had three lodgers. These were men that worked in the Moat pit beside ma father. There wis the three lodgers, ma father, and ma brothers Davie and Peter – all worked in the pit.

There were no pit baths then. They all had tae come home and ma mum had the tub in the middle o' the floor wi' the hot water in the pot. She heated the water on the fire. It wisnae a range, it wis jist an open fire. She did a' her cooking and heating o' water there. There wis no boiler, jist a great big black iron pot full o' water. She had to heat the water for the baths several times over – there were the six men: ma father, two elder brothers, and the three lodgers.

The three lodgers a' came frae the west. When the pits closed in the west they a' came through tae Roslin. There wis Andrew Petty, ah think he came frae Wishaw, and the other two, Danny Teague and Sandy Tweedie, came frae Tarbrax. They came through to Roslin for work. Ma mother took them in because they a' did in thae days. All the neighbours had lodgers as well. That wis quite a common thing in Roslin, and the lodgers tended to be young fellows. Ma mother cooked the meals for the lodgers. They ate their food wi' our family. Well, ah think they got fed when they came in frae their work. They a' got washed and the men a' got fed. But we were fed before that and then a' the men got theirs.

Oh, it must have been terrible for ma mother. And, ye know, she always wis dressed wi' a clean white apron on for them comin' in. When ye think back on it ! Mind, ma father worked hard in the house. Oh, he was interested in cooking and he helped ma mother. He always did, even before she died. We didnae really have a garden, it wis all back greens. Whatever spare time he had he worked in the house, cleanin' and polishin' and all that.

The three lodgers were friendly fellows, oh, it wis jist like wir own family actually. They were mostly on day shift. Ah can remember ma father bein' on different shifts but not very much. Generally he wis on day shift. Ah think ma father and ma brothers and the lodgers were a' sort o' on regular day shift – they had tae be. Oh, our three lodgers werenae married in thae days. Actually, one o' them wis married frae ma mum's hoose tae a Burdiehouse girl. Ah remember the wedding but ah wasnae at it. He didnae come back tae us once he was married, oh, no, that wis it. Oh, they had their own place tae go tae. And then ah think Danny Teague wis goin' wi' a girl in the next block o' hooses tae us. He got married tae that girl. But then we were movin' house tae Wallace Crescent, and the remainin' lodger he went home tae Wishaw. That wis about 1928–9. We didnae have any lodgers in Wallace Crescent.

At Wallace Crescent it wis four houses in a block and ah wis downstairs. These were new houses built. The houses belonged the Coal Board.[27] There wis two bedrooms, a livin' room, kitchen, a bathroom and a flush toilet. It wis smaller than our house at Rae's Buildins because we only had the two bedrooms at Wallace Crescent. But we didnae have any lodgers there. Oh, it wis different a'thegither, Wallace Crescent, and it had electric light and a range. The range had tae be polished, that's a horrible thing. Oh, when ye think back now it makes ye wonder how ye done it. But Wallace Crescent wis a big improvement on Rae's Buildins.

Before we had the three lodgers at Rae's Buildins my Uncle Will Kemp, ma mother's youngest brother, used to have friends coming tae stay wi' us. Uncle Will was in the First World War. He wisnae married when he wis in the war because he used tae send ma mum, ken, money home. He sent money and she saved that up for him. And when he come home from the war she put him into business wi' this money which she had saved up. He bought a fish van, a motor van, and he used tae sell fish. Then his

older brother John and him bought this big motor van for a fish
and chip cart, which they done very well out of. They were based
in Loanhead. And when Uncle Will wis away in the war he met
thir men, two London chaps. They were policemen. And after
the war they promised tae come and see him, and they cycled
from London, the two o' them. And he gave them ma mother's
address, of course, and when they came tae the bottom o' the
Killburn Brae there jist outside Roslin – the water out the pit
used tae run underneath the road – they stopped there. They
didn't know they were as near the village. They stopped and had
a wash and they couldn't get over it that the water was hot. It
wis comin' up from the pit, of course. So after that, when they
got married, they used tae come wi' their wives to stay with ma
mother. We were still in Rae's Buildins then. Ah cannae mind
now how we a' slept. But the visitors had the best room. Oh, ah
think only one couple came at a time. That's what it was. Oh,
they were big fellows, bein' in the police, but they didnae have
any families. And ma mother and father used tae take a holiday
wi' them, like they used tae take them out. Ma uncle used tae
come wi' the car and take them away every day, away tae Ayr, a'
these different places. So ma parents got around a wee bit then.
That would be in the 1920s.

Oh, ma father would likely get holidays before the war but we
never went anywhere as children – a day here and there.
Burntisland we used tae go tae, Portobello, Kinghorn, just for
a day out. Well, ma sister and I went to ma aunt's and stayed
there for a day or two. She lived away up the Pentlands, her
husband was a shepherd at Loganlea, between the two reser-
voirs. And that wis lovely.

Ah went to Roslin primary school. Ah liked the school, I liked
arithmetic. Ah wis off quite a lot wi' bad throats and that when
ah went to school first. Ah had a bad stomach. And ah had done
well when ah went back after havin' ma tonsils out, and the
teacher Miss Shearer wis very, very good and she used to help
me. She wis marvellous. And ah won this prize at school and ah
got a lovely book for it, *Bunty of the Blackbirds* and it wis about
Guides. And ah treasured that book. Ah read quite a lot as a girl.
Ah never joined the library. Ah don't think there was a Roslin

village library then. I used tae buy all the magazines and things like that for girls.

I sat the Qualifyin' exam and passed it. But I wouldn't go to Lasswade High School. Ah don't know, ah jist wisnae interested. Ah had no notion to go to Lasswade High School. Ah didn't feel that ah could keep up wi' that. Ah was sort o' shy. Ah wouldn't feel at ease wi' strangers. See, we were never away from home.

Ah never joined the Guides or Brownies maself. It wis because ma dad used tae say, well, the older boys they got uniforms for the Scouts and everything for them and, of course, they were only in them once and wouldnae go back. By the time it came tae me he said, 'I'm no' buyin' a uniform. You'll be like the rest o' them, you'll no stick it.' So that wis it.

Ah never had any particular ambitions as a girl at school. If ma mother had lived ah don't think ah would have been out working. Ah would have stayed in the house wi' her and helped her to run the house. Oh, ma mother's death brought a big change in ma life. Ah left school as soon as ah was fourteen.

As ah say, ah liked walking and the countryside. Ah loved workin' outdoors. When ah was at school we used tae go on a Saturday morning to Dryden Farm. Mr Martin wis the farmer there down at Dryden. We got paid 2/6d. for four hours, from eight till twelve. It wis only maybe two Saturdays or somethin' like that. It wis jist a' for fun, ah think, really. Ah think we got to keep the money as pocket money.

When ah left school ah wisnae supposed tae be goin' oot tae work. That wis ma mother's wish, and ma father wis keepin' that wish, ye see. He didnae want me tae go out. Ah didnae work efter ah left the school because ah used tae go out tae the fields and work, jist odd jobs, at Langhill Farm, up at the top of the hill from Roslin to Bilston. Well, Jean Haig, the woman up the stair next door at Wallace Crescent, she used tae have a gang worked on farms. She wis a sort o' contractor. She used tae collect the workers and take them up. They were girls like me who'd left school that went up, oh, they were married women as well. Ah jist went now and again – jist the tattie pits, gatherin' the potatoes, and threshin' mill. Ah did odd jobs on the farm for a few months. Ah think ah started in the Dalmore paper mill jist aboot before Christmas 1934. The girl upstairs in Wallace Crescent worked in the paper mill, that's how ah got the job. Ah aye jist fancied goin' there, well, jist a notion efter you leave the school. Ah said tae her, ah said, 'Is there any jobs goin' ?' She says, 'Ah'll see.' So she came back and she said, 'You've tae start on Monday.' Ma father wis angry. But ah jist said ah wis goin' and that wis it. Ah wis quite determined and he gave way. And he wis quite pleased efter that. Ah had no notion to remain in the house. Ah wanted to get out and do a job outside.

At Dalmore mill ah started on the shavins. Well, that wis – ye werenae supposed tae dae it – crawlin' under the cutters to get the shavins out. It wis very dangerous. It shouldnae have been dangerous if things had been done properly. Ye were supposed tae bring them out wi' a long stick. Well, if an inspector came the metal guards were put up that prevented you from crawlin' under. It wis quicker tae crawl under. Well, it wis jist the other women showed ye what to do. At first ah wis nervous. Ye jist got on wi' it. Ye were supposed tae pull the shavins out. Ye know how the cutters are goin' and they take the edge off the paper. Well, these have a' got to be pulled out, bagged, and taken up to the baiter house, where they mixed a' the pulp and everything. Well, these shavins went intae that. Nothing wis wasted. Ah didnae really like that job. Och, well, ye'd tae trail oot in a' weathers away tae take this stuff up to the top o' the mill. Ye put it intae sacks then ye took it in a barrow, and then come back and gathered more. That wis ma day's work.

Ah wis on the shavins, oh, then ye got shifted on tae the cutters. It wis a step up. Oh, ah preferred that work. It wis easier, no' dangerous, no' really, Oh, ye got cuts, ye got cuts on your fingers right enough, paper cuts and that. Oh, our fingers often got cuts. We had them wrapped up a' the time. We used tae jist take a bit o' the sticky paper and pit it roond to save our fingers from bein' cut. The management didnae provide you with protective gloves or anythin' like that.

Ah worked on the cutters about a year, ah think, and then if there wis a vacancy up the stair ye got taken upstairs. Well, it wis the overhaulin' upstairs. Ah didnae go on the overhaulin'. Ah went on the balin' – tyin'. Ah jist fancied the balin', ah asked tae go on that. The balin' ye were jist puttin' the wrappers on the table, puttin' the string down first, the wrappers, then you lifted your ream o' paper, put it on and tied it. It wis always a ream, a ream at a time, 500 sheets. It wis heavy work. Well, ye'd tae heave it up on tae the top o' the barry – no mechanical aids, no lifters, ye did it all by hand. Oh, it wis heavy work. We were tired at night.

Twenty-past six we started till five o'clock, ah think it wis. But ye got an hour for your dinner and ye got ten minutes in the mornin' and ten minutes in the afternoon for a cup o' tea. There wis no canteen there. Ye ate your food in the brosie, they cried it. It wis only a tiny wee place, wi a couple o' forms and a bench. And it had a wee coal fire thing where ye could make a cup o' tea. Ye couldnae really cook food there, well, ah believe ye could heat soup or anything like that but we never ever done anything like that. We'd take a piece wi' us, and that wis it. We'd make some tea for ourselves. And then we got our dinner when we came home at night. At the mill ah think the men used tae jist eat their piece where they were. They were mainly women when we were havin' our piece in the brosie. But, ye see, if they were locals they wid go home for their dinner. It wis only the likes o' us from Roslin that travelled.

We travelled on our feet to Dalmore mill – we walked ! It took, oh, aboot twenty minutes, ah think. From Roslin we went up The Beeches road – it wis lined wi' beech trees on either side – and doon tae the Cleugh, up through the fields, it wis a right o' way really, an earthen track between two fields, and ye went up there and then ye came oot at the top o' Auchendinny Brae. That wis the quickest way from Roslin. There would be aboot fifteen o' us a'thegither, men, women, girls and boys, walked that way to Dalmore, maybe two thirds women and a third men. We never a' walked thegither, ah went up wi' ma friends. There wisnae a lot o' us. Oh, we were away frae the house before six o'clock, we started work at twenty-past six. Oh, ah wis up back o' five. We walked home that way at night and got home about half-past five. It wis a long day. Oh, some nights we went tae bed early – ten o'clock. If there wis nae dancin' on we'd have an early night.

Catherine Smith

There were maybe aboot two hundred worked at the Dalmore mills when ah wis there. They were on shifts. Ah don't think there wis any women on shifts. Ah wis always on day shift.

There wis no union in the Dalmore mill. Ah don't remember anybody in Dalmore who was in a union. Ah think the union came in jist after the war. As far as ah know there wis no union there before the war, we never had a union up there. Ah remember ma father sayin' to me as a girl that there should ha' been a union.

Ah widnae say there were anybody frae Roslin worked in Esk Mills paper mill. Well, it wis usually Valleyfield or Dalmore. It wis easier tae get tae Valleyfield than Esk Mills from Roslin. Never anybody went tae Esk Mills from Roslin. It wis a' Penicuik folk that worked in Esk Mills. But there were Roslin folk ah remember worked at Valleyfield: oh, aboot half and half, ah wid say, worked at Valleyfield and Dalmore.

As ah say, it wis a long day workin' at Dalmore. But, oh, we were out dancin' nearly every night! By the time ye got hame and had a wash and got changed you were right. We went tae the Masonic Hall or the Miners' Institute in Roslin, the Tryst at Milton Bridge, Loanhead Town Hall, Rosewell Miners' Institute, and Penicuik Town Hall. Oh, aye, we went dancin' nearly every night. It wis ballroom dancin', oh, it wis super. It wis good fun, we jist had a good time. Ah went tae the dancin' frae ah wis fourteen, jist after ah left school. Well, ma father didnae like me goin' away from Roslin tae the Tryst or that. He didnae mind us dancin' in Roslin. Ah wis beginnin' to get a bit older by the time ah went to Loanhead, Penicuik, or Milton Bridge or Rosewell. We walked to Rosewell – down through the Glen and up. It would take a good half hour and then back again later at night, sometimes quite late. And then ah wis goin' wi' the party by that time – ah had met ma future husband! Ah wis aboot fifteen when ah met him first.

Winchin' wis quite common jist after you left school. Ah well, ye jist used tae go oot and meet at St Clair's corner in Roslin. The young lads used tae meet there and then we used tae come up and have a talk wi' them. Two or three nights a week there would be a group o' them there. Most o' them were miners and then, ye see, they had the Institute tae go tae – billiards and everythin' in the Institute that they used tae go tae. Oh, the girls didnae parade up and down. If you were passin' you had a blether wi' them.

On a Sunday night the done thing wis everybody went up the Penicuik road. Ye couldnae get movin' there on a Sunday night on the main road from the Country Inn at Roslin road end up tae the Tryst at Milton Bridge. That wis the Penicuik road, and ye walked back and forward and back and forward there on a Sunday night talkin' tae a' the young men. Oh, that wis the done thing on a Sunday night. Everybody went up the Penicuik road. Boys and girls they jist walked there from Roslin, Penicuik, Auchendinny, Loanhead. Oh, ye walked everywhere. Even if it wis rainin' ye went, oh, there wis some o' them would have umbrellas, right enough. But the rain didn't put us off.

It wis jist the one side o' the main road, the side opposite Glencorse barracks. Crowds – a hundred, two hundred easy. Ye couldnae hardly get movin' ! So ye met at the dancing and on a Sunday night, and that wis the recognised thing. That wis in the 1930s. If you had a steady boy friend ah dinnae think we went unless they werenae playin' fair. Well, if a girl had a steady boy friend she'd be out wi' her boy friend, wouldn't she ? She wouldnae really go to the Penicuik road on a Sunday night. It wis only those that werenae very serious or were playin' a double game that went there ! The Penicuik road was jist fun but also to look for a boy friend or a girl friend

Oh, we used tae go now and again tae the cinema if there wis somethin' special on. Loanhead wis the nearest. There wis never a cinema in Roslin. Ah didnae go much to the cinema, ah preferred the dancin'.

As ah say, ah wis aboot fifteen when ah met ma husband first. He wis a Roslin lad, he jist steyed doon the road. We met at the dancin'. He'd worked in the pits at the Moat and then he worked in contractin', building contractors. When ah got married ma husband wis in the army. He wis called up – Royal Engineers – jist before we got married.

So ah worked at the balin' at the Dalmore paper mill right till jist afore ah got married in October 1940. They werenae gettin' the orders from abroad then, wi' the war. Well, actually what happened wis aboot a month before we were married the boss at the paper mill came and said, 'Cathy, they're peying off a' the merried women. So are ye goin' tae cancel the weddin' ?' Ah said, 'No way.' So ah says, 'Ah'll jist look for somethin' else.'

So a friend and I went in and got a job in the rubber mills – the North British rubber mills at Fountainbridge in Edinburgh. About a month before ah wis married ah started there. The rubber mills were horrible, horrible, horrible. Ah worked for a fortnight and then ah wis off ill, ah, well, ah had a bad stomach. Actually, it wis a good department ah wis in – golf balls – but ah hated it. Ah mean, ye wore white overalls and everything. But the people werenae nice. They never spoke to you. It was horrible. It wis a terrible atmosphere. Ah don't know why that wis. Well, ah think there wis a sort o' wee bit snobbishness. They were a' sort o' well dressed and everything in that department, ken. And ah wis a country lass and then ah wis a bit shy and then ah wisnae keepin' well at the time either. Everything wis against me. Ah jist didnae like it. And then of course when ah came out at lunch time to meet a friend to go to the canteen the smell jist really made me ill. It wis a heavy smell. So that wis it. Ah worked a fortnight and that wis the end o' that. Ah hated the rubber mill for a' the time ah wis there. And then ah went to the bomb factory at Roslin after that.

I'd either to go there or in the Forces. And then when ah wis married in October 1940 – ah don't think they could force you intae the Forces – but they could ha' sent me away to munitions. Ye had tae go to the dole, the labour exchange at Loanhead. And they said to you there, 'You've got to enter war work and you may be sent to a munitions factory in England or somewhere.' And ah said, 'Well, ah've got a job.' Ah had written and asked for a job at the bomb factory. Well, they were lookin' for workers there. So eventually ah got up there to the bomb factory.

Well, there it wis makin' fire bombs ah did, incendiaries for dropping from aircraft. We knew that, we were told, because they had tae demonstrate them up there. We had tae see how they worked. They werenae big things. They were jist tiny. But they took us down the quarry to demonstrate and let us see how they worked. But quite interestin' work it wis.

Oh, well, you were sent to different places to work. We made pellets at one bit, and then at another bit you were doin' celluloid discs that you put on your fingers, varnished them and put them into the gunpowder and put them down to dry. Now these went on top o' the – it wis like a tin, a Brasso tin, a little bigger. Now that was full o' gunpowder. That's still the gunpowder. Then ah think we put the celluloid top on, and then a detonator, and then everything wis on after that. That wis the incendiary bomb, that wis how they were made. Now ah can't remember what the pellets were for. They must have been smoke devices, they must ha' been.

Working conditions were quite good. Oh, very much safety ! When ye went up to the gatehouse ye were searched before you went in, physically frisked a' the time. It wis a woman that ran her hands over you. Ye had a place tae put your cigarettes and your lighter, ye left them there. Ah wis a smoker so ah always left ma cigarettes and lighter there. And that wis you. You couldnae have a smoke until your shift wis finished. Oh, ye had tae be careful. That would ha' been terrible if anybody had smoked durin' a shift. Ah think maybe one or two o' them, maybe on the night shift, went away oot to the gatehoose and had a smoke at break time. You werenae allowed to smoke outside. That wisnae allowed either. Once you were in that wis you till the end o' the shift. You werenae allowed to go outside the gate for a smoke or anythin' else. A few, ah think, on the night shift, instead o' goin' for their cup o' tea, used tae go out tae the gatehouse. It wis wrong because ye had special clothin' on. Well, they might have taken their overall off right enough. I expect they would take their overalls off, because it would ha' been dangerous tae go out. Aye, they would take their overalls off.

Ah wis a heavy smoker, oh, aboot thirty a day. At that time ah wis in aboot ma early 'twenties. It wis an eight hour shift. It wis a long time. Well, ye did find it a strain at first havin' to do without a smoke. But ye got used tae it. Oh, ah had a cravin' ! Ah ate sweets instead. Ah cannae mind if we took sweeties doon to the buildin'. Ah don't think so. Ah don't think we were allowed. It wis difficult but, well, then you were workin' of course and you were kept goin', 'cause you had a tally tae keep up to. You had to produce so many items per shift. You were kept at it. Ye werenae rushin' around but ye had tae keep goin'. Oh, well, you were desperate for finishin' time tae come tae get oot and get a cigarette. Well, when ye worked at the bomb factory ye were bound tae smoke less. You didnae jist smoke the thirty a day in a shorter time ! You would save a bit o' money too wi' that.

Ah cannae mind what the wages were. Ah wis on three shifts, six to two, two to ten, and ten to six. Ye jist carried on from one shift to the other each week.

Ah don't think there'd be a hundred women and girls from Roslin at the bomb factory when ah wis there. Fifty ah wid say. There were a few men there as well – no' as many men as women. The women were mainly war workers only. There was a few – ah would say maybe a couple up the top mill – that had been there before the war. Ken, they would sort o' tell what we had tae do.

Ah finished up there – well, the bomb section wis closed jist when the war finished in 1945. Ah finished then because it wis closin'. So then ah went straight doon to the carpet factory, which ah hadnae been in before. They were startin' up the carpet factory again in Roslin Glen. And then when ma husband wis gettin' demobbed he didnae want me tae work. So ah packed that in right away. It wis the done thing then – if you were married, you didn't work. And ma husband wis a great believer in that.

Oh, the carpet factory wis new tae me. It wis less interestin' than the paper mill or the bomb factory. Oh, ah wouldnae have worked in it for very long, ah don't think. It wisnae ma cup o' tea at a'. Ah wisnae in there a year, ah don't think, a few months. Then ma husband wis demobbed. He says, 'Get packed in afore ah come hame !'

Ah never went back tae work again, no' until ma daughter had been a while at school and then ah took a part-time job – house work at Fairmilehead in Edinburgh, jist in the mornin'. Jist everybody was doin' it and that wis it. Ma husband wis workin' away a' the time. He wis up north most o' the time, in the Highlands – hydro-electric work. So it didnae interfere wi' him at all. He only came home about once every fourteen days. Well, by that time things had altered, there were more married women goin' oot tae work.

Lookin' back, oh, ah liked the paper mills better than anything. Well, they were payin' all the married women off in 1940. They werenae gettin' the orders from abroad then, wi' the war. Ah actually went back tae the paper mill tae see through it no' that long since. Ah got the shock o' ma life. There's no workers ! They're standin' watchin' the computer. Ah couldnae believe it ! There's no heavy liftin', nothin' at a'. It's a' done by machine. The shock o' ma life ! And Dalmore's the only paper mill left oot o' the three at Penicuik.

MARY MURRAY

Ah didnae want tae go tae the pooder mill. Ah wis nervous aboot explosions. But ah liked the pooder mill.

Ma father, ah think he belonged Tarbrax in Lanarkshire, and ma mother as well. Ah wis born in Tarbrax on the 2nd o' February 1914. Ah don't remember much aboot Tarbrax. Ah wis jist young when ah came through here tae Poltonhall and Rosewell, say five or six year auld, ah think, jist aboot the end o' the First World War.

Ma father wis a miner. He worked in the shale mines at Tarbrax. And then we came through here tae Poltonhall in Midlothian, down at Dalhousie there, and he worked up at the coal pits at Whitehill colliery at Rosewell. Ah think his father, ma grandfather Henderson, was a miner too. Ah can remember him as an old man. Ma grandmother and him came frae Tarbrax and they bade at Tranent. Oh, he wis a great old man, grandfather Henderson. And then ma grandfather MacDonald, ma mother's father, and granny MacDonald they bade here in Rosewell. They came frae Tarbrax as well. He wis a shale miner. Work, ah think, wis . . . So they a' come through here tae work in the coal pits.

It wis jist a room and a kitchen, ah think, we were in at Tarbrax. Ah think that's a' they were. The houses they were in rows, miners' rows. The houses didnae have a street name, no' that ah can mind o', it wis jist numbers. Ah can picture our house a wee bit. Ye had tae come outside for the water, a tap, ah think it wis. Ye had tae come out and carry the water. It wis jist paraffin lamps, nae gas or electricity. There werenae anything – ah dinnae think that was thought about then. Ye had a big bath at the fire for baths. Ah cannae mind if ma mother had a range there. Ah think it wis jist the fire, she jist had tae do a' her cookin' on the fire. Ma mother didnae have a job, she jist looked after me and ma brother Robert, two or three years younger than me.

Ah cannae mind o' us flittin' through frae Tarbrax tae Poltonhall. At Poltonhall we were at the Chesters. That wis a row o' houses right down there. They were wee-er houses than what they are now. It wis jist room and kitchen then. It wis a miners' row again, on the main road tae Rosewell frae Bonnyrigg, facin' oot on tae the main road. It wis really stone built houses. Ah think we had tae go out tae a well in the street and get the water – which used tae be the same up here at Rosewell. Ye'd tae go oot tae the well wi' the pail and get it filled wi' water, ken. Ah think it wis gas we had, gas lightin', at Poltonhall. Well, we had tae use the oil lamps first, ah think. It wis the same arrangement wi' baths: the tin bath in front o' the fire. Ah think it wis a kind o' range we had down at Poltonhall.

Ah cannae mind how long we were at Poltonhall. Ah don't think we were long doon there. We moved up tae Louisa Square in Rosewell first. That wis No.8, a room and kitchen. Then we went frae there across tae Victoria Street, No.26. Ah wis still at the school when ah wis in Victoria Street.

Ah was at the school for a wee while when we were at Tarbrax. Ah didnae like it ! Ah can remember – it must have been for talkin' – ah wis standin' there in the class room in the corner ! If ye were talkin', ye know, ye were stood out in the school. The big hall wis in the centre, the classes were a' roond aboot. If ye talked ye were put in your corner ! Ah wis put intae a corner one day. Ah had tae stand in that corner for ages, for talkin' ! Even although ah wis jist young there are certain things you do remember.

When ah wis at Poltonhall ah never went tae school. There werenae a school doon there. It wis either Bonnyrigg or up here at Rosewell. We didnae go to any school until we flitted up here tae Rosewell ! Ah went to Rosewell school. That's the Prodestant school, ma parents were Prodestants, Church o' Scotland. And the Catholic school's further down the road – St Mathew's. There were quite a few at Rosewell school doon there when we came. But it wisnae as big a school as it is now. It's been a' jilted up. The front wis a' old, ye ken, and a' the back an' a', and it wis a' renovated up, ye ken. Mr Lee he wis the headteacher. He bade in the school house, down the road a wee bit from the school. But it wis a nice school, that's one thing ah can say. Ah liked the school, it wis nice. Some days ye would enjoy the work and other days ye widnae. If ye were sittin' puzzlin', wonderin' what it wis and then the teacher would shout, 'Come on now, come on !' Ye ken, shoutin' tae us a', and then ye would a' gie a wee bit look at yin another. We maybe didnae ken the answer and ye would be puzzlin' your brains tae get the answer tae what she wis, ken, tellin' ye. Some wid get it, and some widnae get it. But she didnae bother. 'Now,' she says, 'come on. Think, think, think again !' And ye'd tae get the thinkin' cap on again. Oh, dear ! The teachers wis a Miss Hanley and a Miss Gordon, and Miss Hanley cycled frae Roslin every day. Miss Hanley cycled on that bike for years tae the school frae Roslin. She wis a good teacher. And ah think there wis one or two came frae aboot the town – Edinburgh. There wisnae an awfy lot o' teachers at Rosewell school. That wis the only one in Rosewell, apart frae St Mathew's.

We left school at fourteen. We wis gled tae leave, some o' us. Ah think ah jist passed the Qualifyin' exam – jist, ah think. Ah could have went tae Lasswade. Ah didnae want tae go tae Lasswade. Och, ah wanted tae leave the school and get a job. When ah says, 'Ah'm goin' tae get a job,' ma mother and father they jist says, 'Right.' So ah got a job in the carpet factory in Roslin Glen.

Tae get the job in the carpet factory ye had tae go down the Glen tae see Hanley, them that had it, ye ken. He wis the manager. Well, there were a lot o' folk in Rosewell village that worked in the carpet factory, ye ken. And they used tae tell us, 'Oh, it's a' right, a guid job,' and a' that, ye ken. So two or three o' us when we left the school we went across and we got the job. Ah had tae wait a wee while, ye ken, there were no vacancies when we left the school first. But we always knew at the factory there wis always jobs there. And after that we got in and quite enjoyed it.

Well, you made up the numbers in bundles. When they

printed the drums that wis numbered, and they had a disc wi' the number what that drum wis, and the cords wis on it. This wis ma first job, givin' out the numbers to the girls that were on the printin'. They wid ask ye for the bundle o' numbers. And one o' these numbers there wis a cord on them. Ye jist put it over the wool, tied it on, and that wis how they knew that one wis for this drum, ye know. They kept the drum and the pattern a' in one.

Ye gave the numbers. And then after that ye could get on tae maybe the reelin'. There were bobbins that were there and you could make them intae hanks, or whatever they wanted them. And then ye were boxin' the drum for your partners – two drums. Ye'd tae put the boxes intae the machine for them and this yin. And that wis the colours that they wanted. They shouted oot, and the boxes were a' marked wi' their number and ye kent the colour.

Then after that, if ye were good enough at it and that ye could get on tae the printin' itself. And that's how it went. You started there givin' out the numbers – that wis the first job that ye got. Then ye could get intae the reelin'. This wis hanks that were there, and ye could reel them on tae the bobbins, ken. And then ye could get a job on the printin'. That wis your next job.

Say the yarn that ye had thingmied wis a' the one colour. That wis a plain drum. That wis put roond the drums. They were a' in bobbins. And the different feet o' the drums: there wis small ones, aboot four feet, ah think they were – ah cannae mind now – but ye could get them up tae twelve feet, fourteen, sixteen, and fifty-two feet.

They were about another bit, in fact, and this wis a' in bobbins, and when they came off the drum they were put into the heaters tae dry, put into thir frames. They were taken oot when they were dry, and the women that wis on the settin' had big frames. A' thir bobbins were put on in the order that they should be for them makin' the pattern. As ah say, it wis a pattern like a rug. A' thae were there. They were put on tae thir things and they were a' made on tae bobbins. And that's what ye went for, tae get intae the place where they put them on tae bobbins, tae get them tae fill your drum. And that wis it.

Ah wisnae workin' long on puttin' thae numbers on. But ah

done the reelin' for a while. Ye jist sort o' worked up. If there wis drums ye could maybe go and ask, 'Could ah go . . . ?' Or your gaffer would tell ye ye could get on tae a drum if ye wanted. Ye moved frae one job tae another. And then ye got on tae the printin', and that wis you workin' a wee bit mair, gettin' a wee bit bigger pay, ye know. But it really wis fascinatin' tae see how it wis all done. Oh, ah enjoyed the work in the carpet factory.

The wages when ah first began, oh, what wis it now ? Was it twelve shillins or something ? It wisnae much. Ah cannae really mind, but it wisnae much. But we were quite happy. We were comin' hame wi' somethin'.

Ye started at eight o'clock and ye finished at, ah think it wis five. We got a break for our dinner, och, it wid be half an hour anyway. There wis nae canteen, we had tae take a piece with us then and a flask o' tea. And then there were a woman there after a wee while and we could get tea, she made tea for you. There wis nae canteen, we'd jist tae sit where we worked, we jist had tae sit there. Ye didn't get a wee break mornin' or afternoon, jist your dinner.

Well, we had tae leave Rosewell at aboot half-past seven o'clock in the mornin', tae be across there at Roslin Glen for eight o'clock tae start. We had tae walk, we jist went right round the road. The factory was this side o' the Glen. Oh, there wis a good crowd went over frae Rosewell. We jist a' met and we went across the road in the mornin'. It took us twenty, twenty-five minutes maybe tae walk. We always gave oorsels, say, aboot half an hour. There were some men – weavers – they went. As far as ah know all the weavers in the factory were men. As it came later on ah think there wis women. They were weavin' as well. Ah cannae say ah remember any women weavers who lived in Rosewell. Oh, they didnae say anything at the factory if you were a wee bit late. We werenae quartered. No, you see, we were workin' on wir own when we were doin' the drums, ye see – depends on how many ye had done in a day.

Oh, ah wis in the carpet factory for quite a while. Ah cannae mind how long. Ah wis there for quite a while. Then they were kind o' short o' orders. And by this time the war wis comin' on. We got paid off for a wee while. And frae the carpet factory we went tae the town – Edinburgh – intae the rubber mill for a wee while. We got in there makin' the rubber capes for the babies against gas attacks. Ken, the capes a' jist come up, buttoned right up to their chins, and the wee hoods. Well, that's what ah wis on anyway for a while.

But, oh, the smell o' the rubber ! Brrrhhh ! Oh, it wis terrible. It wis terrible, it really wis. Ye jist got the fumes and it jist – as if it wis puttin' ye away, wi' the smell off this stuff. Oh, ah felt faint. Oh, they were a' like that. Ye would hear one o' them, she'd say, 'Ah'm no' daein' ony mair o' that ! Ah'm no' daein' ony mair o' that !' Yin o' the women that were there said that. Oh, the smell wis . . . Ye were jist sort o' a' intae it. The rubber – it wis aye there, a heavy smell.

We got the bus frae here in Rosewell, we got it right in tae the rubber mill. Ah think we had tae pay something but no' the full thing, and it brought us back at night. There were a few frae Rosewell, and then they picked up at Bonnyrigg, Dalkeith, for the rubber mill. Ah think it wis eight o'clock we left here – or half-past seven, there tae start at eight. We got our dinner break and then oo worked on tae five o'clock. Ah think it wis jist half an hour we got for our dinner. We jist ta'en somethin' wi' us tae eat. We'd jist tae stop where oo were, aye, and have it. Oh, ye couldnae eat it for the stink. Ye thought ye were tastin' the smell o' the rubber. Oh, the rubber got intae everythin', the smell o' the rubber !

We didnae get paid very much ! Ah cannae mind what oo got but we didnae get very much. Well, in the carpet factory ye made your wage wi' what ye done – piecework, ye ken, how many drums ye ta'en off and that. That's how ye were paid. But in the rubber mill – oh, no. Ah think it wis jist a set wage they had for ye bein' there. You definitely didn't make as much money in the rubber mill as in the carpet factory.

Ah think we worked there on a Saturday morning, ah think we did. But ah didnae lest very long there, a matter o' months, no' as long as a year. It wis jist before the war started, ah think. Aye, it wis jist startin' then.

Oh, it didnae lest long at the rubber mill, oh ! Ye would have your piece. Ye ta'en it oot and couldnae eat it. It wis the smell.

We left the rubber mill and some o' them frae the village that were there gave up as well. Ah think that wis when ah went tae the powder mills. It wis jist after the war had begun.

Ah went down there tae see if there were any jobs ! We went across, two or three o' us went across. We heard they were lookin' for workers. So we jist went across and we got started. And we were feared tae go, wi' it bein' the gunpowder ! We were nervous o' explosions at first, but efter we started we never thought any mair aboot it, ken.

There were some people in Rosewell who worked at the pooder mills when ah began there. Oh, there were a lot frae Rosewell started efter that, ken. Ah forget half o' them. Ah remember Sarah McPaul, she bade in Rosewell, and Isa Taylor. She wis a Rosewell girl. Ah think we a' started aboot the same time – so many. Ah remember Betty Ferguson. She bade in the Glen, Glenside. There were houses down there, right along the water. And Will Crozier, he bade in the Glen. Oh, there were a lot frae Rosewell. Ah'd say there would be aboot ten walkin' down in the mornin. And there might have been others on different shifts that ah wouldnae see.

Willie Mitchell and Andrew Miller, that wis the two foremen that were there. Willie Mitchell bade there. They had a wee house at the top. Well, we were jist like here, and his hoose wis up there. It wis within the gunpowder mill, it wis sort o' up on this wee road that came up frae the main road. And we could come oot and see his hoose up there. Andrew Miller ah think he bade in the Glen. That wis the two foremen there. They were the foremen we had tae deal wi'. They kept an eye on our work. They werenae bossy. Ye'd get Andrew Miller: 'Come on ! It's time youse wis started your work !' In the mornin', ken, he wis sittin' in the rest room. 'Come on ! Come on !' And they'd shout, 'Right, Andrew ! We're comin' !' 'Come on ! Come on !' And they'd be shoutin' tae. But it never used tae bother us.

And ah remember Frankie Lorimer frae Carrington. Ah think he wis on the cart takin' the pellets away. But he wis killed on his motor bike in a road accident comin' tae his work. They were on the carts, the men, ye know, the horse and cairt. They came and ta'en away the pellets that we had made.

'Oh, Ye Had Tae Be Careful'

That's what ah wis doin', makin' pellets. It would be for blastin', ah think. Some o' them were for smoke screens, they made smoke screens wi' them. They never used tae say what it wis for. It wis jist, 'That's what ye dae. That's the job, go on wi' it, and watch what ye're daein' !' The foremen didnae explain what we were daein' it for. We jist made the pellets and cordite for incendiary bombs. Ye got this muslin cloth. Ye'd tae cut it tae fit this frame and there were nails on it, and ye put it on, and then ye put the four bits o' wood on the top and screwed them in. Then your cloth wis damp, the muslin stuff ye had on, and ye had tae paint that wi' the powder, both sides, and jist tae leave it tae dry. And that wis cut up for the bombs. That's what it wis. It wis jist, ye know, the plain cloth, and yet when ye painted the mixed up powder on it, let it dry – half dry, it had tae be kind o' tacky before ye put the powder on, ye did this. Ye sprinkled the powder both sides, shook it ower, shook it. That wis it ready tae go intae the steamer.

Ye had tae watch what ye were daein', ken. For we were jist in wee huts, two in each hut that wis the usual. Ah know there were only two huts where we worked at the top end o' the mill, right up at the top. It wis usually Betty Ferguson and me together in one hut. We got on fine.

Ah don't think there wis anybody hurt when ah wis at the bomb factory. Ah wis never injured maself. Oh, ah'd run a mile if ah heard about them ! To start wi' ah felt nervous. You'd aye tae watch and ye couldnae gaun oot wi' the shoes ye had on. When ye went intae your buildin', afore ye went in ye stood on the platform, ta'en your own shoes off, put them in a box, and then put the ones ye worked in the buildin' wi'. These were special shoes. Ye couldnae gin oot off your platform wi' the boots ye had on in the buildin'. If ye went oot ye had tae change your boots. Ye had a pair o' boots for walkin' frae the buildin' up tae your hut. Ye had tae change them tae get in. And then when ye came oot ye had tae put your powder boots intae this locker, and put your other yins on for walkin' the road home. And ye used tae get some o' them runnin' up and doon wi' them on – the boots that they worked in the thingmy wi'. Honestly !

Ye couldnae smoke there. Ye could have a smoke at the gate

before ye came in in the mornin'. And that wis it. Ye had tae leave your matches and cigarettes at the gate. There wis a gatehouse and a watchman there. Ye werenae searched when ye went in tae work, no' really. Ye'd jist tae put them up, ken. What ye had ye jist put it intae the wee boxes that were a' up on the wa'. Ye jist went in and ye turned oot your pockets and stuck them in tae yin o' thir. Some o' the men yaised tae gaun oot at dinnertime tae the gate. Ah mean, that wis the only time they got oot, unless they went away up the back and maybe had a fly smoke there. Ah dinnae ken ! Ah dinnae think they would dae that. Most o' the workers were quite careful. Well, ye had tae be.

The mess room wis where we ate our food. It wis quite a nice place, ye know. It wis sturdy, ken, it wisnae jist a flimsy hut, quite a well built hut, quite comfortable. That wis away in frae the gate. Ye had tae walk quite a distance tae get tae the mess hut. That wis where we went to get our piece or our dinner. They had cooked food there, a canteen, but, och, it wisnae up tae much. We used tae a' take oor ain piece and that wi' us. If they were makin' chips ah've seen us, ken, gettin' some chips. And ye got tea or coffee there. Oh, aye, they were quite good, ken.

Ah cannae mind when we started in the mornin': was it seven o'clock or seven thirty ? It's that long since. Ye had a steady shift. If ye were on day shift it wis frae seven tae – what wis it again ? Oh, ah cannae mind. We worked back shift, oh, for a week, ah think it wis. For they had an order tae go out and we had tae get it thingmied up. There wis a rush on for that. But normally we jist worked tae four o'clock. The women didnae work night shift.

Ah don't remember feeling well off when ah worked at the pooder mill. Oh no ! Ah've no idea what ah got paid there – none ! It's a long time ago. Ah think the wages were a' jist aboot the same as in the carpet factory or the rubber mill.

There wisnae very many workers at the pooder mill when ah worked there. Oh, it wisnae a hundred. Ah would say maybe about fifty, if there wis that. See, ye were a' away tae your buildins. The only time ye seen them wis when they came in in the mornin', walkin' in tae the gate, or goin' oot at night. Ah dinnae ken where they worked, what buildins they were in, or what they were daein'. Most o' the folk ah knew were frae Rosewell, that ah came down the road wi' in the mornin'. The workers wis jist Rosewell, Roslin, and there were one or two frae Penicuik and ah think there wis one or two frae Loanhead.

Ye had tae walk tae the bomb factory frae Rosewell. Oh, there were nae short cuts tae it ! Ye jist followed the Roslin road right roond, past the carpet factory and along tae the powder mill. It wid be a couple o' mile onyway to the gate. And then when ye got tae the gate ye had away up tae the other end tae walk. Ye had a good bit walk. And ye walked back at night. When ye got home ye fell asleep, wi the smell o' the pooder on ye ! A smell ? Oh, wis there no' ! It wis a heavy smell. Ye were goin' like this wi' the heat wi' the fire. Ye had tae change the powder mill clothes when ye got home.

Ah mind yin o' the air raids at the powder mill. There were air raid shelters but we had tae go frae here away doon aboot two or three hundred yards tae get tae it. The hut that ah worked in wis away up at the very top. And when the sirens went ye'd tae come oot o' there, change your boots, come away doon the road, right doon tae the canteen again. The shelters were a' in this big field. But we had the furthest tae go – four o' us and two that worked in the bottom hut, that wis six o' us. We had tae go a' that road right doon. And we had tae get our boots changed and away doon. The rest were a' piled intae the shelters by the time we got doon. They should ha' had yin further up ! Well, this time we a' came runnin' and Willie Mitchell's shoutin', 'Come on !' Him and Andrew Miller were shoutin', 'Come on ! Come on !' And we come doon the steps and yin o' the lassies slipped ! We were a' in front o' her. Ye see, Jenny wis startin' tae go doon, and, oh, it wis deep, and here she come in runnin' at the back. And here the wey she come in her feet jist went like that frae her – it wis kind o' icy. Well, she ca'ed the hale lot o' us right down. We a' landed on top o' yin another at the bottom o' the shelter ! Nane o' us wis hurt. We couldnae get up for laughin' ! We got a fright at the time. The feet at the back jist went and ta'en the whole lot o' us right doon ! Oh, God, we had some laughs, right enough. However, there were naebody hurt.

Mary Murray

Ah worked at the powder mill till we were paid off, ah think it wis near the end of the war, it wis no' far short o' it. Ah wis there about four or five years.

After that ah worked up there at Rosslynlee in the hospital. Ah wis the matron's maid. She lived in a flat there. Ah attended tae her, cleaned her sittin' room and that, ye ken. Ah jist got her food in the kitchen and took the food up tae her. That wis a' cooked for her. Ah got married after the war. Ma husband worked at Rosslynlee. He came frae Langholm. He wis store-keeper and he sometimes drove the bus when they were short. Oh, ah wis at Rosslynlee quite a while, till ah retired.

Ah liked the job at Rosslynlee. The rubber mill ? Whoooph ! No ! But ah liked the pooder mill. It wis a guid job. Ah liked both the job and the workers. Oh, the workers were a' nice, ken.

ELLA GRAHAM

Actually, you see, I never wanted to work in the powder mills, because when I was seven there used to be explosions, and the girl next door to me, Peg Lauder, she was killed there in 1925, along with Pim Arnott from Station Road in Roslin. And ah can remember, because Roslin wis a close village, and when ah come out the school that day everybody wis round the doors. And ah got up to the chemist's shop there and somebody said tae me – well, it wis Cathy MacMillan, I don't know where she is now – but she said, 'Ye know the person next door tae ye's been killed – Peg Lauder.' And it wis a blow, ye know, ye were close tae folk round about. She wis only 25.[28] And I always said that ah would never go tae the powder mills. But then the war war came and ye jist drifted in, ye know. Because I had been in service before that. Well, it wis jist ma mother. She said, 'I think you should jist go to the bomb factory.' So ah went up and got this job at the bomb factory.

Well, ma father was a weaver in Roslin carpet factory. He was born in 1887 in the Glen cottages – they belonged to the carpet factory – and he died on the 12th of March 1952. Ma father was a hard worker, and ah think he wis always doin' things for other people, people who weren't so strong as himself. And that's what happened. He took a stroke in at the carpet factory. He was brought home actually at five o'clock and he was dead at seven. We were vexed. He wis jist 65.

Ma father was one of eight and they were all born in Roslin Glen. After he left school I think he was in the carpet factory at first, and then he went to the army. I think in those days there wasn't much going for them, ye know, and the army seemed to be a good place to go for to be well disciplined and that sort of thing. Ma father had an older brother who was a major in the army and another younger brother who went into the army during the First War. They would just have a small house in Roslin Glen, so it would sort of take care of things if the men went out into the army, you know. So ma father was in the army before the First War. He was a Regular in the Royal Artillery. Ma mother was a Londoner and he met ma mother when he wis at Woolwich, ye see, because they were married in 1913.

Ma dad was in France during the First War but he was wounded and he was home in October 1917. So that's how I came on the scene, you see, well, I was born on the 1st of May 1918. I was born in Roslin Glen in a single end, and I was christened in Roslin Chapel on the 19th of May 1918.[29]

Ma mother wis a Londoner, a Cockney. Ah think she'd been in service a bit. But there wis a big flour mill disaster down in London – ah think it wis Silvertown. Ma mother wis actually in the factory at that time, and that had been a dreadful experience for her. She used to talk about the Silvertown disaster.[30] I think ma grandfather in London wis a docker. Ma mother said it wis a bit rough and ready at her home. Well, there wis eight of them, too: four brothers and four sisters. But there wis something good about ma mother's family. They never sat at the table without saying their prayers and taking their cap off whenever they came into the house and that.

Ma mother and father had a flat in London, but ah think ma grandfather Mason was keen for ma father to come back up here to Roslin again. So they gave up their flat and came to Roslin Glen after the First War. When she came up to Roslin ma mother'd worked in the tea-room. It was the Lawrences' tea-room up about where the chemist is now. And ah heard her saying that she worked there for a while, an odd job. She never had a full-time job.

After he came back from the war ma father'd worked in the Moat pit at Roslin for a while. And then he had an accident – broke his ribs or something – so he went back into the carpet factory, where he was a weaver.

Ma grandfather worked there as well. Ma grandfather Mason actually belonged to Dalmeny. He wis born somewhere there. He wis an illegitimate son of the Masons who had a farm at

Amisfield Mains in Haddington. We never had any contact with them. Ma father did – ma grandfather used to take him down there. Ma grandfather Mason died in 1917. He died quite young, too. He was only about 58. Ma father was upset because he couldn't get home for his funeral from France.

But I remember ma grandmother Mason. She was a widow for a few years. Ma aunts stayed with her but they went away to Australia after a number of years. Grandmother went to ma other aunt in Roslin and that's where she died. But she wouldn't be that old either.

I was the oldest in our family. Then there was Polly, John and David. We were all born within about four years. There wis a year and a half between ma sister and I, there wis only a year and a fortnight between Polly and John, and then ma brother David was about a year and a wee bit after that. So we all grew up together in Roslin Glen.

Well, ah wis there till ah wis five – it was a single end, with no inside conveniences or nothing, I can remember it a wee bit – and then we moved up to Glenside, which was that block of eight carpet factory houses there overlooking the Glen. Well, at Glenside there wis only a room and kitchen. But ours had a little bit made off it, a wooden sort of place off the kitchen. We called it the scullery. Ah think some of the head ones in the factory had been in that house. The dry toilet was up in the coal cellar, away at the back. And about 1928 or '27 they put in the flush toilets outside and a sink in the house, because it was all outside at that time. There was no running water in the house when we first went there. There was a well outside between us and our neighbours the Lauders – that girl that was killed at the powder mill. And there was a well round the back for the ones at the back. There wis eight houses, terraced. There were two upstairs at each side, and there wis one at the back at the bottom, and one at the front at the bottom.

For lighting in the house we just had a paraffin lamp – no gas or electricity then. Ma mother was a wonderful cook and baker and, well, she had to light this wee fire under the oven. It was an open fire and a swee on the top. There was no water tank, we had nothing like that. You had to boil a kettle. She used to light this wee fire under the oven and she used to bake on a Friday. And we had all the children sittin' on the seat, because she made a bread pudding with all the bits of bread and that, and they all got a bit of bread pudding.

We didn't have the washhouse at first. They built that at the same time as the toilets and that. But she used tae just have the tub on the floor, ye know, and the washing board, and scrubbed the clothes like that. Ye know, we don't know we're born now.

We had a tin bath. And ma mother, ye know, in these days they were very fastidious, and we had this tin bath. And on a Friday night ma mother used to get ma sister and I through to the fire – the boys were through in the room. And then we were bathed and then we were sent to the room, and the boys were brought through and bathed. Friday night was bath night, and you got your hair washed.

In Roslin Glen we had the stank to play in. We never had to sort of look for something to do. You see, we were always in at night at dark.

We went to live at Glenside just about the same time ah started the school. I can remember goin' out the gate to Roslin Public School. Oh, ah liked the school and ah liked the teachers, ah got on well with the teachers. They were very nice. They were all misses – there were no married teachers, of course. Ah liked essays and that. Ah remember we were taught very young to spell and write well, and ah wis quite young when ah remember the teacher holding up this sheet and it was mine, and she had V.G. written over it. And then I had the medal once or twice. And then we had a minister at Roslin Chapel who wis very good at helping us. I remember one of the teachers – she wasn't such a nice teacher – and ah had done ma sums and ah had made a wee finger mark, and she had put a big red mark round it and wrote 'Dirty!' And of course ah had been in at the parsonage on ma way home from school and the next day ah wondered why the teacher asked me to come out and she rubbed it all out. The minister had gone to her and said when the work was well done and written well she shouldn't have done that. It was nice to have somebody that cared like that about you! He was a very fine man that minister, Mr Johnston.

At Roslin school there wis quite big classes. There wis a lot of children in the Glen, and they came from Rosslynlee to Roslin school. Ah think Rosslynlee's a good three miles. It's a long way for a five year old. The ones from Rosslynlee would come in soaking wet. And of course the classroom had an open fire in the corner with a guard round it. Sometimes the wee ones used tae wet their pants, and the teacher used tae tae them off at the back of the classroom. And sometimes ma mother used to take the children from Rosslynlee – they were from the hospital workers' families there – in at our house at Glenside if it was snowing and make a cup of tea or cocoa for them. They had quite a few families up at Rosslynlee, they were biggish families. It was a long walk for them, ye know. They wouldn't do it now, ah don't think.

Ah took the scarlet fever when ah wis ten – the only one in the Glen and Glenside to take scarlet fever beside that water. So I missed quite a bit of schooling, and ah came back and ah managed to get up. The gala day started that year, it hadn't been going from the First War, and they started the gala day. So I was about fourth or third in the class by that time – I'd pulled myself up. But I had a chum Evelyn Blanche who lived at Leebank poultry farm, which is just up the Lee Brae, and she was a very clever girl. She and I were always equal. The schoolmaster's daughter was always top and Evelyn and I were always equal. But that year Evelyn wis top and she should have been the gala queen. But her father – Evelyn was brought up with her father and her aunt, her mother had died – wouldn't let her be the queen. Ah don't know what it was. It was a shame, because Evelyn was a lovely girl, and her aunt was a dressmaker.

I was awful vexed that Evelyn never went to Lasswade High School. Her dad wouldn't let her. You see, most people stayed at Roslin school till they were fourteen. To get to Lasswade, which I did, you had to have 70 per cent in the Qualifying exam. So there wis only about four or five at the most that got that out of about 35 to 40 pupils in my class. Well, Evelyn Blanche passed the Qualifying but her dad wouldn't let her go to Lasswade school. Ah don't think it was because of expense, well, she wis the youngest of four. She had a brother and two sisters who were working. So ah don't think it would be that. And then her aunt wis a dressmaker. She could have made her a dress. You didn't pay anything to go to Lasswade school. You got a free ticket for the bus and everything. No, it wis jist that he didn't want her to go. It wis a shame. Ah don't know whether her dad was one of these strong sort of, ye know, was it some kind of Labour . . . ? A strong socialist, I would say.

Well, the others who went from Roslin to Lasswade school with me, there wis Betty Hughes. She's no longer here in Roslin. And then there wis Jean Gillies, who's away through in Fife somewhere now. And I think there wis Tom Russell, who was drowned in the war, and Jean Grant, who went to Canada. That's about all that went. Ah think that wis normal. And the rest of the class stayed on at Roslin school till they were fourteen and just left, ye know, and got jobs where they could get them. There was no staying on at school much. You were sort of judged at that age. Well, there wis some in my class at Roslin that wanted tae go to Lasswade but the teacher, ye know, it wis kind o' nasty. There was a girl Small and her brother wis a sanitary inspector, which was a high job in the council in those days. She was one of those who came from Rosslynlee, she walked from Rosslynlee. So this girl Small hadn't passed the Qualifying but she wanted to go to Lasswade because her brother had been clever, ye see. And she put up her hand but the teacher laughed and said, 'Oh, you can't go.' But she shouldn't have laughed about it because, ye know, ye always get a family where some are clever and some are not. It was a humiliation for children who didn't pass the Qualifying.

So in 1930 when I was twelve I went to Lasswade school. Ah wis there for three years, till ah was fifteen. I went into the commercial course for the first year and I got the book-keeping, and then I went into the other course where I got languages. Oh, I liked my English and, well, I was quite good at maths. I liked music. I was in the choir when the junior bit of the old Lasswade School wis built in the 1930s, while we were there. Ah didn't really like geography and history. Ah liked the French, I wis good at French, but I didn't like Latin. Of course, we were taught grammar, you see. Before we left school in Roslin at twelve you could write an application for a job. You were taught to do that kind of thing. And that was useful really.

I didn't like Lasswade school as much as Roslin. I didn't like sports much and they had sports – hockey and that sort of thing, which you had to take part in. And of course, Lasswade wouldn't be such a close . . . You know, you were with pupils from Bonnyrigg and Lasswade and Loanhead, and they were more advanced because some of them had had French before they came there, you see. We hadn't had that in Roslin.

Well, ah wis there at Lasswade for three years, till ah was fifteen. Times were hard and at the carpet factory where ma dad worked they were on short time. They didn't get paid for holidays or anything. And ah felt that ah couldn't go any further at school anyway. So ah left the school after three years and then ah got a job at The Thicket, which is a big house up at Roslin, in service. Well, ah had taken a course at school in, ye know, shorthand and . . . a commercial course. But I wasn't upset, not really, that I wasn't able to use those skills in a job, because most people were in the same boat. Ye know, there was nobody round about Roslin Glen and that – and there was a lot of children, maybe seventy-odd between the Glen and Glenside – and I don't remember many of them getting to Lasswade school even. So ye were jist quite happy to be working, quite happy to be helping, because even although you were only getting £2 a month in service it wis quite a lot of money.

I had taken shorthand and typing at school but I didn't think of getting a job in an office. I didn't get a job in an office till I was 42 years old ! There were some girls in my class at school who went into domestic service. Most of them went to the factories – the carpet factory or the gunpowder mill – ah think. Well, we always sort of thought, ye know, sometimes they swore a lot in the factories. You know, it was that sort of company. Ah didn't have the notion for the carpet factory. Ah chummed a girl that wis in the factory and she was always moaning about it. In domestic service ye had to have manners and that sort of thing.

Well, ah got a job at The Thicket, in service. That was in 1933. The Thicket is the name of the house. It's away up at Roslin Castle station. There are three houses and it was called

Carr's Avenue. They were quite big houses – ten or a dozen rooms, oh, quite a lot. It wis called Carr's Avenue because it used to be Carrs there before Mrs Forbes came. Mrs Forbes came down from Turriff to there. She was a canon's widow. Her husband had died – he choked on a fish bone actually. And she had three children. Ma mother had been goin' up and helping. So it was really ma mother that arranged for me to start work at The Thicket.

Well, it was jist as a table maid, because Mrs Forbes had a cook and a butler. I had also to help with her three children, because they had a governess who was Norwegian and of course if there wis any lessons that they couldn't do I used to help them with their lessons. So there were four of us servants. I was the youngest, oh, by far the youngest there.

Ah lived in at The Thicket. And ah got up about six o'clock in the morning. We started work at half-past six and you were sort of on duty till ten o'clock at night. And you got two half-days off a week. You didn't get off till three o'clock in the afternoon really on the half-days. So we were working six days a week. So at The Thicket you had not very much time to yourself, jist your two half-days. And then of course I used to get out for the church on a Sunday because Mrs Forbes' husband had been a canon – but she herself went to Old St Paul's in Edinburgh more or less.

Oh, in the morning we would start, well, I would get a note on the table to take up hot water for Mrs Forbes for her to get a bath. Then you had the stairs to start with, you started with the stairs. You had half the work done before breakfast, and then you went on till ten o'clock at night.

Ye put in their breakfast and then you had yours. We had maybe about half an hour for our breakfast. And then when they got their lunch and ye took it through to them, well, we were sort of taking our lunch in between carrying, you know, first course, second course, to them. We had to take our lunch in between serving Mrs Forbes. They had dinner, ye see, at what we call lunchtime, they had it then. And they had supper at night. We didn't get a break at supper time, it wis jist the same again as at dinnertime. You just took your food as you could get it. So as a girl of fifteen I was really working from half-past six in the morning to ten o'clock at night, about fourteen and a half hours a day, six days a week. There were no recognised meal breaks as such for us. It wis a long day. Ye can't credit anybody doin' these hours now.

I was paid £2 a month there. Wages didn't rise every year like they do now. We jist got the same wage. We were paid by the month. Ah think ah just gave that £2 to ma mother and ma mother gave us something, the odd shilling or so. If we wanted anything, ye know, she would give us the money for it.

And I remember ma dad's brother died, the one that wis an officer in the army. He was up in Elgin, and ma father got a telegram to say that he had died suddenly. And we had no money, but ah had taken out a Post Office book, ye know, when ah got the job at The Thicket. And ma dad wanted to go to the funeral up in Elgin. He had his sister, who was quite well off – she had no family – but we were very independent. So I drew the £2 – ah had £2 saved up – and ah drew that out ma book to let my dad go to the funeral, which I never regretted because I had good parents, ye know. And then another thing ma mother used to say – my grandmother in London had a bad leg, you see, for years, it was an ulcer or something – and ma mother used to say, 'Now sometimes maybe send a half-crown postal order to your granny.' So we used to do that – all off the £2 a month, you know.

Mrs Forbes was a very uppish person, you know. Ah remember ah wis there about three days and she said to me, 'The breakfast was three minutes late this morning.' Ye were jist kept on your toes all the time. Everything had to be on time, oh, there wis discipline at The Thicket, very much so, very much so.

Ye had a list on the wall of your duties and everything was itemised right down. And you had fireplaces to do, because it wis jist coal. You see, they had no electric in the house at that time. So everything was done jist by shovels. And what electricity they had was made outside in the garage place. It wis Noble that has the garage in Roslin that used tae come up and fill up the accumulators and things that made the electric. But later on they got the electric put in.

Domestic servants were all living in at that time. And it was £2

1. Men and women workers at Roslin gunpowder mill, *c*.1880. Courtesy Mr George Campbell, Roslin.

2. Workers at the mill and a horse and cart on the bridge over the River North Esk, *c*.1890. Courtesy Mr George Campbell, Roslin.

3. Two men with a barrel of gunpowder outside one of the huts or houses (probably 1910–1930). Courtesy Roslin Heritage Society and Midlothian Libraries.

4. The internal railway that ran on wooden rails at the gunpowder mill, *c*.1890. Courtesy Roslin Heritage Society.

5. Two workers, probably boxmakers, at Roslin gunpowder mills, *c*.1930s. Courtesy Roslin Heritage Society and Midlothian Libraries.

6. Women workers at the gunpowder mill and bomb factory during the 1914–18 War. The two men at left in uniform were almost certainly naval inspectors. Courtesy Midlothian Libraries.

7. Roslin gunpowder mill workers wait at Roslin Castle Station for a train to take them on their annual outing, c.1914–20. Courtesy Midlothian Libraries.

8. Some women workers at the gunpowder mill, *c.*1914–20. Courtesy Midlothian Libraries.

9. Workers at the gunpowder mill, *c.*1900–14. Mr Hargreaves, manager, back row right; Peter Grant, cashier, back row left. Courtesy Midlothian Libraries and Mrs Davidson, Roslin.

10. Uniformed gateman and other workers at the entrance to the gunpowder mill in Roslin Glen, *c*.1920–30. Courtesy Mr George Campbell, Roslin.

11. Workers electioneering at the gunpowder mill works council elections, 1929. Courtesy Midlothian Libraries.

12. Miss Cairns, laboratory worker, at the gunpowder mill, *c.*1910–20. Courtesy Mr George Campbell, Roslin.

13. The gunpowder mill office, 1937. The flags and bunting were for the Coronation of King George VI. Courtesy Mr George Campbell, Roslin.

14. Workers formerly at Camilty explosive works return home to West Calder after their day's work at Roslin gunpowder mills, 1940s. Courtesy Mr George Campbell, Roslin.

15. Houses in Roslin Glen, with Roslin Chapel in the background at the top, c.1930s. Courtesy Mr George Campbell, Roslin.

16 & 17. Roslin gunpowder mill workers and their families on the works annual outing, *c.*1950. Courtesy Mrs Mary Murray, Rosewell.

18. Men workers, 1944, in the blackpowder section of the Roslin gunpowder mill and bomb factory. Back row (left to right) : (unknown), J. Fairley, (unknown), A. Nichol, H. Fairley, J. Reid. Middle row (left to right)): (unknown), A. Dippie, J.Brown, J. Fleming, (unknown), J. Whittaker, D. Smith, W. Grossart, A. Higginson, (last two both unknown). Front row (left to right): W. Milne, R. Waldie, G. Leadbetter, J. McMillan, D. Leadbetter, J. Fulton, J. Main, J. Forsyth.
Courtesy ICI Ltd., and Mrs Elizabeth McCorry.

19. Women blackpowder and messroom workers at the Roslin mill, 1944. Back row (left to right): B. Steel, V. Mannion, C. McArthur, Elizabeth McCorry, S. Neil, E. Higginson. Middle row (left to right): M. Richardson, D. Gilder, J. McLay, B. Kerr, J. McCall, L. Urquhart, J. Whittaker. Front row (left to right): N. Archibald, A. Wright, C. Inglis, (first name unknown), Mrs Bamber, R. George, E. Hepplewhite, (unknown - from Rosewell). Courtesy ICI Ltd., and Mrs Elizabeth McCorry.

20. Women workers at the Roslin gunpowder and bomb factory, 1944. The man in centre of front row is Mr McCorquodale, works superintendent, and the man at left of back row is Andrew Millar, foreman. Courtesy ICI Ltd., and Mrs Elizabeth McCorry

21. Women workers in the bomb section, July 1944. Back row (left to right): Jean Cairns (Rosewell), Ella Delaney, Doreen Ramsay, Agnes Clark, (unknown - from Rosewell), Elizabeth McCorry, (unknown), (first name unknown) Sinton (from Auchendinny). Middle row: (left to right): Mary Bain, Betty Hunter, Cathy Davie, Bessie Naismith, Babs Milne, Bessie Brown, (unknown - from Rosewell). Front row (left to right): Chris Smith, Dolly Hannah, Nora Comrybog, Mary Murray, Nettie Bolton, Helena Affleck, Nan Richardson, Lizzie Grant. Courtesy ICI Ltd., and Mrs Elizabeth McCorry

22. Women workers in the bomb section, and white-coated government inspectors, at the gunpowder mill, 1944. Back row (left to right): Margaret Dowers, (unknown), (first name unknown) Russell, (first name unknown) Wilson, Martha Leadbetter, Mrs Gregg, Sarah Dyet, Betty Ferguson. Middle row (left to right): (unknown), (a mother and daughter from Rosewell, names unknown), Mrs Wallace, Mrs Bennett, Nellie McAvoy, Jean Scott, Nan Paterson. Front row (left to right): Mrs Smith, supervisors, names unknown), Mr Millar (supervisors, names unknown), Jess Leary. Courtesy ICI Ltd., and Mrs Elizabeth McCorry.

23. Women canteen workers at Roslin gunpowder mill and bomb factory, 1947, with two foremen, Willie Mitchell and Mr Gargan. Courtesy ICI Ltd., and Mrs Elizabeth McCorry.

a month at the Thicket but then you had your food. And I was lucky – The Thicket was a good food place.

Ye got paid for your holidays. We got two weeks' paid holidays. But Christmas and New Year didn't really come into it, ye know, in these days. It wis jist another working day.

Well, of course, at fifteen years you've plenty energy. I mean, at fifteen or that sort of age you've got plenty of energy and you don't think about work, ye know. I never remember feeling tired then. And of course you were never off sick. If ye had the cold ye jist worked on. There was no sick leave or anything.

I had a room at The Thicket and it wis outside the house. You went round the back and there wis two doors, and one wis the downstairs room and one wis an upstairs room, and there wis a well between it, like a big well with a top on it. Betty, the daughter of the house, had had this room. So they gave me that. It wis quite a nice room – of course, it wis a nice room compared to being at home at Glenside, where I had always had to share a room with my sister. It wis a lovely room at The Thicket. Ah had jist a wee oil lamp in it, and that worried me because we always slept with the lamp lit in the Glen. So I thought, 'I'll light it.' But one night I thought, 'I'm frightened it goes on fire.' So I stopped. Ah wasn't really nervous about being out there on ma own at The Thicket.

When Mrs Forbes and her children went away on holiday for a fortnight, I was left there alone. You see, the cook and butler they were a married couple, and they got their holidays – a fortnight – and then ah got mine at a different time. So ma father wouldn't let me stay in that house myself for a fortnight. So he went up and stayed at The Thicket for the fortnight and ah stayed down at home at Glenside. It wasn't far. To stay in that big house myself for a fortnight at the age of fifteen or sixteen wasn't on.

When I left The Thicket – I was there for two years – I thought about going to nursing. As a girl at school I don't think I'd ever had ambitions. We jist took every day as it came, ye know, and we didn't think about the future much, I don't think. But ye got your lessons at school and ye took them seriously. Your parents encouraged you, and we only had an oil lamp at home but you did your lessons just the same. So when I left The Thicket I thought about going to nursing. But my sister Polly was working at a house at Seafield crossroads, at the back of Bilston. Polly was a cook, always a good cook. She didn't go to Lasswade High School, but she was a good cook. And so the girl working beside her at Seafield had left and ma mother said, 'Well, there's a job up beside Polly.'

And this was an American lady, a very nice lady, Mrs Todd, at Seafield. Her husband was a lawyer. She came from Pittsburgh. Her father was in the steel mills. But very different in her outlook, you know, and very generous, very generous. She was a cripple and then she broke her hip when I was there. Well, I was seventeen when I went there and then by the time she became sort of in her bed most of the day – she stayed downstairs in a bed, not upstairs – and after she broke her hip and she came home from the hospital she brought a nurse for a wee while. I used to take over when the nurse was off. Then the nurse left and I just took over altogether. But I enjoyed it because Mrs Todd was such a good person. So I ended nursing her actually till the night she died.

Well, she jist had ma sister Polly and I as servants. I did the house work and looking after her, and ma sister did the cooking and a bit of the washing. We had to do a bit of washing there, too. Some went to the laundry, and some was washed.

I was living in at Mrs Todd's, too. The wages weren't high – £2 a month, the same as at The Thicket – but then you had your food and she was so good to us in other ways. I enjoyed it because she was such a good person. And again I was lucky: Mrs Todd's was excellent for the food. The food was very good, because they just sent the biggest they could get – the biggest turkey at Christmas, you know. And Mrs Todd was really a great person to work for. Well, the police station wis built there, and she used to let us bring the chaps in, you know, at night just for eating, more or less. They enjoyed the food ! My sister Polly was a good cook and baked and everything.

Both at Mrs Todd's and at Mrs Forbes' we always started the day before breakfast by saying prayers. We knelt on the floor in front of the chairs. Ah had the same long day at Mrs Todd's as at

The Thicket. Of course, ah wis up at half-past six because she needed early morning treatment and that. And then she had to be washed and all that. And ah washed her again about ten o'clock, ye know, to go to bed. But then she used to let us out to dances, and she used to get Mr Todd to come home early. They had dinner at night, and he came home early so we could get the coffee dishes done, and then she sent him to take us down to the dances. Dances used to be whist drives and dances and they went on till two o'clock in the morning. So we went to the whist dances. She would send us out to all the dances in Roslin. We used to get the folk to phone her up and tell her the dances were on, and she'd send a taxi for us. And Mrs Todd was a dear soul, ye know. When ah went in after a dance she'd be still awake and she'd say, 'Did you win a prize ?' – because often she gave the prizes ! For our birthdays she'd buy us a coat or shoes and we had frocks and everything bought for us, and Easter eggs even. We never wanted for anything. I used to go out in the car with her. She wis a wonderful person. Ah couldn't stop talking about her when ah went to the bomb factory because she had been such a nice person. Ah missed her.

I had two half-days at Mrs Todd's. I had Tuesday and Thursday as half-days, and every other Saturday or Sunday. And ma sister Polly got it the same, so we got an extra half day there after a while. Well, I had Thursday and either Saturday or Sunday, and ma sister Tuesday and either Saturday or Sunday. We didn't need a lot of money. We only went into the pictures maybe in Edinburgh on a Saturday. It was cheap – 4d. return in the train. A shilling would just about cover the outing.

Ma sister Polly had started work in Roslin carpet factory, she would be two years there and she would be sixteen when she went to Todd's as a cook a year before I went. Cook in domestic service was a fairly senior job, and ma sister was quite young. She wis great though, she could cook. But it wasn't such a difficult job at Mrs Todd's as ah would say it was at The Thicket. Mrs Forbes there came through and made up a menu every Monday morning and, ye know, it was all the different things. And then her children were on something where they didn't get brown bread, and they didn't get white bread, and they didn't get meat. So it was quite difficult for the cook at The Thicket. But Mrs Todd just had pretty ordinary cooking, ye know. And then she became a diabetic, so that was kind of difficult. Her stuff had to be weighed.

On a Saturday, as ah say, we went to the pictures. And then ah chummed a girl that wis in the carpet factory. And at night when ah got ma half-day from service ah used to meet this girl and we used to walk over the Rosewell road and we used to meet the chaps, young miners, from Rosewell coming towards Roslin. So we had a blether with them, you know. That's how I met ma husband ! And the road was dead quiet, ye know. They just walked in a row across the road, and we – more than us – used to walk over and chaff them on the road. This was a sort of custom, I think it was. It was more or less a chaffing, you know, just sort of you were in groups and ye just had a good laugh. Well, it wis only on our half-days that we could go out, ye see, at night. The young fellows probably went out for a walk quite a lot at nights. There was nothing else to do, you know. And then on a Saturday, as ah say, we went to the pictures and a lot o' the young chaps used to go to the pictures as well on a Saturday so you got to know them in that way.

We walked up and down the main road from Bilston to Penicuik once or twice on a Sunday night. And then the soldiers at Glencorse had wee cottages out along the side of the road and they used to come to the wall. And I think a lot of the girls used to have a blether with them, and then ye walked up and down the road. But we tended to go from Roslin in the opposite direction – towards Rosewell. That was another sort of recognised courting or meeting place. But eventually we met these two chaps quite a lot, ma friend and I, and one o' them wis Jimmy, the one that's ma husband. So that's how I met him.

Ah don't think there wis that many girls in Roslin that married anybody from Rosewell, except me. Ye know, ma friend didn't marry the other chap that came over from there with Jimmy. At that time there wasn't any feeling that people in Roslin were better than people in Rosewell, or vice versa. Ye jist felt ye were all one more or less, well, all workin' people, ye know, because there were miners in Roslin and miners at

Rosewell. At Rosewell there wis jist really the brickworks and the pit, and maybe one or two big houses with domestic servants. But in Roslin there was the pit – the Moat – and the carpet factory, the gunpowder mill and the bomb factory, which wis separate.

But, ye see, ma husband was at the pit in Rosewell from when he left school, because his father was killed in the First World War. When his father was killed in 1916 in the east, at Gaza, Mr Hamilton, the colliery manager, or whoever it was, came down to ma husband's mother and told her they were allowed to keep the coal company house on condition that the two boys went to the pit.[31] But that was the only way Jimmy's mother was allowed to keep the house. And ma husband at that time wis only two years old and his brother wis four. But as long as the boys went to work in the pit . . . So his brother became an engineer in the pit and Jimmy wis a joiner in the pit. And then when Jimmy's time wis out he got a job in the colliery time office wi' Mungo Mackay or one o' the Mackays.[32] But ma husband said that when they got word that his father had been killed in the war – he was said to be missing at first – your pension stopped or something. And an invalid aunt stayed with them who had nothing either. However, the minister's wife must have got to hear about it and she put up some messages, as they say, to keep them going till they got sort of sorted out. But it wis hard, ye know. They were very reserved people, Jimmy's family, because they were Irish, ye see. Ma husband's father and mother belonged to Northern Ireland. So they were a little bit out there as well, staying in Rosewell, though Rosewell was known then as Little Ireland.[33] But they were very quiet people. They came from Ballymena, I think, in Northern Ireland over to the pit at Rosewell. They were a Protestant family. But they got on well with the Catholic people in Rosewell.

I don't remember in those days any division at all among people in Roslin over religion. In fact, on a Sunday night the Salvation Army band used to come down from Penicuik and play at the Original Hotel at Roslin, and the churches all had evening services there. So that all came out about the same time and they used to all stand round at this band and sing the hymns, which was rather nice, ye know, that they all joined together at the end of the day. There were very few Catholics in Roslin when I was a girl. In fact, there wasn't a separate Catholic school, they didn't go to Loanhead or anything, and they stayed at school with us in Roslin. They jist stayed in the class and they didn't take Bible with us or anything. Well, ah can remember in the Glen once – of course, they all went to the church more or less, some of them, but we went regular, you see, we were regular Chapel goers – and ah remember one girl said to me, 'Of course, you're Christian.' ! She meant Episcopalian. We got on well together really. There wasn't strong feelings between Catholics and Protestants. One girl sort of bullied me once, pulled me down Jacob's Ladder in the Glen. But, you see, ma mother jist gave me a note to the school and the headmaster took the girl into the room along with me, and he took the belt out and he belted it down on the desk. And he said to her, 'The next time you do that . . .' And I had no more trouble.

Ah was at Mrs Todd's at Seafield till she died. I was there five years and she just died suddenly one night. That would be 1940 when she died. Mrs Todd's husband decided then he would get an elderly housekeeper, because ma sister Polly and I were two sort of, you know, dancing girls. Then ah went to the bomb factory at Roslin. Ah went voluntary, ah wasn't called up to go. I asked for a job there and I got a job. Well, it wis either that or the Services, you see. So at least there you were at home. But ah wasn't actually called up. Well, it wis jist ma mother. She said, 'I think you should jist go to the bomb factory.' So ah went and got this job at the bomb factory. Actually, you see, I never wanted to work in the powder mills, because when I was seven there used to be explosions and the girl next door to me, Peg Lauder, she was killed in 1925, along with Pim Arnott from Station Road in Roslin. Peg wis only 25. And I always said that ah would never go tae the powder mills. But then the war came on and ye jist difted in, ye know.

Well, when ah started at the bomb factory ah went in and the man said, 'Ah'll put you on the wrapping.' And the wrapping was actually a cardboard piece of paper that you put shellac on, and you had a round piece of pressed powder, and you wrapped that up, tucked it all in. And then it was taken next door and they put it into a cartridge and put the top on. And that wis where the signal cartridges were used by the navy. So ah wis on that for quite a while.

But sometimes ah wis sent to other jobs. Ah made the bags for that gunpowder to be put in at one time. And then ah wis sent to weigh cordite up near the office place. Ah got this wee job on the scales. And ah wis also on, ye know, making the discs, the pellets, and ah wis on the Northovers. The discs or pellets, it wis a strip of cambric and it had been done with some kind of glue and then the gunpowder put on. And you had a hammer, a wooden hammer, which you punched these discs with, for to be used for other things, you know. And some bright spark told me that that was the hut in which I was punching these discs where somebody had been killed during the First War ! Somebody was always cheering you up, you know ! The Northover projectors, ah think they were used for tanks, the Northovers.[34] They were sort of funny wee jobs. You had to fill these wee sort o' plastic caps. You put them under a hopper and filled them. They were fiky to put in but you managed them and you'd to do quite a lot, about 2,000 or something a shift – you had sort of tallies to do, ye see. And then sometimes we filled bombs – metal containers and you filled that with gunpowder. These were small bombs that were dropped from aeroplanes. You just sort of went where you were asked to go. But this wrapping was the main job ah had.

Ah had a good time. Ah wis only on two shifts. A lot o' them were on three shifts. And then what happened was we were on the one shift, and then instead of doing, I think it was a six-day shift, they decided to do a five-day shift and a seven-day shift, to get the Saturday off, because that suited them to get the Saturday off. So we decided on that. Ah mean, it wis voted on so we had a five-shift week. It meant that church people like myself could go to church on Sunday.

Well, we started at six in the morning and we finished at two in the afternoon. That wis a short day to what we were used to in domestic service. And we got half an hour for our breakfast. I think that wis all we got really wis the one break. It wis about nine o'clock, and we used to get up for that. Then we worked straight through from about half-past nine to two o'clock. And then on the other shift we started at two o'clock till ten. We got jist one half-hour break in that time, about tea time.

I was put on a night shift one night and I met one o' the gaffers goin' up the hill. Ye see, there wis three gaffers. And it wis Willie Mitchell that I met in the car going up the brae on the Sunday night, and he said, 'Where are you goin' ?' Ah says, 'Oh, ah'm goin' out on the night shift.' He says, 'Oh, you're not supposed to be on night shift. Go back home.' So I was sent back home. It must have been because the work I was doing you weren't on night shifts. So I had only done the Saturday night shift. I was quite glad ! I didn't like night shift. I had that one night, and eating in the middle of the night. I said, 'Oh, I don't like this at all.' But again ye had to do it if you were on the shifts. Some of the girls worked three shifts.

When ah started at the bomb factory in 1940 my wages were £2.5.0. per week. After we decided to do a five-day shift and a seven-day shift we got extra money. So it ended up that one week we got £2.5.0. and we got £4 for the other week. It wis quite a lot of money. It wasn't piece work, it was jist time rates.

Actually, the wages were quite good, you know. Ma sister Polly worked in the bomb factory, too, but she gave up the smoke floats. She couldn't stand it because it wis very, very dirty on the smoke floats. It wis white powder that they used and it used to get into your skin. She said they didn't even have masks at first, and then they got masks. But eventually her husband had come back from the B.E.F. in France after 1940 and had got a job as a military police down in England. So she went away to join him. They tried to put her off at the bomb factory by sayin' there were no jobs down there but she went down and got into Short's, the aircraft makers, down in Rochester in Kent. And of course there she got about £4–odds a week, and she said to someone, 'What good wages you have. We just got £2.5.0. up there at the Roslin bomb factory.' And they said, 'But what about your danger money ?' She says, 'Oh, the £2.5.0. included the danger money.' It wis jist the same !

At the gate at the bomb factory you were searched at the

beginning of every shift. It was quite necessary really, you know. Well, I think really sometimes they sort o' knew the people that smoked and the people that didn't smoke. So it wis more or less the people that smoked that had to leave their cigarettes and that and they had to go out there at the gate to get a smoke. Ah didn't smoke myself: ah smoked for a week before ah went to the bomb factory and then ah never smoked again – I got a packet o' Woodbine and that finished it ! They never really touched you at the gate, you know, you jist said that you had nothing in your pockets. Oh, they didn't frisk you or anything like that.

The thing is that you didn't think about the danger, you know. I had always had this dread, but once you were there amongst other girls you never thought of the danger of it. And safety precautions were always taken. We had shower facilities and all that laid on for after your shift, because you had to change your clothes coming in and going out. We wore special boots and sort o' tweed skirts and a blue jersey and a black sort of fireproof overall and hat. That was all issued to you, you didn't have to pay for that.

On a Friday you washed up – or a Saturday, whatever was the last day of the week. You'd to wash out all your building with a pail and water. And sometimes we used to take the pail into the building beforehand, ye see. But when Willie Mitchell, the gaffer, came round he used to say, 'Get that pail out of here!' We were not supposed to have it there because it was metal.

We were all in different buildings, ye know, because ye had to be kept separate. They wouldn't allow sisters to work in the same building; you had to work in different buildings.

But we did things, you know, that we shouldn't have done, like piercing ears and that with a needle ! It was a great fashion to get your ears pierced. And of course the girls used to bring a cork and a darning needle and pierce it. Well, ye see, that wis metal. They shouldn't have had it, we weren't supposed to have any metal at all. And we started this ear-piercing. However, when we were doing it one day the girl fainted and we'd a job gettin' her round. And then the one that did the piercing she fainted as well. So we got them all round before anybody got to know about it.

Then there was somebody brought a tank up once to the bomb factory. Well, we made the Northover projectors. Ah think they were used for tanks, the Northovers. So we were all given a bit shot in this tank inside the bomb factory. It wis a big tank. Ah don't know how, but it wis brought up there and ah remember we all got into it to see the inside of it and that, ye know. Ah don't know if that would maybe be a wee bit dangerous, a tank inside the bomb factory. But it wis quite interesting.

We had concerts up at the bomb factory sometimes, E.N.S.A. concerts. And we had a film sometimes.

Ah don't think there was any trade union in the bomb factory. Ah don't think ah joined a union. And the factory was very strict, ye know. You couldn't take days off. You'd be sent for if your attendance was . . . You weren't sort of allowed days off or anything. It had to be something serious. So most of us were never off our work. The ones that if their husbands were in England and got home on leave, they would get off for that, ye see. But otherwise you were never off your work. Oh, you were sent for to the office if you had taken days off without proper permission. They were quite strict about it. I don't know if they would have paid you off. The only thing is they could have said, 'Well, there'll be no wages if you're off', ye see. I don't remember anybody being sacked for absenteeism. I know them that were sent for once or twice when they were off, but nobody I know of wis sacked.

We got two weeks' paid holidays at the bomb factory in the summer, two consecutive weeks. Ah think we got Christmas Day and New Year's Day. We never had gone away on holiday as a family. Ma father got one week Trades Holidays – the first week in July – from the carpet factory, but it was unpaid. So ma mother used to say, 'It's a week's idle time.' With four children it would have been quite an expense for my parents to go away on holiday. But as children we loved going to Portobello. It was really nice, we enjoyed that. Ma father didn't get Christmas holidays or that, just the unpaid Trades Week. Actually, the best job ma father had – the carpet factory closed for a while during the war – was when he got a job as a watchman in the Second

War in the powder mills. And he had that for about four years, and that was the best job he ever had. But then when the powder mills closed after the war he had to go back to the carpet factory again.

Ah remember at the bomb factory we had an old inspector. He was for the navy. He liked a drink. He wasn't very nice to some of the inspectresses we had. He come into our building one day and we had our things on the tray that we had wrapped, you see. I don't know if some of them hadn't stuck down properly but he started picking at them and throwing them about. And of course ah've always been the kind of person that would speak up if it was necessary. So of course I said, 'Do you realise it's explosives you're throwing around ?' And he says, 'Nothing to do with you, girl.' I think the girls in the hut next door were all enjoying it, you know, somebody speaking up. Ah wis sent to the office but ah jist told the manager that the inspector wis throwin' the stuff about and it wasn't right, because we were to be careful and that. Oh, he was a bit of a bully, the inspector. He wasn't a nice man at all. There were different inspectors for different things. They were naval and air force and army people. But the inspector was for the navy, and he wis inspecting these things. Well, he could have been slightly tipsy at the time, I don't know. As I say, he wasn't a nice person. He wasn't very nice to some of his own girls, ah know that. They wore blue. They wore different coloured overalls from us. We had to wear fireproof clothes. But the inspectresses had jist overalls, and there wis blue for the navy, ye know, khaki for the army, and so on. Oh, they weren't W.R.N.S.[35] I think they were employed actually by the bomb factory people, and the inspector was in charge of them.

During the war German planes came over the bomb factory. You see, they had huts up at Eddleston in Peeblesshire. That's where they stored the gunpowder, in huts up in the hills there. But we had air raid shelters that we used to go into. You went down into them, they were sunken into the ground. Ah remember being in them once or twice, but not very often. And, ye see, there's another thing: ma mother's family in London they were bombed out, and ma mother had ma cousin with three children and another cousin with three children, and her own brother and his wife – all come up to Glenside at Roslin. And our neighbour at Glenside got a little money for giving them accommodation, to cover sheets and that sort of thing. So between ma mother and our neighbour we put them up. But ma mother did all the cooking and she was still in that two-roomed house. And one of ma cousins from London actually got a job at the bomb factory for a wee while sewing, ye know, mending overalls and that. But we had all these people up from London, and then they would go home, and then it would get bad again and then they'd come up again. It wis a bad time.

During the Second War there was just one person killed at the bomb factory. He was a Mr Malcolm, and he was the second husband of Mrs Manson, whose first husband was also killed there. He was killed in the bottom mill, of course. Oh, there were quite a few deaths in and after the First War. Mr Manson was killed then, and there wis a Robison killed in the same explosion. And ah think the one in 1925 where Peg Lauder wis killed and Pim Arnott, there was another girl by the name of Glass, from Bonnyrigg, badly injured. But she recovered, I think. And then ah think there was a girl Gargan killed in the bomb factory during the First War. Because ah remember being sent to that house or hut to work in and that's where she used to work. Oh, it was quite a dangerous job, the powder mill and bomb factory. When they heard the rumbles in Roslin it used to shake the houses and everyone ran out the back and they could see the puff of smoke and they knew it was the mills. And I've always remembered that day in 1925, because I remember Mrs Lauder, Peg's mother, dressed in black, goin' away at night. They'd be goin' in to identify them possibly at the Infirmary in Edinburgh. It was terrible. Peg Lauder was just a young person. She wasn't married. And there had been an explosion not long before that, and she was chaffing somebody and she said, 'Oh, well,' she said, 'it's not ma turn yet', or something. And then that happened.[36]

I think there would be about 500 worked in the bomb factory when I was there. Some of them were long term people, ye know. Most of them had been in the powder mills, whereas people like myself were there jist for the war. There were three shifts and there wis quite a lot of people because we were all in different buildings, ye know, because ye had to be kept separate.

There wasn't more men than women There were a few men, because most men would be called up, and there wis a few men on the presses and that sort of thing, pressing the gunpowder. And then we had the ones that were overseers, of course, and inspectors. But the other workers were mostly women.

At the bomb factory we didn't have much contact with the workers in the gunpowder mill. The only thing is we used to have meetings. It was a committee meeting or something they used to have up in the house at Eskhill. And we used to go down the woods and across and up to Eskhill to these meetings. But that's the only contact we really had with the other mill people. They worked down there. They were basically making powder, ah think. There were quite a lot of men in the powder mill. We knew quite a few of them that worked there. They lived in Roslin.

The bomb factory wis a great place. You had your rough and ready ones but ye had a mixed crowd. There were people at the bomb factory that had never worked before. They never needed to work. But they had to work during the war, ye see, so they came to the bomb factory. So you had a mixture of very refined people along with your usual ones. It wis a happy place, but some days you were upset because somebody, a Services person, had been killed that you knew. And then another day they'd a' be sittin' singin', ye know, jist workin' and singin'.

When ah worked at the bomb factory ah got married. Ah got married in September 1942. Jimmy had been called up earlier in the war. I got a telegram from him the one Saturday to make the arrangements for the wedding the next. And I had a bike so I cycled down to Lasswade wi' the banns, and did all the necessary work. We got the cake, and we got Mrs Young, who had the tearoom at Roslin – she did a steak pie and that, because it wis all rations then. And I had a wonderful wedding. In a week I arranged it all maself. Jimmy got home on embarkation leave on the Friday and we got married on the Saturday. We were married in Roslin Chapel. So we had a nice wedding and we jist had a night at the Empire Theatre in Edinburgh, as it was then. And ma husband went away on the Monday and ah never saw him for four years after that.

And then of course before the end of the war we were paid off at the bomb factory. When the war in Europe phased out – April '45, I think, after that push, ye know, across the Rhine into Germany – they decided to pay off some of them. And of course it was done on an age limit. So I wis jist on the age limit to be paid off. I was 27 and that was the limit. They decided to pay us off, the ones that were 27. The foremen weren't very pleased because most of us were the best attenders, you know.

But we were paid off and they told us that we could go to the Eveready battery place at Dalkeith, where they made batteries. But ah didn't go there. Ah went to the buroo and they gave me a job down at Kevock at Lasswade, blood testing for the Ministry of Agriculture and Fisheries. It wis for hens. But it wis only temporary. While I wis on that job Jimmy, ma husband, got home on leave for three weeks but he had to go back to Italy again. That was 1946 and that was the first time he'd been home for four years, since we were married. And then of course we were paid off at Eskgrove, Kevock, about the end of '46. And ah thought, well, the only thing ah could do wis to go into the carpet factory, which was near home and which ah'd never worked in. After ah got married in 1942, you see, ah stayed on with ma mother at Glenside till after ma husband came home from the war. So I decided to go into the carpet factory for jist a few months. And I went there and I got a job in setting the wool, which was quite a nice job. It was big rollers and you had bobbins of wool and you put them on, and then you ran this roller back and it sort of set the wool the way it should be. And of course they used to get fed up when it got near the end of the bobbins, and they would say, 'We'll just wrap them off and tear them off and take them home and burn them.' So we had to smuggle these bits o' wool out. But it wis quite a nice job. But it was very cold in the factory, oh, it wis a cold place to work. Ah wis sittin' beside a heater, a tin heater that used to blow out as much draught as heat really.

Ah left the carpet factory as soon as ma husband came home

at the end of '46, ah just left. In those days you didn't think about working once you were married. The war was exceptional. Even teachers they left work when they got married. That was the done thing in those days. So I just left the carpet factory.

Housing wis a real problem at that time. Ma husband's parents at Rosewell and mine at Glenside only had two-roomed houses. So what happened wis ah had to stay between Rosewell and Glenside, because I'd put ma name in for a prefab in Roslin but ah didn't get one there. So ah put ma name in for Rosewell. Sometimes, jist off and on, jist maybe weeks, ma husband and I weren't living together: ma husband stayed in Rosewell with his parents and ah stayed with mine at Glenside. And then we managed to get a prefab at Rosewell. And they were nice wee houses, only they were aluminium – they were cold. And a garden to yourself. Oh, the kitchens were marvellous – everybody was looking in the windows and saying, 'What lovely kitchens you've got' – and nice big bathrooms. It was the first time we'd actually had a bathroom. We'd never had a bath really, except of course when we were in service – we always had baths there. Ah remained sixteen years in that Rosewell prefab, then we came to Roslin.

I've just got the one son. He went to Heriot's. Ah hadn't thought about this sort o' thing but the Women's Rural started in Rosewell. Ah wis the first treasurer there, and they were all talking – the farmers' people – about their sons sitting these exams. They said, 'It's only five shillings.' And my son was doing well at school in Rosewell. So he sat the exam for Heriot's and he got accepted. He wis twelve. He didn't get a bursary. But at the same time through the Rural this girl who was the head one in Gestetner's at Stafford Street in Edinburgh, she says to me, 'Ah'm needing a part-time person for the cardex. Would you be interested ?' It wis £3 a week, and ah went from Rosewell to the West end for £3 a week. And that practically paid all my son's fees and his train fares at Heriot's. And eventually it wis £6 a week when we got equal pay.

I was at Gestetner for seven years part-time. And I did typing during that time and stock-taking, stock book, the wages, well, ever so many things there. So ah learnt a lot at Gestetner. Ah wis always grateful to that girl because she put me on the office ladder, ye know. And then ah left there eventually because there wis a coachworks in Roslin at the back of the Penicuik Road, and they were needing a person to do the office work. So ah got that job. That wis only £4 a week, it wis part-time, but ah saved on bus fares. And then ah learnt the wages there. So ah did that for about six or seven years, and then I went up to The Bush estate to the plant breeding and ah got a job in the chemistry department there. However, ah wasn't very keen on that job, and I had an accident with acid. Then ah saw this advert in the *Evening News* for the civil service for clerical assistants – and it wis up to age 59. Ah had to look if ah wis seeing right. So ah sat the exam – that's where ma Roslin School education came in, because it was the English grammar, the arithmetic and things like that, and it just suited me down to the ground – and so ah learned that ah had been accepted. Ah wis 56 then. So ah got into the civil service, first of all in the Economic Planning Department in Old St Andrew's House then I got this job with the development department graphics group, a job as a photo-typesetter on this fabulous machine which was new at the time. Ah got so good at it ah could do even slides for some of them giving lectures. So ah worked in the civil service for nine years. It was the most enjoyable job I ever did. When I went into that job it wis about £25 a week, and when I left it wis £80–odd a week. Ah kept that job till I wis 65. It wis a great way to end ma working life because, well, ah get a pension from that whereas I would have got nothing before that.

My son went through the university and took an Honours degree in geography, which I hated when I was at school. He's got a good job and he likes travelling. He does hill walking. He's been at Katmandu and been up Mount Kilimanjaro. So we never got any further than Portobello but ma son's made up for it!

JANET PEEBLES

It wis in 1941 anyway ah went tae the bomb factory, it must have been in the late summer, I think. Ma father was killed in the April, and I'd had ma callin'-up papers and I'd went for an interview for the W.R.N.S. Ma sister had went for something else. And ma uncle Jim Bell, he was ma mother's brother, worked in the powder mills at Roslin. So he got us a job up there – without even askin' us ! So that's where we ended up, me and ma sister.

Ah wis born at Loanhead in June 1919. There were six girls and one boy in ma family. Ah wis number 5. Ah had a sister – she's still livin' – then ma brother, and then another two sisters and then me. Then there were two sisters below me.

Ma father was a miner. He was brought up on a farm. He bade away in Nether Shiels, no' far frae Stow. But he hadn't worked on the land as far as ah know. He worked in the Dalmore paper mill. And he was on the horse and cart, ye know, taking the paper back and forward. He must have took it intae Edinburgh. Well, ye see, he got married and needed the money. And there wis more money in the pits in these days than what there wis in the paper mill.

Ma father wis really self-educated, I would say. He left school early. He widnae have much education. But he wis a great reader. We had a dictionary and he read it frae end tae end. He worked for the miners. They had a Federation, they called it. And it wis great, it did wi' their health. If they were off work ye got so much. It wisnae very much. It looked after the Miners' Institute and a' these things, run the Institute.

Ma father wis killed April 1941 in the Ramsay pit at Loanhead. A hutch ran away and he grabbed it and went down. Oh, that wis a shock. I'd be twenty-one then. We got £300 compensation, that's what ma mother got.

Ah went to school in Loanhead. Ah left school when ah wis fourteen. Looking back now ah wish ah'd had the chance to carry on at school. Oh, ah'd like to have went to Lasswade School and learned languages. But ah wisnae disappointed when ah left school, ah jist accepted it. I had one brother, Bill, and he wis an engineer in the pits and his manager, the head engineer, was awfy good. And he got him tae Heriot Watt. Ah don't know if it would be day release or jist night school, but the books that he had tae buy – well, money was spent on that. Well, ye see, long ago a girl left school and got married and kept house and that was it. And the money wis spent on Bill. There were six girls and one boy, Bill, in our family. Well, Bill remained in the pits through his working life and eventually he wis a colliery manager. He ended up in the Lady Victoria colliery at Newtongrange.

So ah went straight into work when ah left school in 1933. First job I worked in a shop in Loanhead. It was a hairdresser's and confectioner's. Ah used tae go in at nights on the Saturday before ah left the school. Well, I had a paper round before that. I used to go wi' papers. But ma sister worked in the draper's shop in Loanhead and she heard they were wantin' a girl in this sweetie shop and hairdresser's. And she had me workin', she made me go intae this shop. She got me this job there – makin' sure ah was goin' tae work! But the sister that got me this job she would ha' stayed on at the school, too. She didnae want tae work either. But she didnae get. It wisnae in the fashion for her either.

In the sweetie shop and hairdresser's I started at half-past eight in the mornin' and finished at half-past seven at night – other than that it was nine o'clock at night. That wis Monday to Saturday. Saturday you worked till ten o'clock at night. But there wis a law came out no' long after ah started workin', so ah got a half-day on a Tuesday and a mornin' off on a Wednesday, and ah got away at half-past four on a Thursday.[37]

The wage there wis ten shillins a week, which wisnae much. They got a lot more in the paper mill. But I wis quite happy. Oh,

I didnae feel tired, never thocht anything aboot it at a'. It wid be two years ah wis in the Loanhead shop.

Then ah left there. There was a traveller, ye see, and this traveller he got me this job in a fruit shop in Penicuik – MacDonald's. They wanted an assistant and ah came up tae this shop in Penicuik. It wis a poorly paid job and ah had fares, too. Ah travelled up and down on the bus, ninepence a day return it wis. Ye started at nine, finished at seven, ah think it wis, six days a week. A half-day on the Wednesday. So the hours were maybe a wee bit shorter than at Loanhead but not much. But, oh, young as ah wis ah knew it widnae pay. The fruit shop wisnae busy enough. Something tells ye that ye're no' goin' tae last long. Ye have tae increase your wages, ye see.

It wid jist be about a year, I think, I wis there. Then ah left there when ah wis about seventeen and I worked in Woolies at the east end o' Princes Street in Edinburgh. That wis a good job. It wis the manager, Mr Bach, that interviewed me for the job. The supervisor wasn't available that day. It wis a bus strike, it wis the month o' May and it wisnae nice weather. There'd been snow and ah had a trench coat on that had been ma nephew's, and ah went in wi' Wellie boots on for the interview. Mr Bach asked me what ma father did and ah says – ah'd been warned – ah says, 'He's a collier.' Ah hardly knew what that meant, by George ! We always spoke aboot miners. And Mr Bach says, 'Does he work ?' Ah says, 'Yes.' He says, 'How many of a family has he got ?' And ah told him. He says, 'Are they workin' ?' Ah says, 'Yes, they're a' workin'.' 'Well, ye know,' he says, 'some o' these men they get their family workin' and they won't work themselves.' He says, 'Does he drink ?' 'Oh,' ah says, 'he likes a pint.' Nothing wis said. And he asked me if ah knew the banker in Loanhead, Mr MacMurray. Ah says, 'Oh, ah know him very well.' So ah did, ah knew him well when ah worked in Loanhead. 'And who's your doctor ?' Ah says, 'Dr Gunn.' He says, 'I know Dr Gunn.' Ah says, 'Well, the first house he ever came intae in Loanhead wis ma mother's house.' And he always called ma mother Ting-a-ling, because Bell wis her ain name. He wis jist makin' a joke. And he always wis awfy good tae ma mother, Dr Gunn. Two days after the interview ah wis told ah wis gettin' a job. MacMurray the banker came tae tell me. Mr Bach had been speirin'. He wisnae interested in written references. So that's how ah got the job in Woolies.

That wis a good job. It wis better paid, oh, about twenty-five shillins a week. That wis a good wage for a girl. Well, ye started at nine and ye finished at seven, half-day on a Tuesday. Eight o'clock at night on a Saturday. That wis your hours. It wis quite a long day but that wis quite common, they were standard hours.

And ye got 2/6d. o' a rise every year. Ah started in March – that wid be 1936 – and ah got a rise in June: 2/6d. And it wis a girl frae Penicuik – well, she wis a woman, and ah said ah'd got a rise – she says, 'Away and tell Mr Bach, the manager, ye got a rise.' See, nobody'd tell you you were gettin' a rise. We used tae call Mr Bach Little Hitler. He wis like Hitler ! But he wis broad and a wee moustache, ye ken. And ah went up and ah asked tae see him. And ah said, 'Ah got 2/6d. in ma pay packet that ah didn't notice.' He says, 'Everybody gets 2/6d. on their birthday up to a certain age till they've got so much money – whether they deserve it or not.' That wis the law, in Woolworth's anyway. So occasionally ye used tae get an extra 2/6d., it wis always 2/6d. extra he gave ye. Maybe twice a year I would get it. I had quite a good pay. I had over £2 when ah left Woolies and went tae the bomb factory in 1941. I had as much at Woolies as some o' the men had when ah think about it ! And then, ye see, I got extra bonuses all durin' December. There wis a limit tae what they could give ye for wages, unless you were a foreman. So they gave you bonuses durin' the four weeks in September. Everybody got a bonus of five shillins for workin' overtime, and ah got extra. There were two or three o' us got quite a lot extra. But ma mother got that. Ma mother was quite pleased tae get it. Ah mean, a big family to look after and no' much money comin' in.

Ah wis well looked after at Woolies. Ah mean, it wis a good place tae work. Oh, there must have been about a hundred workers there, mainly young girls. Oh, there wis one or two older ones. Ah mean, if ye were in there and ye worked, ye were there for life. It wis that kind o' job.

Well, ah didnae think it wis hard work, no' really. Ah wisnae exhausted at the end o' the day. The hours were quite long but ye didnae think it. And ye were standin'. In these days there wis supposed tae be seats for women. Well, there wis a wee turn-up stool at the back, away under – but if ye were caught sittin' on it . . . disciplined. Oh, no, ye didnae get the sack. The manager, Mr John Bach, wis a man that watched ye. And ah wis maybe fortunate it wis him that gave me the job. So he took an interest in me.

You started on the counter at Woolies. Then you were a chargehand and then you were a floorwalker. The floorwalkers at Woolies wis women. And then there wis always a man over them. The men – ah don't know what they called them, but ah think they were jist trainee managers. When ah wis there there werenae any women that became trainee managers. Ah think it would come, though.

Well, it wis a' girls on the counters but there wis men in the basements – storemen. There were big stores o' goods down below there. Ah don't think there were any cleaners. Ye did your ain cleanin'. That's what ah dinnae understand. Nowadays nobody does the cleanin' in the shops. And there wis a brass rail up the stair and ah used tae clean that brass rail, quite happy tae do it. You weren't expected tae do it – anybody could do it – but the cleanin' stuff wis kept in oor coonter, the stationery counter at the bottom o' the stairs. So ah used tae clean the bannister. It wis only done once a day.

Ah always worked at the stationery counter in Woolies. That wis all ah did. They didnae have a policy of moving you from one counter to another.

There wis no trade union at all in Woolies. Ah don't remember any of the girls being in a union.

It wis quite a lot o' money tae find for the bus fares from Loanhead. If ye got a season ticket it wis four shillins a week. I suppose the cost o' travellin' wis somethin' tae think about but it wisnae tae me. It wis a job. And it wis quite a well paid job for a girl at that time.

And then before the war came in 1939 – he wis a very clever man – Mr Bach our manager said that things were goin' tae be scarce. They were tae order everythin' up. See, ye had big ledger books for each counter, for each department. And some things in the books were never ordered, other things were. And he said, well, things were goin' tae be scarce. So ah wis made like a stock clerk, that's what they called me. And ye had tae go round wi' thir books and ask them why this wasn't ordered, why that wasn't ordered. Ah said, 'Well, you must order it.' Well, some o' them were quite good. But there was one girl in the haberdashery, she knew what wid sell because she wis comin' up in years – she'd maybe be forty. She knew what they could sell and what they couldn't sell. But ah says tae her, ah says, 'You must order all these things.' And she wouldnae do it. Ah says, 'Well, ah'll have tae report ye.' So ah went and telt Mr Bach. But he knew she wis a good worker anyway. But he had her up and she had tae order things that you would never have dreamt on buyin'. But this wis for when things were scarce he wis on aboot, and he wis good. He foresaw the coming o' the war.

Mr Bach had a son and a daughter. The lassie used tae come intae shop, and in these days before the war ye had tae wrap everything – get the money and then wrap it. And she'd give ye the money and she wanted the stuff without wrappin'. Ah said, 'No.' And if some lassies at the counters didnae know who she wis she wis up and telt her dad. Mr Bach's son never did that. But his son wis killed in Norway in the war. It wis awfy sad. He wis an awfy nice lad.

I'd be there five years at Woolies. Oh, ah did like workin' there. Then in 1941 I had ma callin-up papers and I'd went for an interview in the W.R.N.S. Oh, ah wisnae apprehensive, not really, about ma call-up. Ah didnae think much aboot it. Of course, it wis the times, there wis a war on, everybody wis goin'. Ah didnae have a medical examination, jist an interview for the W.R.N.S. There wasnae anybody in our family in the navy, ah jist fancied the W.R.N.S. rather than the A.T.S.[38] or the W.A.A.F.s But ah never went to the W.R.N.S. Ah never got any further than ma interview ! Ah think the interview wis held in Rose Street somewhere, in Edinburgh. Ah cannae remember. Ah might be wrong. Ah think it wis in Rose Street, because ma other sister, older than me, she had tae go too and she wis goin' tae go tae the Air Force. But she wis a dressmaker. So they suggested to her she could sew parachutes. Of course, that never came tae anything either. We jist had this interview. That wis it.

Well, it wis ma uncle Jim – James Bell, ma mother's brother – he worked in the powder mills at Roslin. And he wis at ma father's funeral, he wis awfy good tae ma mother. He must have mentioned tae ma mother that he would, so he got us thir jobs in the bomb factory – without even askin' us! He wis lookin' after us. Well, ma father had just been killed and Uncle Jim wouldnae want his nieces sent away from home. So we jist had tae toe the line and go up. The jobs were there. We jist went up and ah got the job. It would be June, July 1941. Ah wis jist twenty-one.

So then we were put on different shifts. Ma two sisters Bessie and Jessie – Bessie wis the dressmaker and she wis older than me, and Jessie wis younger than me – went to the bomb factory wi' me all at the same time. But we didnae work in the same hut. We were on different shifts! We never worked thegither, funnily enough. Maybe there wis a policy o' makin' sure that relatives weren't . . . in case o' an accident. It could have been. Ah never thought on that.

Well, at the bomb factory, they didnae make the actual bombs. They made the detonators for big – it must have been big massive bombs. They couldnae even test the detonators up there at Roslin Glen. And they made small hand grenades. How they were worked ah don't know. They were long canisters. We filled them and dumped them down and put the tops on, and a bit sticky tape tae keep the top next tae the thingmy. And they took this sticky tape and took the top off and ye dumped it on the ground and it went off. They were called hand grenades. They had a name, ah don't know what the name wis. So they must have dumped them and then threw them. Ah couldnae think what they were usin' thir grenades for. They must have worked! Nobody explained them tae us. We were jist set on tae doin' them. And then they made smoke floats for the navy and then dumped them in the water. They were horrible things – smell! That wis hard work. Ah wis on the smoke floats for a wee while. And, oh, sometimes ah made Verey lights. You went and helped out if they were needin' anything. If one wisnae busy ye went away somewhere else.

Jist the two people worked in the hut where ah wis. We packed the bombs and put them away. And if they werenae busy in the packin' ye went up tae help them tae make them. And there wis, I think it wis three in that hut. But they were a' divided off, if ye understand. They were a' separate huts, jist big huts, made of wood. There wis a big long one in the middle. About six or seven big huts, ah think. And then the smoke floats were separate a'thegither, if ah can mind right. Ah'm no' very sure.

But the bomb factory wis separate from the gunpowder mills. The gunpowder was in the valley and we were up on the top o' the hill. We didnae really have any contact with them down there.

The bomb factory was up at Roslin Castle station, on the Penicuik railway line. The factory wis close to the railway line. It wis I.C.I. that owned the factory, part o' the I.C.I. gunpowder works.

I've no idea how many workers were at the bomb factory. Ah think there would be less than a hundred on each shift. Ah think there would be between 100 and 200 workers a'thegither. Ye see, we were three shifts. Usually ah wis six tae two and two tae ten. What was it ma sister did ? She wis on three shifts. It depended on the work ye did, ye were either on two shifts or three shifts. I think there were some o' them on jist one shift. The night shift workers would be ten till six in the mornin'.

There wisnae very many men in the bomb factory, very few. They were mainly women workers. They had a shift foreman and then the head, the other foreman that wis above. There wis a foreman, then Mr Thomson, ah think he wis the heid yin. Ah dinnae ken what he wis, the manager, ah suppose. The senior men were all gunpowder mill folk. They were brought up tae look efter us. There werenae any women in senior positions. We had a foreman, Andrew something. Ah cannae mind his name. He wis awfy strict. He wis the union man, tae. Andrew was a right union man. Ah couldnae tell ye which union it wis. I've an awfy feelin' it wis the Transport and General Workers. But it didnae seem tae connect wi' makin' bombs anyway. We were a' wantin' tae be in the union. It wis the first time ah'd been in a union.

Ah cannae mind what the wages were. Ah think it would be about the same as Woolworth's. It wisnae quite £3 then because we got a rise. Ah think it might be something like £2.10.0. a week. Ah think it wis £3 before we left at the end o' the war. It wid be as much as ah wis gettin' in Woolies, but no' what ma sister Bessie was gettin' for a dressmaker – she had less as a dressmaker, an awfy poor pay. She wis better paid at the bomb factory. Ah suppose the war wis a relatively prosperous time at home when we were a' working. I suppose it would be. But ma mother wis lucky. We always had work. We maybe didnae have much money but we were always employed, every one o' us.

Oh, they were very strict about safety. Oh, aye, ye had tae check in at the gatehouse, and anythin' on ye – cigarettes: ye werenae allowed cigarettes or matches. At the gate they didnae really search ye. They actually took ye at your word really. They shouldnae really but they did. And they know who the smokers are more or less. But ah never knew anybody that took matches. Ah will say that. Ah don't know if anybody ever did. But ah never knew o' it. Nobody went by the gatehoose withoot leavin' their matches and their cigarettes – if they had them – as far as ah know. Most people were honest about that. Ah wisnae a smoker myself.

And ah think it wis the girl on duty at the gate that time she got intae trouble. She let these E.N.S.A. concert people in. This man wi' them he said he had no cigarettes. And he comes on and he lights up a cigarette in the hall ! Oh, we were a' awfy angry because the girl at the gatehouse would get the blame. She wis supposed tae search, ye see. Oh, we were a' angry. The man could see that. He wis taken off the stage. He wis a comedian or a singer, supposed tae be amusin' us by his way o't. There wisnae much amusement then. It wouldnae ha' caused any harm. But it wis the principle o' the thing.

Ye had tae change a' your clothes. When ye went in tae work ye went intae the changin' room and ye put this black skirt on and a black jacket thing. It wisnae cotton they were made o', it wis heavy stuff. Horrible hats ! Oh, they were horrible ! The hats wis made o' some kind o' – when ah think now it might have been fire-proof material because it wis thick and shiny. The hat wis like an old fashioned cook's hat, ye ken, jist a cap thing, a bonnet. And boots, jist lacin' boots, leather boots. They didnae have iron studs, nothin' like that. You were supplied wi' them, ye see, and if you went out your hut you put on big rubber boots which were kept outside the door. Ye stepped intae them if ye were goin' anywhere.

Oh, aye, the precautions were strictly enforced – except when the air raid siren went. Then everything went for a Burton ! When the siren went ye had tae go out. They had air raid shelters, ah think they were made o' brick. So we dived intae these. If there wis thunder or lightnin' ye went up tae the canteen, ah think, for that, thunder and lightnin' – the air raid shelters for the bombs. Ah wisnae nervous about thunder and lightnin'. Once just ah remember bein' in the air raid shelter. The siren went. But the works wis never bombed, no, no.

There wis a canteen at the bomb factory. You got your dinner there. Ah cannae mind how long we got. Ah think it wis jist half an hour. Ah dinnae think we got a tea break. Ye jist stopped for your meal. We always got a cooked meal at the canteen. It wis another big widden hut. It wis like a wee hall, tae be honest, ye know. Ye went round the counter and got your meals and you sat at the tables.

Tae get tae the bomb factory we walked from Loanhead up through Dryden woods, up through Roslin and up the hill. We left aboot half-past four in the mornin', aye, half-past four in the mornin'. We were always in plenty time for oor work. I've no idea how long it took to walk, it must have taken half an hour anyway or an hour. We'd be up there half-past five, ah think. It'll be three miles. It wis no' a very pleasant walk. There wis always three o' us usually walked up together and walked back again at the end o' our shift. There wis Nell Buchan – she's dead now. Whae else wis there ? And then there wis a miners' bus used tae come round so we got it tae stop. But it only stopped on a Saturday, because it wis early on a Saturday. Even if it wis awfy wet we went jist the same tae the bomb factory. Ah remember once it wis snowin' and when it snows the road intae Roslin gets blocked, ye know. And we had tae go up and round the long way. You know this – the men didnae go ! The girls went but the men didnae go. Two men frae Loanhead, they widnae walk. Oh, that gave us an extra distance tae walk that day. We were away early – soaked when we went in. But everybody walked tae the pooder mill, ah think. They walked frae Rosewell, jist walked, rain, hail or shine. The Auchendinny girls walked up the railway line, ah think, well, they knew when the trains were comin' so it would be quite safe.

Ah worked at the bomb factory from 1941 right to the end o' the war. Well, ah'd got married in 1943 and ah carried on to the end o' the war. Ah don't think ye were allowed tae leave somehow, ah think ye were tied to your job under labour restrictions.[39] But ah jist left when the war finished. Ah don't know when the other ones a' left. But they were paid off pretty quickly. Ah gave up workin' a'thegither at the end o' the war. Ah never had another job after that. Ma son Jimmy wis born in 1949.

But lookin' back ah quite enjoyed the bomb factory. Ah suppose ye felt ye were doin' something worthwhile. Ah didnae think much aboot it ! Ye jist did the job.

LYDIA NEIL

But then ah got married, and of course it wis durin' the war, and ah stayed at home, because ma husband wis sent tae the army. And then we were called up for munitions. We all got notified we would be put to the A.T.S. or the ammunitions. And then we were put to the ammunitions down at the powder mill at Roslin. There were eight or nine o' us frae Auchendinny a' went.

Ah wis born in Auchendinny on the 19th o' December 1918. Ah had two sisters and a brother. They were older, I'm the youngest. Ma sister Agnes wis the oldest, then Sarah, and then Alex, but he died quite young, then me.

Ma dad wis a head machineman in Dalmore paper mill. Well, he wis in the mill frae ever I knew him. Ah never heard him say he'd worked at anything else. He wis born in Chirnside in Berwickshire. Ah don't know how he'd come tae move from Chirnside tae Auchendinny but, oh, he'd be quite a young man. He went tae school at Chirnside.[40] Ah couldnae say, ah'm no' sure if he wis away in the First War. Ah don't know about ma grandparents, ma father's parents. Ah wouldnae remember them. They were dead by the time ah wis growin' up.

Ma mother's parents were dead, too, by the time ah wis growin' up. Ah couldnae really say where ma mother wis born. Ah jist knew when ah wis born in Auchendinny she wis ma mother, ye know. She didnae talk about her early days. She didn't work in the paper mill, well, ah mean, she wis jist at home a' the time. We were as a family. She never mentioned what she'd done before she got married. Ye see, these things ye should really maybe go intae but when you're young you don't really.

Ah wis born and grew up at No.8 Evelyn Terrace in Auchendinny. There were sixteen houses in Evelyn Terrace. Out o' those sixteen families ah cannae remember any who didnae work in Dalmore paper mill, no' really. They were a' in the paper mill that wis in Evelyn Terrace. They were mill houses, they belonged Dalmore mill.

We had a good house in Evelyn Terrace. And you knew all your neighbours, ye know, ye knew all your neighbours in Auchendinny and ye helped one another. But nowadays ye dinnae see the neighbours: they're workin'. In those days when women got married they gave up their jobs. They had tae look after their family. Single women worked in the paper mill but married women, oh, they didnae work once they got married.

Ah went tae Glencorse School. Oh, ah liked the school. Ah mean, we never got holidays or anything like they get nowadays. They get chances now that we never got. We had tae walk frae Auchendinny tae the school, run home – half an hour for your dinner – and run back again. Now they get school dinners and everything. There were no school dinners wi' us. We went home every day for our dinner. Ma mother wis ready for us and then we went back to school. Oh, ah couldnae say that ah disliked anything at the school. Ah quite like biography, you know, writin' about that – history, famous people. But we learnt mental arithmetic but now the kids dinnae learn that ! Well, ye hear them, they've got their computers. They cannae count. Ye go intae a shop and they've got a paper and a pencil and ye've got it counted in your head afore they get the thing written doon. Oh, it's terrible nooadays ! Of course, its changed days.

Ah never had ambitions at the school, tae work in domestic service or become a nurse. We never got any chance. Ah left the school when ah wis fourteen in 1932. At that time there werenae really a lot o' jobs goin', ye know. Ah left the school on the Friday and ma father had us lined up tae go intae the Dalmore mill on the Monday mornin'. That's what happened.

Just after ah'd left school and started in the mill ah tried tae get a job in the Penicuik Co-op. They had a Store in Auchendinny. In fact, the Store's still up yet in Auchendinny. It's like a wee hut now but that wis oor Store. We jist came out from 8 Evelyn Terrace four doors up and ye were at the Store. They used tae want, ye know, people in the Store at that time. Ye had tae sit exams and we used tae go and sit exams. Well, ah mind one time there were maybe a bit o' a kick-up because the girl that got it her dad wis on the Store board ! So we hadn't an earthly chance whether in the exams wir sums wis right or no'. So ah jist accepted that ah would work in the paper mill.

Well, all the men that used tae work in the mill their family used tae get intae the mill, ye know, if they couldnae get another job. But ah quite enjoyed the mill. At Dalmore ah wis on the cutters first. Well, the paper went through this machine and ye had tae sort o' what we ca'ed keppin' it – catch it, ye know – and put it intae . . . it wis like wooden pieces and it fitted intae these sizes. On the cutters you just got so much an hour for your pay, you weren't on piecework.

And then after that, ah wid be about seventeen, sixteen-and-a-half or something, ah wis on the overhaulin', overhaulin' the paper. You were on piecework there. Ye made your own pay. Ye had tae lift what they called reams. It went intae a ream, 500 sheets. And it wis heavy ! And then ye overhauled it and ye took all the waste out. And ye had tae make sure it wis perfect. If ye didn't ye wis called up by the manager. Oh, we used tae get reprimanded: 'If that goes away again and comes back as a complaint you're for it', ye know. But, oh, we never let on tae them. There wis nae punishment. You were jist reprimanded. And sometimes the paper wis really bad. Some weeks it wis terrible, it wis really a lot o' waste. So ye jist had tae make the good wi' the bad. Ye didnae throw out all the bad paper. Ye got quite good paper at times. And, ye see, on the overhaulin' there wis quite a few that what they called they lumped the paper. Instead o' takin sheet tae sheet – it wis greed tae make a big wage – they wid take two or three together, and they didnae know if there wis a bad sheet: it could be a torn sheet or a bad sheet in between. You had really tae look at each sheet. Ye used tae overhaul the sheets one at a time and if ye thought there wis something no' right about it ye would look at it and ye would put it to the side. Oh, it wisnae very often the paper wis poorly made at Dalmore. It wis quite good paper at Dalmore. But some days there wis a lot o' muck. But if ye wis doin' it right, sheet by sheet, ye didnae need tae get intae bother. But, as ah say – they called it lumped – they used tae lump the paper for tae get, ye know, more pay. They would take several sheets at a time and then it wis hidden in there. At the overhaulin' ye were paid at the end o' the week by how many reams you done.

All the cutters and overhaulers were women at Dalmore mill. There wis a foreman in charge o' the cutters – not a forewoman. And there wis a foreman in charge o' the overhaulers and he wis an awfy man ! Walker wis his name, we used tae cry him Old Walker. Now ah cannae mind his first name. We used tae say, 'Oh, here's Old Walker comin'.' Oh, and he said, 'Come, come on, get on wi' your job, get on.' Oh, he wis aye pushin' ye on. And if ye asked away half an hour early: 'Ye're not goin'. Ye'll be goin' for a pair o' shoe laces likely,' he used tae say tae us – and we never got away. Oh, he wis an auld . . . !

Mr Wallace wis the manager there. He never bothered us. But if there were a complaint and ye saw Mr Wallace comin' through, ye'd say, 'Oh, oh, here he comes.' He'd get us a' together, ye know, and he'd say, 'I've had this complaint back. This'll have to stop.' And, oh, they got a reprimandin'. And ye a' shook. Ye were wonderin' if he wis goin' tae say it wis you, you, or you. But he wis quite a good boss, quite a good manager. No, he wisnae bad. Wallace never come near unless there were a complaint at the paper. But Auld Walker – we cried him Auld Walker !

Auld Walker, oh, well, ye see, he said he wis the boss. He wis the boss and you had tae . . . Ye darenae ask away, ye darenae ask away. Oh, he wis strict that way. Oh, he wisnae liked, he wisnae liked. He wis the foreman o' the overhaulin' a' the time ah wis in the mill. He lived at what they call the station, Auchendinny station.

But ah don't remember anybody gettin' the sack at Dalmore, no' when ah wis there. Oh, you got a right reprimanding.

Mr Wallace wis the manager and there there wis an assistant manager, ah'm no' awfy sure o' heez name. Then there wis the foremen o' the departments. Well, Mr Davidson wis one. He stayed in the Terrace beside us but he's dead now. He wis the foreman o' the machinemen. And then there wis Auld Walker, he wis overhaulers, he wis for the women up the stair. Then the man that wis foreman tae us when ah wis on the cutters wis Mr

Gowans. Well, he's away, he's been dead for years. Then ah think there wis Mr Gillan – four or five foremen.

The paper at Dalmore it used tae go away abroad, ye know, it used tae be shipped out overseas. Oh, it had tae be good paper that wis sent. It wis writin' paper, well, they made wrappin' paper an' a', but there wis writin' paper, too, all kinds o' paper. It wasnae jist one kind o' paper. But not bank note paper: it wis Valleyfield mill that made it. Ah cannae mind o' them usin' rags to make the paper at Dalmore.

When ah started in the mill in 1932 when ah wis fourteen it wisnae highly paid. Ah got 6/8d. a week. Then we went on to fortnightly pays; it wis 13/4d. Well, we handed over the pay to ma mother and ye got half-a-crown pocket money, ye know. But ye could go one or two places wi' that half-crown.

We started at half-past seven in the mornin' in the mill and ye worked tae five. Ye even worked on a Saturday, ah think it wis half-past seven tae half-past twelve. Ye got home for about half an hour for your dinner, and we used tae run up the brae at the mill and get wir dinner, and run back. It wis jist like bein' at school, 'cause your parents wis in, they knew you were comin' home. There wis nae tea-break then. Ye worked straight through from half-past seven. Well, we got wir dinner at quarter to one. It wis a long mornin'. And then you were there till five, Monday tae Friday, and Saturday till half-past twelve. There wis nae tea-break on Saturday mornin' either.

In overhaulin' you were standin' all the time. You could sit when you were at the cutters. But at the overhaulin' you were standin' a' the time. And you had heavy lifts, ye know. Ye had tae lift the paper, overhaulin' it, and then ye had tae lift it up and take it to them that wis countin' it, like intae the reams. And ye carried what ye thought wis about 500 sheets over to them at a time, maybe four or five yards away. It wis heavy. But, ah mean, ye were young then and ye never thought much about it. Ye used tae wear low-heeled shoes for standin'. It wis your own shoes. And you had tae wear your own overalls and that. Ye didnae get overalls or nothin' like that. Up the stair at the overhaulin' they were wooden floors, downstairs it wis cement maybe. We used tae sometimes stand in our stockin' soles, ye know, durin' the

summer if it wis hot. Oh, it wis quite hot in the mill. Ye were
never cold. Ah cannae mind o' any o' the older women sufferin'
frae varicose veins wi' the standin', no' that ah know of.

Well, at the cuttin' machines it wis noisy. The machines wis
goin' a' the time. And then the big machines wis jist through
from ye, ye know. It wis a wee bit away frae ye, the big
machines. There wis a wall or partition that shut off some o'
the noise.

Oh, there were quite a few workers at Dalmore mill, countin'
the men – maybe more than a hundred. The number remained
much the same all the time ah wis there. The numbers o' men
and women were jist about equal, ah think, when ah wis there,
something like 50 or 60 men and 50 or 60 women. People didnae
come and go at the mill, they stayed there for their working lives
– till they got married if they were girls or retired. Oh, no, there
werenae a big turnover o' workers. They jist started and they jist
stayed there. There were older women worked there when ah
wis there, they were older than us, a lot older than us. They'd be
in their fifties. Maybe half or jist under that o' the workers lived
in Auchendinny. The biggest half ah knew stayed in Auchendinny. Most people living in Auchendinny worked in the Dalmore paper mill, that wis the place for Auchendinny ! But there
wis one or two frae Penicuik, there wis some frae Milton Bridge,
and there wis two girls came in frae Roslin. Ah mean, ye were
taken on if there wis a job there for ye. The mill wis busier some
times than other times, depended on the number of orders.
Nobody wis laid off when we were there. You always had work.

Oh, we never got holidays, no that ah can think of, oh, no, no,
nothing like that. The mill never closed down. We didnae get
holidays off and paid for. Ah think we got Christmas Day, aye,
that wis a holiday but we didnae get paid for it. And, well, ah
mean, ye were off on New Year's Day but ye didnae get paid for
it, no' that ah can think o'.

We – the women – never wis asked tae join a union at
Dalmore. Ah don't know if the men paid the union or not.
Ah didnae join a union, as far as ah can mind .

As ah say, we handed over the pay to ma mother and ye got
half-a-crown pocket money. But ye could go one or two places

wi' that half-crown. We used tae go to the dancin'. Ah loved the dancin'. We used tae go tae Penicuik on a Saturday night. We liked it. It wis the Cowan Institute then, it's the Town Hall now. Oh, it was only about a shillin' or 1/6d. tae get in. And we used tae go to the Tryst dancin', that's at Milton Bridge. We used tae pay 6d. at the Tryst. It wis cheaper there ! Ye didnae go through the week dancin' – ye didnae have the money. We were at the dancin' and that's how ah met ma husband. He wis in Valley-field paper mill.

At the Tryst dancin' the soldiers from the barracks at Glen-corse went. People at Auchendinny they used tae say, 'Oh, the barracks.' And we used tae walk down the Graham's Road alongside the barracks. And they used tae say, 'Oh, the soldiers.' But ah can safely say we walked that road from the dancin' and everything and never once were we . . . never once, no. Jist once we were comin' down the road and somebody touched us on the head, and there were soldiers at the back o' the wall. And we started tae run and we thought, 'Now they'll come out o' this big gate and they'll get us.' But no – never bothered ye, never bothered ye. Ah mean, the barracks wis there from ever we were anything. It didnae bother us, it didnae bother us. And then we used tae go to the barracks when they had their sports day on. We were invited tae the sports day. It used tae be a great day at the barracks. Well, none o' my friends that ah went with they never had any dates wi' the soldiers. Ye could go tae the sergeants' dances if ye wanted. Ah never went tae dances there, ah wis never in the barracks.

Ah used tae knit and sew, ah enjoyed that. And ye used tae get good books tae read, decent books, no' what they read nowa-days ! Well, there wis a shop, a paper shop, jist at the bottom o' the brae frae us. Then there were another paper shop at Milton Bridge. You could get papers and magazines there. Ah still get the *People's Friend,* that wis one ah got. We used tae get the *Daily Record* and the *Evenin' News,* and we used tae buy *Women's Weekly.* And ah used tae like cookin'. Ah learned cookin'. Ah could aye cook when ah got married ! Ah could cook and bake.

Ah wis at the Dalmore mill nine years till ah got married when ah wis 22. That wis 1941. As soon as you got married you stopped working, well, ye didnae go back tae the mill then. Ye did it o' your own free will. Of course it wis durin' the war, and ah still stayed at home, because ma husband wis sent tae the army. Peter wis called up no' that long after ah wis married. He wis in the Reconnaissance Corps. Ah wis jist at home no' very long, a few weeks. And then after ma husband got called up ye had tae take a job – wartime. So ah wis put to the ammunitions. Ah didnae want tae go. We had tae go. We were made tae go. We all got notified we would be put to the A.T.S. or the ammunitions. We got no choice. We jist got told that we were tae go to the munitions. And then we were put to the ammunitions down at the powder mill at Roslin. There were eight or nine o' us frae Auchendinny a' went. And there wis three o' us anyway frae the Dalmore mill.

Ah wis on the incendiaries in the bomb factory tae start wi' – ye know, they used tae drop these, tae light up places: flares. And then ah wis on the high explosive bombs after that, for the Air Force and the navy. Well, wi' the flares ye had tae put this certain stuff in and they were round, ye know.

Ye had tae be careful, even ye werenae allowed tae have rings or anything. We werenae allowed wir weddin' rings nor nothin' on us. No jewellery nor nothin'. Ye used tae forget you were married wi' your ring, when ye were on a' these shifts and takin' them off. And ye used tae sometimes no' put them on and forget ye had them !

Oh, they had tae be careful, oh, aye. If you had gone outside and got a wee stone it would have caused a spark and we could have a' been blown tae bits.

Ye had special overalls, special boots and special caps. Ye left them in the powder mill. Oh, ye werenae allowed tae take them outside. We wore our own ordinary clothes tae walk tae work and come back. Ye had tae wear this certain clothes ye got. We had a fireproof skirt, a fireproof overall, and the skirt and overalls wis to oor ankles. And then we had boots, firewear boots, and then we had the fireproof caps. And ye werenae allowed outside the buildin'.

Oh, no matches or cigarettes. Ye used tae get searched, ye

know, if they thought ye had anything on ye. They didnae search ye physically. Ye know, our foreman used tae come in and he'd say: 'Stand there. Shake your skirt. Shake your overall.' And then, 'Take off your cap.' And ah says, 'Well, he can shake me any time,' ah says, 'ah've never got anything.' Well, the only time ah wis searched wis not for that. There wis money goin' amissin' wi' purses. And we were at the canteen – you went tae the canteen for your break, ye see – and this lassie, in fact she wis in our department at that time, says, 'Oh, we're goin' tae get searched, goin' tae get searched.' Ah says, 'Well, they can search me now,' ah says, 'ah definitely know ah haven't got it or took it.' And ye know this, she says, 'Ah'll have tae go out tae the toilets.' And she came back and she had put the money in the purse in a cistern. Of course, they got searched. Ah, but she wis caught out, she wis caught out. She wis a Rosewell lassie. And she got the sack.

In the incendiary section, well, there wis two lassies in the one place. And the same in the bombs, there wis two o' yiz in the bombs. Ye were never alone, ye were never on your own, for safety reasons. There wis always two. And then the bosses would come round at night and they were tappin' on the door and ye had tae dim the lights, let them in, then put the lights on. Well, ye had the lights and it had a sort o' cover, a wee shade, and ye see, when ye put the light out this cover used tae come over the light and there wis no light got out your buildins.

We were on three shifts. Ah wis on day shift, night shift and back shift. Well, we started on the back shift, we left Auchendinny at one o'clock. And on the night shift we had tae leave at twenty minutes tae nine or quarter tae nine tae get there tae shift your mates. But we were up at half-past four in the mornin'. We went out Monday tae Friday on wir day shift and ye started back shift on the Saturday, two till ten. And then you were night shift ten tae six in the mornin' on the Sunday. Ye were out on the back shift and then ye were on the night shift on the Sunday, and finished on the Saturday mornin'. Then ye went on tae day shift. Ye got a Saturday afternoon and Sunday off every two or three weeks it was. It wis long hours.

Frae Auchendinny, well, we were up at half-past four in the

mornin' and we left Auchendinny at five o'clock and we had tae walk tae the bomb factory. And we went down what you called The Ditches, down past Auchendinny farm. And then we got on tae the back end o' the Firth road and on to the railway. And we had tae walk a' the railway, through the tunnel and everything ! Pitch dark ! Oh, we were frightened ! Ye walked along the railway and ye came out at the station, well, it wis near Hawthornden. Go in tae the Hawthornden station and you came off, and then you jist went this wee brae and you were at the bomb factory. It wisnae far tae walk once ye were off the railway. Well, say we left Auchendinny at five o'clock we got there for about twenty minutes tae six. It wis a good forty minutes tae walk, and comin' back. That wis the quickest way. Well, ye had tae go up intae Roslin tae get a bus. And then ye had tae walk frae Milton Cottages doon tae Auchendinny. So we were jist as well walkin'. And it wis cheaper, of course.

We jist had tae walk. See, goin' away at five o'clock in the mornin' there were no buses. Ye had tae go. There were no buses, not even goin' intae Roslin. And if ye did get a bus ye had tae walk away down the powdermill brae, down Jacob's Ladder and away up the hill on to the Rosewell road tae get tae the bomb factory. So we had tae walk. Oh, wintry ! Snow !

There wis quite a few o' us walked frae Auchendinny. Ah wouldnae have gone if there had only been another one. Ah would have been petrified. And there were one night we were comin' through the tin tunnel and there wis this awfy hammerin' on the outside. We thought, 'Oh ! Oh !' We were frightened tae come out at the other end. We didnae see anybody and we had tae come up a wee hilly bit and go over a stile, a fence, tae get through oot o' the wood, on tae the road. And we were gettin' over the fence and ah'm sayin', 'Ah'm no' goin' first and ah'm no' goin' last.' And ah wis gettin' over the fence, ah wis in the middle, and here thir lads that had tried tae frighten us in the tin tunnel came and, oh, we were petrified ! We were runnin' half up that hill tae get on tae the road. But they never touched us. They were only havin' a laugh, sayin', 'Oh, we'll frighten thir yins the night.' That wis the only time ever. They werenae Auchendinny laddies. No, we would have kent them if they were Auchendinny

lads. They wid come frae Hawthornden or Rosewell or somewhere. They knew us. And, ye see, wi' us bein' in the tin tunnel
we took a wee bit longer tae come oot. By Jove ! Well, it wis
always called the tin tunnel. It wis a' made o' tin, ye know, and it
wis pitch dark. Ah don't know why it wis made o' tin. It wis the
tin tunnel frae ever we knew. And, oh, it wis pitch dark ! And ye
couldnae put a torch on, ye see, in case o' the blackout. Ye had
no torches. Ye used tae jist sort o' feel your feet goin' along the
sleepers. It wisnae so bad if the moon wis shinin'.

There werenae any trains passin', no' in the early mornin'. But
ah mean, if ye happened tae be in the tin tunnel there were sort o'
wee bits ye had tae sort o' go intae and hold yersel' in for the
train passin'. Luckily, that never happened tae us. The train never
passed us in the tin tunnel. Ye had an idea o' the times o' the
trains. We seemed tae time them, ye know, we seemed tae be
there before the trains wis comin' through the tunnel.

And then on a Friday we used tae get the train on a Friday, on
wir day shift back intae Auchendinny station. Well, we hadnae
far frae Auchendinny station tae walk. And the train used tae be
packed wi' A.T.S. Ye had tae stand. That wis a' the A.T.S.
comin' intae Glencorse barracks. That wis the admission day for
them. Oh, they looked at us – ye know, they used tae have their
fur coats on and shrugged their shoulders at us when we came in
the train. Oh ! They were lookin' down their noses at us. And
they were the scum ! We went tae the church on the Sunday
because we were on night shift. And they were a' sittin' out at the
wooden huts at the A.T.S. camp – the North Camps is jist up
there at the church at Glencorse – and they were a' sittin' out wi'
towels round their head. They were a' gettin' searched – for lice !
And they were the ones wi' the fur coats that turned their noses
up at us ! Oh ! They looked down their noses at us ! They were
the A.T.S., the A.T.S. We done harder work than they ever done,
ah think.

Ah remember when the Germans were bombin' Glasgow ah
wis goin' out on the day shift and ma dad says, 'Ye're no' goin'.
Ye cannae go in that. Ye're not goin'.' Ah says, 'Ah'll have tae
go.' And a crowd of us set off frae Auchendinny. And we had tae
throw wirself down on the bankin' ! The shrapnel wis flyin' !

They were aimin' for the powder mills, ye see, and they dropped a bomb but they were a bit off. And, oh, the huge hole ! No' on the railway, on the field jist across from that. That wis on our way tae work.

And the flares, they dropped them twice in Penicuik.[41] It wis the barracks they were after. But they were off their track. We used tae get the signs at the bomb factory for when the Germans were comin' over the Forth and then ye were tae get prepared – untie your boots, get ready tae run. And we had a wooden locker right outside where we went intae our huts, and ye had tae take your boots off and run tae the shelter when the sirens went. And it wis quite a bit away down, away at the bottom o' this road. We were in the shelter a few nights, well, maybe no' all night but quite a few hours. They were underground shelters. They had been built specially for the war. Oh, they werenae jist ordinary shelters. Ah mean, if the Germans had got the powder mill we'd a' been blown tae shreds ! The powder mill wis never actually bombed. But they were aimin' for it, they were aimin' for it. Ah mean, on that embankment they werenae that too far off it. But they went off their target. They were nearer this side o' the railway we went on tae than nearer the bomb factory side.

And when the German bombers were comin' over the Forth ye got a signal. And then when they were comin' this way, ye got the red. Well, that wis when ye had tae be ready. Ye had tae jist get your boots, take your boots off, and down and intae the shelter. Ye didnae get any warnin'. There wis a blue light in each hut. They were a' the same. Every one had the same. And that let you know when the Germans were comin' over. That wis the first warnin'. And then the second light they were comin' nearer. And if they were comin' nearer over the Forth ye got the red light. But sometimes ye got the two lights. But they got them turned, ye know – the bombers were sent back – and ye hadnae tae run tae the shelter. Oh, it wis frightenin' for us.

The men that wis the foremen there, ye know, and some men that used tae bring it to ye if ye had tae get things intae the hut or anything, they used tae knock at the hut door and ye had tae shout. 'Who's there ?' and dim your lights – 'cause, ye see, ye didnae know if there wis German planes comin' across or no'.

Oh, as ah say, we were in the shelter a few nights. Well, maybe no' all night but quite a few hours. And the workers that wis on ma shift there wis quite a lot o' Rosewell workers. But, ye know, they were good company and that. And there wis two on ma shift especially – Bernie Gallacher and Betsy McGeary – oh, they were beautiful singers ! Oh, they were beautiful singers. And they used tae sing *Ave Maria*. And then Betsy wid sing it in Latin. Oh, they were beautiful singers ! They entertained us in the shelter. Bernie used tae be one o' oor foremen. Oh, dear, he wis a lad !

We had a canteen, aye, we used tae get a break. We finished at two. We used tae go and get a break for jist aboot ten minutes and get a cup o' tea. There wis a woman in the canteen, in fact, she came frae Milton Cottages, and she wis one o' the workers wi' us. And on a Saturday afternoon workin' a back shift, they thought they were doin' good, they got us thon E.N.S.A. concerts. It wis tae break the monotony on a Saturday, the back shift Saturdays ! Well, ye see, ye were finished at two. And, oh, they were a load o' trash ! Oh, ah think they jist picked them up off the street. But ye used tae get them at your break. Ye used tae go for your break, say, at tea-time on the back shift. And ye used tae get this E.N.S.A. concerts. Oh, dear !

Oh, there were quite a few workers in the powder mills. There wis a lot frae Rosewell. And there were Roslin, and there were the Auchendinny ones, and then there wis some frae Loanhead, and then some o' them that wis round about, say, the Glen and that, ye know, at Roslin. They all worked in the powder mills. Oh, there might have been about a hundred workers – jist about the same as at Dalmore paper mill. Oh, there were a lot. There would be more women than men, oh, aye. When ah first went to the powder mills, well, ah knew one or two Roslin ones. And then ye got tae know a' the Rosewell gang. Ye know, they were a' on different shifts. But ye got tae know them as you were comin' out your shift and they were comin' on. Ye got tae know each other. We had good lassies on our shifts. It wis good company. And they were a good set o' lassies frae Rosewell.

Ah didnae feel tired working in the powder mill wi' these long hours and the walk tae work and back again. Ah mean, well, when you're younger, ye see – we'd only be about 26 – and at that time, well, ye were quite young. Once on the night shift, it used tae be a Wednesday, ah got so fed up wi' the night shift. We used tae get up early and we were up in the afternoon and we used tae go intae Edinburgh, buy wir tea, and we used tae go tae the Palais de Dance or go tae the Empire Theatre – hear Vera Lynn in the Empire, in our time.[42] And we went tae the Palais this day and this person that walked with us by Milton Cottages, they were comin' up for us: 'Would you like a dance ?' And they says, 'Ah didn't know the Old Age Pensioners wis comin' the day.' We never went back again ! They insulted us. We were young but there wis three o' them, quite older than us, and ah thought, 'Oh, that's the finish o' us goin' tae the Palais.' Never went back. We used tae go tae a theatre or something like that.

Well, sometimes you were tired. You were comin' in, well, see off the back shift it wis about quarter tae eleven before ye got in, and ye were shut in all day. And we used tae get wir supper. And this policeman – he wis the policeman for a' round about Auchendinny and Milton Cottages – he used tae come and see us on the back shift and say, 'Ah'll meet ye and we'll go a walk.' And we used tae go a walk wi' this policeman. What was his name ? Aye, we used tae say he wis takin' us because he wis frightened ! And he used tae take us a walk and we used tae go away up, ye know, up tae the high road, what they call the Minister's Brig, that wis the minister's manse, goin' on tae the Biggar road, the high road. We used tae walk there off our back shift night, and come back in tae Auchendinny. Well, ye werenae goin' out tae dinner time. But ye couldnae dae that on your day shift, because, ah mean, ye were up at half-past four in the mornin'. Ah often wonder how ye done it. Nowadays they widnae do that. Ah tell ma family that and ye tell the younger generation. They'll say, 'Oh, that wis in the aulden days.' Ah'll say, 'No' sae much o' the aulden days. Ah wisnae auld, ah wis only 22 !'

Oh, they werenae highly paid at the powder mill. Tae be truthful ah couldnae tell ye exactly what ah got paid. Ah didnae join a union, as far as ah remember. We didnae pay union. There might ha' been a union man, but, ah mean, we were never asked.

'Oh, Ye Had Tae Be Careful'

If it wis near the time and ye wanted away from the work for anything, well, ye had tae ask. In fact, there wis one or two times their husbands came home on leave – no' jist mine, but there were a few of us – and we never got off on leave. We were comin' in off o' back shift and they were on leave. Then we were maybe goin' oot on nightshift and they were on leave ! We got nothing like that, no concessions at all. That happened tae me once or twice when ma husband came on leave, aye, we didnae get leave.

Ah wis at the bomb factory nearly four year. There wis quite a few o' us finished jist before the war finished. They were gettin' less and less, because the war wis really you could say finishin'. Ah didnae go back to Dalmore paper mill, ah stayed at home. Then ma husband wis demobilised no' long after the end o' the war. He went back tae work at Valleyfield mill. But ah didn't go back to work, because then ah had ma oldest daughter jist after that, aboot 1947. Then ah had a son, and then ma youngest daughter. Ah never went out tae work when they were bairns. Ah never went back tae work for years after the war, till ma husband really wis ill for a few year and he didnae work for a few years. So ah took a wee job. Ah wis at the school dinners. Well, ma son wis married and ma daughter wis married, and ma youngest daughter, well, she wis quite a good age. That wis jist a part-time job, ah liked it.

Well, ah quite liked the school dinners, ah quite liked the paper mill, and ah quite liked the bomb factory, too. Ah mean, ye got a laugh in the bomb factory, ye know, wi' them that worked there. Ah enjoyed ma work.

MARION BRYCE

Ma father was a box maker in the powder mills. He started work there in 1893. He wis born about 1878. Oh, ah don't know if he served an apprenticeship or no'. He wisnae a joiner. But that's what he did. He wis a box maker – wooden boxes – there, and that's what the powder went away in, well, tae the magazines. A lot o' it went through like tae different places, through West Quarter way, was it ?, and quarries.

Ah think ma father wis born at Milton Cottages. That wis at the top o' the hill from Milton Bridge, before ye come along tae the cemetery. There were a lot o' houses up there at that time but a lot o' them have gone now. At the far end there are about four o' them. Well, ma father lived in a but and ben at Milton Cottages, and ah think there were about eight o' them in his family.

I'm cried Marion after ma grandmother, ma father's mother. Ah cannae mind o' ma grandfather Bryce or ma granny Bryce either. Ah think they were dead before I grew up.

Ma mother stayed at Kirkhill in Penicuik. Ma mother wis in Esk Mill paper mill, ah think. Well, ma mother, ma grandfather and them it wis an Esk Mill house that ma mother used tae stay in in Dublin Street in Kirkhill. Ah couldnae tell ye really if there wis any Irish connection wi' Dublin Street. But ma mother's father had been a ploughman, ah think. He was on different farms. Originally he came from the Juniper Green side o' the Pentlands. But then they were up in Kirkhill when ma mother and father got married. Ma grandfather finished up in Esk Mill paper mill, ah think. Ah can remember o' him but ah cannae mind o' him that well. Ah never seen ma grandma. She'd passed away by the time ah wis growin' up.

Ah wis born at Milton Bridge on the 4th o' April 1920. Ah had a sister Cecilia, she was ten years older than me, and a younger brother that died in infancy, when there were a bad flu'. He wis only months old. Ma father wis in his bed wi' the 'flu at the same time. And then there wis ma cousin Annie Munro stayed wi' us. My mother brought her up frae she wis weeks old, for Annie's mother had died. Annie wis six years older than me. She wis brought up as a sister.

We used tae stay doon the pend at Milton Bridge, and that house had a kitchen, room, and bedroom. Down the pend there wis not runnin' water and there were outside toilets. Then we moved up intae one in the front – No.7 Milton Bridge – a kitchen and two rooms, well, two bedrooms. So then we weren't as crowded as some families were. Well, there were a wee bedroom and a bigger room, and there wis the kitchen bed. Ma parents slept in the kitchen. There were two o' us – ma sister Cecilia and me – in the wee room, and ma cousin Annie Munro in the bigger room. Cecilia wis married in 1933. At No.7 there wis runnin' water but again outside toilets. But then we got a toilet intae the house after the Second War. We lived in that house until 1975. We were one o' the first tae get the electricity there. Ah wis only about eight year old when we got the electricity in, because our landlord – Alexander Inglis o' Loganbank House – wouldn't put in gas or that for they knew the electricity wis comin'.[43] It wis paraffin lamps we had till then. There wis no bath, no – ye washed up and doon ! We never had a bath at Milton Bridge. We never had a bath till we came tae live in Penicuik in 1975. Ah wis 55 then. Alexander Inglis had a lot o' the estate round about, jist up past Glencorse Church – Loganbank. But he didnae own all the houses at Milton Bridge when ah wis a girl – Smith o' the lemonade works, they had the faraway block, next to the Fisher's Tryst. There were just the two landlords.

There wis a garden at the back o' our house. Oh, it wis a big garden. Ma father wis very fond o' the garden. He used tae show – vegetables mostly. He died in 1935, he wis 57. Well, there werenae a pension scheme at the powder mill when ma father died but they started one after that. Ma mother missed out on that. She had only the widow's pension, ten shillins a week. She had quite a struggle after ma father died.

Ah went to Glencorse School. That wis just up the road at the top of the hill from Milton Bridge. Ah wisn't that fond o' the school, och, no' when ah went first. Och, later, ah quite liked it. Ah liked the arithmetic and composition – oh, aye, we used tae get plenty o' them ! We had ah think an essay every week. We got cookery and we got sewin', ah liked them. Ah wisnae wildly enthusiastic. Ah passed ma Qualifyin'. Some went tae Lasswade – no' very many, very few went on at that time. Ah just remained at Glencorse School. Nothin' stopped me from goin' tae Lass-wade – ah didnae want really tae go ! Ah don't think there were fees there. Ah wouldnae say that they were better off youngsters that went to Lasswade. After the Qualifyin' you had another two classes. You were wi' the headmaster after that. Ah don't think ah would have liked to go to Lasswade High School. Ah knew ah wis goin' tae the paper mill ! And ah left school at fourteen in 1934.

As a girl at the school ah didnae really have any ambitions. Ah wid never have been a nurse. Ah thought frae the very start ah would go and work in the paper mill ! Ma sister Cecilia had always worked in Dalmore mill and ma cousin Annie Munro wis in the mill and ah went. Ah didnae mind that, ah didnae feel unhappy about it. Ye jist put your name in for the paper mill. Ah dare say it could help if you had a relative there that could speak for you. It wid be ma cousin Annie that put ma name down.

Oh, you started on the cutters, the cutter house, where they cut the paper. Ah did that for about a year and a half and then ah went up tae the overhaulin'. Ye had tae be very particular in these days wi' the overhaulin', takin' out any shades and every-thin'. Yin customer we really had tae be particular wi' wis Andrew Whyte, printers, Leith – ah think their place wis doon there at Bonnington. We had tae be very particular wi' their paper.[44]

In the summer ye started at twenty past six in the mornin' till five o'clock at night. Well, ye had a break – an hour at nine till ten, and ye had an hour from one tae two for your lunch, and ye worked tae five o'clock. That was Monday to Friday, then Saturday mornin' from twenty past six till twelve o'clock. That wis the summer, and in the winter ye started at twenty past seven tae half-past five or somethin' like that. Ah'm no' very sure.

We jist walked doon the Graham's Road from Milton Bridge tae the mill. It would be a quarter o' an hour. You thought nothing about going out in the dark and returning in the dark then really. There wis jist Annie Munro and me went from Milton Bridge. Ma sister Cecilia had got married in 1933, before ah went tae the mill.

Ye got a fortnightly wage. It wisnae very much. Was it aboot seventeen shillins or somethin' ? Ah dinnae ken whether it wis seventeen shillins a week. We were on fortnightly wages, so it might have been seventeen shillins a fortnight. Ye got a ha'penny an hour rise sometimes ! The machinemen got aboot tuppence, and it wis only about a ha'penny or that the women got. Ye didnae get your wages in a packet in Dalmore till after the war. If there were a note the silver wis stuck inside and it wis jist handed to you. Ah think ma mother must ha' got ma pay then. Ma father died in 1935, when ah wis fifteen, the year after ah began at Dalmore. It wis when ah went on tae the overhaulin' ah paid ma digs – fifteen shillins a week. So ah must have had seventeen shillins a week. Ma mother let me keep whatever wis left out o' ma wages. And ah got sometimes a shillin' off her ten shilliny pension from ma father died till after the war.

At Dalmore they didnae have a union till after the war. It wis after the war we were in the union. Ah dinnae think anybody wis in a union before the war. Ah don't think any o' the men wis in a union then, no' till after the war.

It wis a friendly sort o' atmosphere in Dalmore mill. There were quite a lot o' the Auchendinny girls there, girls ah wis at the school with. There were no married women workin' there then. When girls got married they left. That wis expected, more or less automatic. They a' left when they got married. There were no married women workin' there.

Oh, there wis maybe about sixty women workin' in the mill. There wis about thirty overhaulers. And then there wis balers that wrapped the paper. And there were about fourteen or fifteen down in the cutter hoose. And there were some in the office. The women didnae work shifts, it wis jist the men. There were two paper-makin' machines goin' at that time. Dalmore wisnae as old as Esk Mill and Valleyfield. And these were bigger mills.

Mr Wallace – Auld Wallace we used tae cry him – wis the manager. In thae days, if Mr Wallace wis aboot, ye had tae be doin' the right thing, ye know. Oh, he wis quite strict. But ye didnae see a lot o' him. If there were a bit paper lyin' he would point tae it. Mr Somerville used tae come through the mill at that time – he wis still the owner when ah started at Dalmore. Ye see, it wis William Somerville & Son.

Ah don't think ah felt tired when ah got home at night from the mill, ah dinnae think so. Ye went away early tae your bed at night then, between nine and ten o'clock anyway.

We walked quite a lot. Ah never had a bike, though ! And ah never fancied the dancin'. There wis dancin' at Milton Bridge in the Tryst hall but ah very seldom went. Ah wisnae interested in sport. There werenae tennis or badminton at Milton Bridge. So it wis more goin' tae the pictures at Penicuik – three times a week. It changed three times a week. Ye usually got the bus there but we often walked home from the pictures. There werenae much traffic on the road and ah went wi' ma friends. Oh, ye were passing the barracks but ye never thought anything aboot it then. It wis tuppence on the bus and a shillin' or nine old pence tae get in the pictures, ah think.

Ah remember the outbreak o' the Second War. That day, well, on the Sunday mornin, when it came over the wireless that the war wis declared, there were conscripts up in Glencorse barracks at that time, and they were up in the church. And we went up tae the church and Rev. Begbie told them frae the pulpit that war had been declared. Oh, well, ah think they were a' expectin' it. But these young lads, when they came up tae the barracks – this wis jist before the war – they had grey flannels and blazers and ah think they had a beret. They were issued wi' that. But ah think an awfy lot o' them, just young lads, that went across tae France or Dunkirk, they never came back.[45]

We met quite a few of them. We walked the main road ! Well, on a Sunday night, ye walked frae Penicuik tae Roslin south road. Oh, in these days, Penicuik tae Roslin south road that's where they a' walked along. That's where an awfy lot o' them met their men – locals, it wisnae jist the soldiers. There werenae sae many o' the soldiers walked the road as a lot o' the locals. That wis the recognised walk for the young people, frae Penicuik doon tae Roslin south road and back up. So that's what ye did on a Sunday night, walked the main road. Well, after the war started ye used tae talk more to the soldiers, ye know, than before. Oh, it wis different a'thegither then.

Ah carried on at Dalmore paper mill for two years after the war broke out. But then the mill went slack. Ah think it wis they couldnae get the material and that – esparto grass, and ah think some o' it wis straw. Well, we were on the dole and that quite a lot in the openin' years o' the war. The war started in 1939 so from then until 1941 we were really slack. There were quite a lot o' us left Dalmore tae go to the powder mills, because they all got a job doon there at Roslin. So ah started at the powder mill in April '41. And then ah wis tae register. Well, ah wis in the lot that wis tae register first – the 1920s. It wis nearer the end o' April ah think ah wis tae register. But ah wis exempt wi' bein' already down there at the powder mills.

Ah wis up in the bomb section. Ah wis on the Northover projectors. It wis a big order, it wis for the Home Guard. But ah never heard o' them bein' used round about here. But it wis a big order. They made them for years. It must ha' got fired frae some kind o' a gun. They would be aboot two inches in circumference. And ah filled thir discs wi' powder frae a machine. And ah cannae mind if it went in next door and they were put into this thing. Aye, ah think it wis next door. We jist made the discs for them. Well, we jist knew the Home Guard used them.

There were one man brought the stuff – materials, the things that ye made, ye know. 'Cause we were in the buildins. There wis a row o' wooden huts in this part for the Northover projectors, and then we went into different huts. And there wis four in ma hut doin' that, and there wis two next door pastin' them, ah, think, and puttin' them in. There would be aboot twelve o' us on that.

Ah cannae really tell ye how many workers there wis at the powder mills. There were quite a lot o' them. On the night shift there wisnae so many. That wis the smallest shift. There wis, och, there would only maybe be about fifteen or sixteen on the night shift – all women. The workers were mostly women. Well, there wis Mary Dudgeon, Julia Louden, Fay Gowans, Ella Delaney, Lily Dippie. Jenny Porteous, aye, she wis on our shift. Elizabeth Dugan wis in the bottom mill though, ah think.[46] She wisnae up in the top mill. There wis some men, one or two men – no' many. They made smoke floats, too, ye know, that wis a big drum. They were put overboard and everything in the navy. And there were one or two men on that. There would be a lot more down in the bottom mill where they made the powder and that. Ah don't know about the bottom mill.

Well, we worked three shifts: quarter to six tae quarter to two, and from a quarter to two till quarter to ten, and a quarter to ten again – the night shift – till quarter to six in the mornin'. Ye checked oot at the hour but ye got that time tae change your clothes. Ye worked the shift for a week – night shift, day shift, late shift, a kind o'cycle like that. We worked one week-end, ah think it wis the back shift we worked that one week-end. We didnae work seven days a week ! But ah cannae jist mind – it's over fifty year ago ! The hours were shorter than at Dalmore mill but in the paper mill ye had that hour for breakfast and an hour for your dinner. Och, well, ah didnae like the night shift. Ah couldnae sleep tae start wi' ! And then by the end o' the week ye were gettin' used tae it. And then you changed your shift again. It wis quite upsettin' really. Oh, at home at Milton Bridge, ye never heard the traffic noise. Ye got accustomed to it. There werenae quite as much traffic then. But we were used tae it. But in the night, if you were lyin' wakin' in the night and there were a lorry comin' up the road ye could hear it away in the distance, away along the cemetery wey, and then it gradually got nearer . . .

The wages at the powder mill were £2 odds, ah think. The one that we worked the week-end we had about £4, ah think. That wis a big pay. But the rest wis jist a' £2 somethin'. But that wis more than in Dalmore paper mill, but no' that much more.

Och, it wis easy work. Oh, ye were at it a' the time.

We had tae take off our shoes and intae boots before we went intae the buildin' in case there were sparks settin' anythin' alight. When ye arrived at the gate ye were searched, actually frisked, well, mostly. Some mornins they missed it but ye had tae see that ye werenae goin' in wi' matches. They had tae leave their cigarettes and matches at the gate. Well, ah never smoked at ma work. Ah dinnae remember anybody bein' caught wi' matches or cigarettes or pipes ever, no' really.

Well, there were an explosion on the bottom mill nearer the end o' the war, ah think, ah'm no' very sure about that. Ah think it wis somebody frae Bilston. Ah think one wis killed. Oh, ye never really got told what caused the explosion. Ah wis on night shift at the time it happened, ah think, and it wis in the mornin'. Ah didnae hear the explosion at home at Milton Bridge.

One night shift we were in the air raid shelter nearly every night. It wisnae awfy long after ah began at the bomb factory. Ah think it wis maybe the Glasgow raids. It wis a' right goin' intae the shelter tae start wi' but it got cold. We were sometimes in there till about four o'clock in the mornin', no heatin', of course. It wis quite a big shelter, doon under the grund. There were more than one shelter. There wis one away another bit. But it wis on the night shift, that wis the shelter we went, away across this field and intae the shelter thing. We had tae run across there tae the shelter – about a hundred yards. When ye got the purple light first that wis the warnin'. And then, ah cannae mind if it wis two lights or three lights when ye were tae go for the shelter. Oh, we didnae change our clothin' but we were supposed tae change our boots. But ah can remember one or two nights we run wi' our boots on, for we could hear them goin' over.

The Germans didnae actually bomb the powder mills. But once when ah wis on the night shift there wis one dropped along no' far frae the bomb factory along the railway. It wis when Penicuik got the incendiaries, and this one was dropped doon in below the viaduct at the Firth. And they dropped them up in Martyr's Cross and one or two up Castlelaw way on the Pentlands that night. Ah dinnae think they were tryin' tae bomb the bomb factory. Ah think we had chased them and they dropped them jist tae get rid o' their bombs on the way home.

Well, the boss came in and he said, 'Oh, there seemed to be one dropped along the Auchendinny wey.' 'Oh, dinnae say that !' But we walked the railway tae get tae work. Ah mind when we walked along that in the mornin' we saw the big bomb crater doon below the bank.

When we walked tae the bomb factory we walked tae Milton Cottages and doon tae Auchendinny and along tae the Firth drive and doon on tae the railway. And we went through the tin tunnel. That wis a tunnel that wis tae keep sparks frae goin' over intae the gunpowder works. Oh, well, that wis what the tin tunnel wis there for. It had been there for years. For ma father, he worked doon at Kirkettle in the First War – he must ha' been exempt wi' bein' in the powder mill – and it wis jist doon below the tin tunnel. The tin tunnel's been away for years an' a'.

Ah would say that walk would be aboot two miles. It would be Roslin Castle station wis jist outside the bomb factory. So we jist crossed over there from the railway. And we walked back and forth there a' through the war. Oh, there were quite a lot o' the bomb factory workers came from Rosewell. They came up the railway an' a' the other way.

We used tae get intae trouble sometimes when the inspector wis on the railway. We were told no' tae do it again. But, well, that meant we had tae walk down intae Roslin Glen and up Jacob's Ladder and up intae Roslin. It wis far longer. That wis the quickest way tae go, along the railway. There wis a train at ten past nine at night, so we usually had tae watch, waitin' till we knew it was away up before we went on tae the railway. And this night we were goin' down on tae the night shift but it wis a windy night, and nobody heard the train. So we jist started walkin' – and it came out the tin tunnel ! And we were jist aboot there ! We slid doon the bank. What a fright we got ! We werenae supposed tae go up the railway. The railway inspectors wis there sometimes.

Then on the day shift we got a train just after two o'clock up tae Auchendinny. That brought us home to Auchendinny station. Oh, ah'll tell ye another thing. Oo used tae come up in that train off the day shift, and there were a lot o' women sometimes on it joinin' the A.T.S. And we got off the train and they would be doon wi a truck tae meet them. And we hurried oot the Auchendinny station, and some o' the corporals or that that wis roond gettin' the A.T.S. used tae come runnin'. 'Come back ! Come back !' They thought we were A.T.S. ! But they used tae come doon and meet them off the train.

Once on the day shift in the powder mill we got the length o' the tin tunnel and we met this man in the tunnel. His hat, ye ken, the peak, wis away doon. And this woman says, 'Oh ! A bloody German !' And oo run through that tunnel ! Then oo met him again two or three mornins after that. They were convalescent soldiers up in the North Camp at Glencorse, and he wis stationed up there. He wis a Scots Guards or something and the peak on his cap wis away doon. But he wis keepin' company wi' a woman doon in Rosewell, and this wis him walkin' tae Glencorse barracks along the railway line ! And we took tae oor heels and through that tunnel ! A Jerry !

Ah think we had a union at the powder mills. Ah wis asked tae join and ah joined. It wis the Transport & General, something like that. The other girls and women they were all in it then.

Well, ah worked at the powder mill frae April 1941 tae '45, jist at the end o' the war. Ah wis on back shift the day o' V.E. Day – the Monday night when war came to an end in Europe.[47] We got home. And ah don't think we were really back much after that. So it must have been about May or June 1945 we stopped there.

And when we left we couldnae jist take a job anywhere. We were sent tae a job. And so about half a dozen o' us were sent tae the roperie in Leith. But none o' us wis wantin' tae go. And on the tram goin' doon we said to the conductor about where wis the roperie. He said, 'Oh, ye're no' goin' there are ye ?' So we never even went tae the roperie tae see aboot a job ! We said, 'Oh, no, we'll no' gaun tae the roperie.'

Oh, well, ah got a job in Auchendinny laundry then for six month. And I jist hated it. Oh, well, they done a lot o' the army washins. And, mind ye, in these days a lot o' people put their sheets and that tae the laundry. The laundry motor went round collectin' them. Well, ah wis on doin' the sheets, ye know, ye put them through in that press thing and ye folded them. Oh, ah didnae like that either. Oh, the steam and the heat ! But, hooever, that wis instead o' goin' to the roperie. And then ah jist got intae Dalmore paper mill after that again. Oh, I wis glad tae leave the laundry. Ah wis the only one, ah think, that went tae the laundry. Some got intae Valleyfield for a wee while. But they a' came back tae Dalmore after the war was over.

We jist went doon to Dalmore and asked aboot a job, and then we were sent for.

Well, ah stayed at Dalmore mill till 1980, till ah retired when ah wis sixty. Ma war years wis counted – ah wis 46 year there, ah think it wis. Ah wis overhaulin' and then ah wis a sampler in the Jagenberg cutter. That was, this paper didnae go to the over-haulers. When it wis a ream a slip came through – ye know, it coonted and that. But it wis wrong every wee while and ah had tae sample that paper. And if ah didnae get anything in it that got passed. But if ye were gettin' like creases and that in it, it had tae go tae the overhaulers.

O' a' the jobs ah had ah preferred the paper mill, ah think, because ah didnae like the shifts at the powder mills. But it wis jist a job really

SHEILA MACPHERSON

Ma' schoolin' finished at thirteen. Ah wis keepin' house then for ma father and two brothers. And ah never worked until the war broke out. Ah wis seventeen the day war wis declared. And then when ah wis nineteen that is when the nineteen year olds were called up for munitions work. So I thought, 'Here's ma chance then. Ah'm gettin' out tae work and earn some money.' And that is when ah went up to the bomb factory. And ah wis there until the war finished.

Ah wis born on the 3rd of September 1922 in Roslin Glen. Ma brother – he's dead now unfortunately – but he wis two year older than me, and ah've got a younger brother Stanley. He's two or three years younger than me. They were born in Roslin Glen, too.

Ma father wis born in Dumfries, and his father was a cobbler. Ma father had eighteen brothers and sisters. Quite a few died in childhood, ye know. But ah remember about nine or ten. Ah remember a' these aunties. When he was six month old ma father went to Maybole – apparently it was famous for shoemakers and cobblers. Then when he was quite young he came to Edinburgh to live, out at Gorgie, and he grew up there. And I think he was one o' these harum scarum types o' young fellows. He went to Canada eventually for work, because things were tight in these days. And he wis in Canada when the First War broke out. When of course that happened he says, 'I must go home and join up.' So he joined up in the Seaforth Highlanders and wis there for the duration o' the war. He must have married ma mother sometime in between, before he went overseas wi' the army. Ah think ma parents met before the war, because ma mother lived at Dalry, ma dad at Gorgie, which wis quite close tae each other. Quite possibly he would know her before he went to Canada.

Ma mother and her family – her family wis about nine, and they were all alive like, I remember seein' all them – lived in Orwell Place, out at Dalry in Edinburgh, but she really came from John o' Groats. She wis born between John o' Groats and Wick and went to the school at a small place called Newton up in Caithness. And the family – ma grandfather and grandmother Manson – it would be the work that would bring them down to Edinburgh, because there was nothing up there in Caithness. Ma mother was quite a young girl then. And ma grandfather Manson was a coal merchant, had his own business – that wis the days o' the horse and cart – and his sons went into the business. Ah remember ma grandparents very well. In fact, ma cousins tell me, 'You're Granny Manson's double.' Ma grandfather spoke with a sort o' Gaelic tongue, sometimes difficult to understand him. Ma mother wis an office worker, a cashier.

And I do remember very much ma grandparents on ma father's side. As ah say, he wis a cobbler when he came to Edinburgh and that wis his job – and a man that wis very fond o' the bottle, ye know. He liked his drink. Ah remember ma father tellin' me that ma grandmother had tae go tae his place o' work tae get the wages before he got home wi' them or there would be no wages.

After the 1914–18 War they couldn't get jobs. Ma father's brother wis in Auchendinny, and he wis eventually the cobbler for the barracks at Glencorse. So ah think it wis through him that ma father came to Roslin Glen after the war, got a job in the carpet factory, and got a house in Roslin Glen and stayed there with ma mother. That wis before ah wis born in 1922, because ma older brother wis born in the Glen, that would be 1920.

In Roslin Glen carpet factory ma father would be what you'd term a labourer, ye know, jist jack of all trades. He used tae mend the wires, some wires, for the weavers. He used tae do a lot of solderin' in the factory, any broken wires and things like that. And what he did – one of the jobs – he wis the gas lighter. In these days it wis gas and he went out early in the mornings, oh, before we were awake, and lit these gas lights in the factory before the workers came in. Ah think ah can recollect the carpet factory whistle blowing in the morning, between seven and eight, maybe eight, ah would think. Ma father would come home for his dinner, oh, twelve o'clock – well, ah'm not goin' tae say it wis an hour. Ah don't remember that. But ah know it wis twelve o'clock. We used as children tae run up and get a carry on his back comin' down the road. Then at five o'clock at night the factory whistle blew again and he came home, finished for the day. And ah think he would in these days work on Saturday mornings, ah think so. Ah don't think his pay wis much, ah think a pound tae two pound, ye know. Ah've heard the others talk about it. That wis the wages then.

Ah can still remember the day clearly that ma two brothers and I were baptised in Roslin Chapel. Ah can still remember goin' intae this little place that wis at the end o' the Chapel. The font's still there today. And that's where we were baptised. Ah must have been maybe, say, four. My younger brother Stanley wis jist an infant. Ma mother wis a great Christian person, a great Christian woman she wis. Ma father's brother in Auchendinny they were members o' Roslin Chapel. And when ma mother came tae live in the Glen – ah think it would be through ma father's brother in Auchendinny – she went tae the Chapel, Roslin Chapel. And ah remember an aunt sayin' tae me, 'If your mother hadn't taken that asthma durin' the First War she would have been in the mission fields.' Ma mother had wanted tae go to the mission fields. Durin' the war ma mother had been a V.A.D. nurse, ye know, and went out helpin'.[48]

The house ah wis born in in Roslin Glen it wis a carpet factory house. They must have built these houses for the workers when the carpet factory opened. There wis 24 houses in the Glen. And ah must say everybody was so close to each other, so friendly. And ma mother wis one o' these people, if there wis trouble they came to her. As ah say, it wis the V.A.D. she had joined in the First War. Ah think it would jist be first aid training she had. Ah don't know much about that part o' her life. But ah do know when we lived in the Glen anybody sick, anybody needed anything done, they came to ma mother. Ye know how ye had tae write a note if you were off school? Ah can remember manys a one came tae her, 'Would you write a note to the teacher ? So-and-so's been off school.' She done a' these sort o' things for them.

Well, the house that we lived in in No.8 Roslin Glen to start with was what you called a single end. That wis the only single end along the front. It wis only one apartment. The beds were in there, the fireplace. You lived in there, you ate there, you slept there. There was no running water, nothing in the house: outside toilets, no running water. There wis a tap where the people went tae, with a bucket, tae get their water. There wis three taps for the 24 houses. That wis one there, and the other one wis quite a bit along the Glen. And the third one – the houses in the Glen wis like an L-shape (and there wis single ends; too, up where the L-shape was) and you went round that corner, which years before that wis called the bleaching fields, and up there there would be eight houses probably – and that's where the other well wis, for these people round there. So one tap for each eight houses. Our household shared an outside tap with seven other households. There wis no running water in the houses, no bath, no shower – nothing. For baths we had the zinc bath in front o' the fire. There would be two or three nights for baths, because you were out playing, but ah think Friday night wis the main bath night. Then eventually, in our second house, No.11, which was a room and kitchen in the Glen, when ah wis still quite young, they built the washhouses at the back. And time without number we had a bath in the tubs in the washhouse. But all three of us as children lived first in the single end at No.8. And then jist two doors along another house – No.11 – became vacant. It wis a room and kitchen and we moved to that room and kitchen.

In those houses in Roslin Glen it wis always dry troilets, and they were outside at the back. The toilets were all in a row. Everybody had their own toilet, no sharing with that. We had wir own toilet. And it wis the men in the factory – two men, a Mr Durie, he wis the horse and cart man, drove the horse and cart; and a Mr Perfect – and they emptied these toilets every week. When ye think about it ! They must have had tae dig somewhere about, I would imagine. But they had that job o' these toilets.

Ah remember before these washhouses went up ma mother

always went into the bedroom wi' this tub, ye know, on a chair, and done the washin' there. And the pot went on the fire tae boil the white things – the big soup pot wis on the fire, boilin' the white things. What a hard life they had, really hard ! Very, very little leisure.

At No.8 the sleeping arrangements were our parents in one bed and me and ma two brothers in the other bed. Ah can't remember if we slept top to bottom or just all in a row, ah can't remember that. Sometimes in these days the older ones or the girls were at one end o' the bed, and the younger ones or the boys at the other. Oh, that wis common ! And, ah mean, we were three of a family. Some o' them in the Glen were seven o' a family, mixed sex, too, but they were in a room and kitchen.

Oh, all the time we were in the Glen, at No.8 and then at No.11, it wis paraffin lamps. Ma father lit the gas lights in the factory but there was no gas lighting in the houses. It wis paraffin lamps right up to the late 1950s when these houses were brought down. No gas for cooking either. There wis an open fire, with a range style, and a wee tank with a wee tap at the side for hot water. And ah used tae wonder how did they have time tae black-lead that fireplace ? Ma mother cooked on the coal fire – well, she done the pots and pans on the coal fire. And she had a paraffin stove where she used tae bake. If she wanted to bake scones or anything they were done in this paraffin oven. And ma mother was always knitting – knitted everything for us – and she would bake things on that paraffin stove. She got all that done.

All the houses in the Glen were just single storey houses. On the L-shape there wis one there with an upstairs – they were single ends in these four places, two at the top and two at the bottom. That wis the only one that had an upstairs, four in that stair.

When we moved to No.11 ma parents slept in the kitchen-cum-livin' room and me and ma two brothers in the room. And we had a bed chair, so one o' us children must have slept on that bed chair.

Every house had a beautiful garden, oh, beautiful gardens ! They were at the front. We had the flower garden at the front.

Then there wis the road, and then there wis the burn, the North Esk.

Almost all the people in the Roslin Glen houses worked in the carpet factory. But for some reason or other there wis in these houses some that worked in the powder mill, down at the bottom, in the powder mill. There wis miners, too, in the Glen cottages. Quite a few worked in the coal mines. They were householders, they were the householders. Maybe at that time some o' the carpet workers didn't want to live in the Glen, maybe they preferred Roslin, ye know.

The carpet factory wis Henry Widnell & Stewart, famous for their carpets, Axminster carpets. And famous for their peacock pattern. And they used tae have outings in the summer, and in these days it wis the train ye went on. They used tae go on the train away to Ayr. Ah remember goin' in 1938 tae the Empire Exhibition at Bellahouston Park, Glasgow. That wis the year before the war broke out. Ah wis there wi' the factory workers.[49] And they used tae take their banners, the peacock banner, and the men wid march wi' that through the place that they were going tae for the day's outing. They always had a banner wi' the carpet. But the peacock was *the* one. Ah think the slogan on the banner wis 'Henry Widnell & Stewart, Roslin Carpet Factory'.

Ah had an accident in the Glen tae ma leg when ah wis two, two-and-a-half, and ah've always had a limp since. And ah can remember the accident as clear as it wis yesterday. The woman next door tae us, Mrs Durie, had a shop in the Glen. And ah must have had a ha'penny or a penny, impatiently shoutin' for the shop – because Mrs Durie was in the house talkin' tae ma mother at the time. And ah wis climbin' this fence, as a child would do, and ah pushed ma knee intae this fence and ah got ma knee stuck. Ah couldnae get it out the fence. Ah think they had tae send up tae the carpet factory for some o' the men tae come down tae get it out. And it was from then – ah must have displaced something.

Ah started school at Roslin when ah wis five and then this knee started tae trouble me again. Ah had jist a slight limp. Ah mean, it didn't keep me back from gettin' around. No, as a child ah used tae run in the Glen, playin' maybe up in the woods – that wis our playground, up the woods, or in the burn, the River North Esk, the burn as we called it. And that's where we spent our days, playin' in the burn or enjoyin' wirsel' in the woods. Ye know, that wis our playgrounds.

And then they put me down into East Fortune hospital in East Lothian. And practically half ma education was in the hospital. But at these·days, ah mean, they never done anything for me – jist rest, jist lying. For quite a long time – ah felt it wis a long time – ah wis lying in bed. And then ye gradually got up for an hour, for two hours, and then ye got up for the whole day. Ye were up at six in the morning till six at night. That wis your all day, they called it, you were up for all day. But, mind, there wis happy memories there. There wis children from all over there. They came from the Borders to East Fortune – none from Edinburgh, they never came from Edinburgh – but all the Lothians and the Borders. And at that time ah liked concerts. We used tae perform for the rest o' the children. We had one teacher, a Miss Fergie. And she used tae teach a' different classes, ye know, she had us all there. And then she taught singing, and we were a' fond o' singing. Ah wis interested in singing and drama. She taught us to put on shows at Christmas time and different things.

Ah wis in East Fortune hospital maybe a year or a year and a half – ah felt as if ah had been in a long time, ye know ! And then ah got out for, oh, a year or a couple o' year. And ma mother died when ah wis ten. Ah'd come home for so long, ye see, and it wis durin' that time she died. Oh, that wis a blow ! Ma older brother was twelve, and ma younger brother was eight. Ma mother had friends in Glenside at Roslin, a Mr and Mrs Gray, and after ma mother died they took me to stay with them. They were good Christian people, ye know. Actually, they were the Brethren. They went tae the Brethren in Loanhead. And when ma mother was livin' we used tae have a night in the week, we used tae go to their house in the Glen for the meetings and singing – the Sankey hymns, ye know. But ah stayed wi' them for a while after ma mother died. And there again it wis a room and kitchen. There wis a son and daughter, and at night time ah used tae sleep wi' the daughter, Aggie Gray. The son wis killed later on in the war. But they were all on their knees every night and said their prayers.

So ah wis there until ah went back intae the hospital again for a couple o' years, and when ah come home ah wis thirteen. And that wis ma schoolin' finished at thirteen. Ah wis keepin' house then for ma father and ma two brothers, looking after the family. That wis from about 1935 and ah never worked until the war broke out. Ah had no option. Ah done the washin', done the ironin'. There was times when ah felt disappointed and restricted. Ma ambition as a girl wis always nursing. You know, you thought, 'When ah grow up ah'm goin' tae be a nurse.' Or ah wanted tae do somethin' wi' the mission fields. And maybe it wis jist through knowing that ma mother might have gone to the mission fields that, you know, you feel you want to do the same. That was what ah fancied then.

Ah started practically from scratch wi' the housework. Ma father wis pretty good, because he had tae do it. He wis practical where that wis concerned. He could cook, he could cook. He looked after us. And then, jist about the beginning o' the war, that's when ma father had tae stop work at the carpet factory wi' a heart condion. And the doctor told him, 'You'll never work again.' Ah wis seventeen then and ah went up tae Dr Waite and ah said, 'Is there nothing ye can do ?' ah says, 'because he's terribly moody tae think that he'll never work again.' Dr Waite says, 'The only thing he'll be able to do is push a pen.' Ma father wis a beautiful writer, ah must say that, but he wisnae an office man or anything like that, not a clerical worker. He'd been accustomed tae work wi' his hands all his life. So he wis at home from about the beginnin' o' the war. Ah think really he wis the type o' person there wis more fear tae know that there wis something wrong with him, and he couldn't do this and he couldn't do that. And ah remember he wis called up to report to some officials about his health, because he wis drawin' off the Assistance Board. And when they examined him they said tae him, 'Oh, ye're fit enough tae climb the Pentlands. Ye'll be able tae climb Arthur's Seat.' Ma father had a quick temper and, oh, he wis really angry then, really angry. And he jist come back really fumin'. But, ye know, in time tae come he did walk the

Pentlands, he did. Ah think the walkin' helped him. He lived till he wis ninety.

Between the ages of fourteen and when you were seventeen, what we got was two shillings pocket money from ma father. Two shillings pocket money. And with that pocket money we went up to Roslin Castle station and for 8d. – old pennies – ye got a return ticket tae Edinburgh. We had tae walk up tae Roslin Castle station, which wis quite a walk up, uphill all the way, a good mile or so. We went tae the Playhouse cinema, what we termed the gods. Ye got there for 9d. And then when the pictures came out ye crossed the street and ye went into the Deep Sea fish and chip restaurant, which is still there today, and ye got your tuppenny plate o' chips. And ye sat there and had them. Then ye went back tae the Waverley station and got the train back tae Roslin Castle. That wis our Saturdays. That's how we spent our pocket money. Two or three of us went there every Saturday night, and that wis a great, great thing, an outing. Either that or it wis tae Loanhead Picture House. They had a picture house then. That wis our week-end. That's how wir youth wis spent then. That wis our days.

As ah say, ah never worked outside the house until after the war broke out. Ah wis seventeen the day war wis declared. Ah wis sittin' in Roslin Church that day, jist after eleven o'clock. Well, during that first two years o' the war ah wis in the Red Cross and ah used tae go round collecting. They had a penny a week for the Red Cross. And ah used to come round Bilston, collecting with a tin, and ah used tae go away up where the bomb factory was, and collect a' these outlying houses, and up and up tae Roslin Castle station for a penny a week for the Red Cross. Ah walked a lot. And then when ah wis nineteen in 1941 that is when the nineteen year olds were called up for munition work. So I thought, 'Here's ma chance then. Ah'm gettin' out tae work and earn some money.' And that is when ah went up to the bomb factory.

We had tae go to the labour exchange at Loanhead. All the females that were nineteen that year had tae report tae their labour exchange. And that's where ah went down and reported. And it wis there that ah said tae them, 'Ah don't think ah'm compelled tae do this, because ah keep house for ma father and ma brothers.' And they said, 'No, no, ye could be exempt.' 'Well,' ah says, 'ah don't want tae be exempt.'

Ah believe ah could have got off through havin' tae keep the house for ma father, ah could have got off under that. But I didn't want tae. I wanted tae go out and work. And ah went up there to the bomb factory when ah wis nineteen. Well, ah jist said to ma father, 'Ah'm goin' tae start in the bomb factory.' And he accepted that. And, ye see, at that time, that's when he had tae stop work at the carpet factory, wi' the heart condition. So maybe that made it a bit easier for me to get out of the house.

We weren't asked tae go to the A.T.S. or the W.A.A.F.s. Munitions work wis for nineteen year olds. We jist were called up and they directed us tae the bomb factory at Roslin. Oh, ah think there wis about half a dozen started the same day as me. There wis Betty Ferguson and Ella Mason.[50] Ella wis what we called Glenside, a block of about eight houses above the Glen.

Ah remember ma first day in the bomb factory. Ah had never been among other . . . you know, such company, grown ups. It wis difficult but ah jist seemed to tone in as you would say, you know, jist accept it wis something tae be done.

When I wis growing up as a girl in the Glen we knew it wis there, the powder mill. You referred tae it as the powder mill. And people living beside us in the Glen worked in the powder mill, not many, not many. Ah can only remember Mr Dave Smith. But we knew the powder mill wis there. Ah never went into it as a girl. Ah mean, we never thought about that. It wis there, and that wis as far as we knew. Oh, it wis a very old mill.

Ah can't say as a girl that ah heard any explosions at the powder mill. But ah can remember when ma mother wis alive and ah wis a wee girl we walked from the Glen up by Gourlaw, away up past Roslin Castle. The baby – ma younger brother – was in the pram, and ah'm sittin' on the top. Ah can remember that walk and it brought us tae the crossroads, the road goin' off for Rosewell, and it was the waterman's house there. Ma mother was friendly with the people there. And ah can remember ma mother goin' tae visit that person there that wis injured in the powder mill. Ah think she lost her hair actually, if ah remember right. And the girl Arnott from Bilston, she wis killed in that accident. Ah knew her sisters as we grew up. They went to the school at Roslin. She would be an older sister that wis killed.

The first job ah went on tae at the bomb factory wis what ye called the Northovers. And that apparently wis for the tanks. Ah can always remember it wis something about six inches high, and jist maybe three or four inches round, and we must have put the powder intae that. Ah think it wis maybe block powder. We got it tae fill intae them, and we had tae fill so many and carry them on a tray and take them along tae the end hut, where they must have packed them. That wis the Northovers, they were called, and that wis for tank usage.

They made Verey lights for the navy and then they made the smoke screens for the navy. And ah wis on a job once – ma husband often says, 'Was it bullets ?' – it wis something about that size, like a brass container, and, oh, jist roond. And ye filled that. Ah remember so much wis the grey powder, and the top – maybe half an inch or about an inch – black powder went intae that. And on that job ye had tae wear a mask for inhaling the powder. Ah do think that's how ah suffer from sinus trouble these days, bits o' powder, the fine dust, goin' up your nostrils. That wis the only job that ah remember where ye had tae wear a mask. It wis a very precise job, ye had tae be precise wi' these measurements. These powders had tae go in there.

And there wis other jobs ah wis on, ah can't remember what it wis. Tae me it wis a job like matchsticks and ye were puttin' powder on them, and these had all tae be counted. Ye were countin' thousands o' them at a time tae put intae something or other, ye know. But ah jist can't remember what it was.

And then ah wis on another job like a pressin' machine, where ye were pressin' like pellets – powder, ye had tae press it down and it came out firm. That wis another job. Ah wis on several different jobs. You weren't moved from job to job at your own request. Maybe they would say, 'Would you go such-and-such a place ?' Ah think you practically learned a' the jobs, ye know ! Ye were on them for a while, oh, ye were on them for a while, because ye got in wi' these girls, ye know, became friendly wi' these girls. A nice bunch o' girls, ah must say.

The gunpowder mill and the bomb factory wis like two separate places. In the bomb factory we didn't have much contact with them down below in the powder mill. We had separate canteens. This canteen on the top wis jist for the workers on the top, in the huts, ye know. They had their own canteen down below. Living in the Glen, ah knew some of the workers in the powder mill, ah knew who they were, but you didn't have contact with them at work, no, not at all. They were mainly men in the powder mill – apart from office workers. It wis a' the females, it wis a' the girls, on the top place.

Ah wis never employed down in the powder mill. The only time ah went down there was when they used tae have a meeting, maybe once a month it would be, and anybody wi' suggestions – they had a suggestion box – and they always picked somebody tae go down tae that meeting. And ah remember ah wis picked once, tae go down there tae the powder mill and sit round the table wi' the managers and that. It wis a man came up from the bottom and took ye down through the woods, a' these wooden steps, a' down through the woods, tae the bottom. It's the only time that ah wis down there.

The gunpowder mill was down in the Glen. The powder mill wis there all the time. Ah think they were there, if ah'm right, for the pits – making powder for that. Ye know how they blasted in the pits. But the bomb factory was there only durin' the war. The bomb factory wis up in the top. They had steps goin' down through the wood from the bomb factory, and a bridge over the water and intae the gunpowder mill. We went up tae Roslin Castle station, up there at the top. And goin' in for the siding for the railway, that's where we went in. And there wis this gate, which was always open, of course, and the wee hut at the gate. And then ye walked further round – not terribly far – ye walked further round tae the huts and intae your changing room. But we were up in the top, and that's where the railway waggons came right in.

There was a siding from the Roslin Castle station line for the waggons tae come in. And ah remember they had a long tunnel – that wis from the First War – the tin tunnel, they called it, for any sparks from the trains, maybe settin' fire tae the dry grass or anything. The tin tunnel wis slightly along from the siding, between there and Auchendinny, it wasn't right at the siding. The waggons that were brought into the siding were to take things away.

I worked three shifts at the bomb factory. But the first job ah went on tae, the Northovers, ah think ah started on the two shifts, the day shift and the back shift. And then after ah had been on that for a while ah got put on tae three shifts – on tae night shift. And, well, up after four in the mornin', ye know, and five o'clock breakfast, because ah had tae walk from the Glen up tae the bomb factory – six o'clock start in the morning. The three shifts were six o'clock in the morning till two, from two till ten, and from ten at night till six in the morning. You worked each shift a week at a time. It wis always a change over at the week-end. Ye were a' these hours: morning one week, afternoon the next, and the night shift. And when ye were on the night shift ye had tae go to your bed durin' the day tae get sleep. Well, at first ah found it difficult, because in the bedroom ye had the washhouse at the back, and that's where they all met and had their wee gossip and talk, ye know, the neighbours. And you're lyin' there tryin' tae sleep and ye heard a' the tattle. At the beginning ah thought, 'Oh, my, ah'm goin' tae take ages tae go over.' But no doubt eventually ye would get intae that system that ye would sleep. But it wasn't easy tae adapt at the beginning.

You were jist getting accustomed to one set o' hours when you were on tae another – week about: day shift, and then on tae the back shift, then on tae the night shift, Sunday nights. You worked day shift on the Monday till Saturday and you finished at two o'clock on Saturday afternoon. And then the night shift started, and you were out at ten o'clock on Sunday night till Saturday morning. And then you started on the Sunday at two o'clock back shift.

On the night shift we all had a wee sleep in the huts. Ye got your head down. After your work wis finished ye got your head down like that for your forty winks. Ye felt ye had tae have that on the night shift. It wis jist the night shift, not the day or the back shift. About three tae four in the mornin', that's when, 'Oh, gosh, ah could sleep now,' ye know. Well, ye hoped the management never knew.

Ah mean, that wis one thing, the management weren't on top of you all the time. Ye had – what would ye call them – girls that came in at certain times. They were checkin' on your work. There were maybe about two o' them on each shift. They wore the sort o' white coats, ye know. And they wid come in and jist sit and blether and watch ye doin' what ye were doin', jist checkin' that ye were doin' it properly. They were jist like a supervisor. We had men there, which we called supervisors, one on each shift, and they came round at some point o' the day, jist checkin'. And ye always had a visit on the night shift, ye know. Ye could always tell what time they were comin' in, ye know. They came at a fairly regular time. They were round each building that wis workin'.

There wis three managers, like works managers. We had a Mr Miller on one shift. And Willie Mitchell – he had a house down at the bottom mill – he lived there. And the other one that we had was a Mr Milne from Penicuik. So ye had these three. Each shift these men came on and they were in charge o' that shift. That wis your shift manager. They came round – but not on top o' ye all the time.

Ye knew that ye had tae be strict wi' your work. Ye had tae be precise wi' your job. Ah know it was very dangerous work. But, ye see, when ah started in the bomb factory ah wis conscious o' that fact. When ah started on the Northovers ah wis really conscious o' bein' in among the gunpowder. And ah did feel, 'Oh, my, ah'll need tae mind ma p.s and q.s here.' You never thought about it, tae the extent that when ye were goin' out tae a dance ye put your rollers in your hair, which wis forbidden. But, ye see, ye got that ye never thought about the danger – and how silly it was, really, takin' a risk. There wis a person that used tae come, an ordinary worker but she had this wee bit higher up that she could check. And they would say. 'There's Ella O'Hara on the go.' And you nipped up and got all these things out your hair before she came in, dreadin' that she wid come in. They always passed round, ye know. But we did that occasionally. Ah know it wis silly. But then ye got over the years climatised tae the thing, ye did ! Ye never thought about the dangers. If there had been an accident that would have been different, that would have been different.

There wis a hut at the entrance, where ye we went in and ye clocked in there. Ye clocked in, and they had the wee doocot places for anybody that smoked – men wi' pipes, everybody. Ye were searched, and these things were put aside. Well, they searched when ye went in for a time when ye first started. But people got tae know ye if ye were a smoker or what, ye know. But they still searched ye roughly tae see that ye had nothing on you, like. Ye left all that there. Oh, ye were frisked. They did check ye.

And then ye had a wee walk intae where they had a canteen. They had the changin' rooms, quite a big changin' room, because there wis a shift comin' off and a shift goin' on. And ye had your hooks there for hangin' your overalls on. And there must have been something tae put your skirt in and your jersey and your boots. Ye carried your boots with ye up and down from the changin' rooms tae your hut, your place o' work.

We were supplied with a black skirt and a black jumper. It wis just a woollen jersey. The skirt wis a sort o' woolly serge material, maybe serge, black serge material. And that wis fairly long, ye know, below your knees like. That's the first things ye got when ye went up there tae work at the bomb factory. You were issued wi' this black skirt and a black jumper and quite a thick overall, which came right down to your ankles. You tied a belt round the waist. And ye had a pair of boots, and a black hat tae pull over your hair. The hat wis made the same material as the overall, a firm sort o' hat, a sort o' glaze, ye know – thick, but not hard. Ye could pull them on. There wis a turn-up brim on the hat a' the way round, and ye just pulled it on, jist a tammy style hat, ye know, wi' the turn-up. The hat wis tae keep your hair covered, because if ye were goin' out, ye would have powder in your hair, ye see. Ye had tae cover all your hair wi' the hat. Ah don't think ah wis ever on a job wi' gloves. But it would depend on what jobs you were doin'.

Now ah wonder were these skirts ever washed ? Wis the jerseys ever washed ? Ah think ye jist wore them and if ye needed a new one ye got a new one. They were never sent away for washin' because, ye see, the gunpowder wis on them wi' the powder.

Well, ye were issued wi' these boots, leather, jist leather uppers and soles, sort o' light weight, and lacin' up, jist like a man's boots, like an ordinary pair o' boots, a short ankle bit there. And no tackets on them, of course – very plain soles, very plain soles. And when ye went intae a hut . . . Jist imagine a square, and a' these huts are round a big grass centre in a square, and the office is up at this end. And on these huts wis a platform, a wooden platform, and a box at the side o' that platform. And tae go intae that hut ye had tae step on tae that wooden platform – a long platform – and take your outdoor shoes off and put these boots on. And your outdoor shoes went intae that box. And then ye couldn't go intae that hut wi' your outdoor shoes on.

But that's a thing ah'm recalling now – footwear. Ah remember them saying, 'Now – boys' shoes.' You either got boys' shoes without clothing coupons or for very little coupons. And we were all into the town buying boys' shoes tae walk up that road tae the bomb factory, ye know, because ye were walking through the snow and the rain and everything and your shoes that you did have were goin' pretty down. And it wis coupons then. And we got boys' shoes, lacin' shoes, and that's what we wore tae the finish o' the war. Ah remember that.[51]

We were very cautious about changin' your boots, and everything had tae be clean and scrubbed out, ye know. And every Saturday, at the end o' your shift, on a Saturday – we worked back shift Saturday, but ah'm jist tryin' tae remember if it wis when ye were on the day shift – ye had tae scrub out that hut, and this platform had tae be scrubbed. And it wis cold water we scrubbed it. Mind, it made it rare and white, it certainly made it white. Your brushes – the handle o' the brushes – had tae be scrubbed, and the shovel – the handle o' the shovel. Ye scrubbed all that. Every week that wis scrubbed – them that were goin' off that shift, every hut, inside and outside. Ye had work benches, ah remember the work benches, and it wis like that brown linoleum that wis on the work tops. And ye had tae sweep out and sluice out the floor. Ye would have tae wash it out some way. But this wooden bit outside the door, a' these slats o' wood, had a' tae be scrubbed. That wis done every week. Ye'd done your shift work and then you had tae do that. That wis additional work that had tae be done. That wis all in your week's work, it jist went wi' the job. We'd stop at a certain time and then get on wi' the cleanin', the washin' and that. Ye had tae do it. It had tae be spotless, ye know.

Well, these years ah felt ye were jist workin', ye were goin' home – well, ah had tae go home and clean and wash and what have you. Ah still had that tae do at home. But ah jist felt you were eatin', sleepin', workin'. That wis your life, ye know. Ye were a' these hours: morning one week, afternoon the next, and the night shift.

The canteen and the changin' room wis all in the one, the one hall, as ye wid say. And then, oh, there wis a hut – a long one there, but divided, ye know, as if it wis intae sections. And then there wis another one running this way, and another one along that way. They were at right angles tae each other. Quite possible that wis for safety reasons – in case of an explosion ye wid be far enough apart, ye know. There wis some distance between each hut. And they had pipes – they must have been heating, ye know – across the ground. The huts had the hot pipes running through them for the winter time. Ah can't say that ah wis workin' and sayin' it wis cold. Ah'll tell ye when ye felt shivery – when ye were on the night shift, and when it come tae three and four in the morning ye were tired. Well, as ah say, we all had a wee sleep in the huts on the night shift.

And we had showers. We had showers for people tae go and have a shower, and the washhand basins, ye know. That wis off the changin' room. Well, if ye were goin' out for a dance or anything – well, me especially – ah wisnae goin' home tae have a bath or a shower, 'cause we had no facilities like that at home in the Glen ! But ye got a shower up there at the bomb factory. Them that lived in Roslin and Loanhead and Rosewell had baths at home. But the showers at the bomb factory wis a good thing for us from the Glen.

Oh, nobody took any risks like smoking in the huts, oh, never.

Oh, that wis taboo that – never any o' that, not tae ma knowledge. Ah'm not a smoker maself but ah never heard o' anybody smoking in the huts. That wis the only time, in the canteen. We had the E.N.S.A. shows. They came on a Saturday night when we went up to the canteen for our dinners about six o'clock. Between five and six you went across and the E.N.S.A. shows came. And ah can remember this night clearly. We were sittin' and ah wis at this end, and the stage where they entertained wis here on ma right. And it wis over the other side o' that ah heard the commotion. This man had taken out a cigarette and a match box, ready tae light up ! So the door wis there tae go through to the changing rooms and the factory girls just whipped him through there. We were a' sittin' wi' wir black overalls on, ye see, and we had a certain amount o' gunpowder on us. But ah don't know how drastic that could have been. The man jist never thought. Ah don't think he wis an entertainer. Ah think he wis one that had came along with them. But the girls were sayin', 'How were you not searched ? !' He must have slipped through the net, as they say, and he should have been searched. But that wis a fright. Well, it caused a wee bit excitement for us, ye know. But he was whipped out there.

Planes flew over a lot, and ye could always tell a German plane had a different sound. Oh, they were very, very strict wi' the blackouts at the bomb factory. They had the black curtain, and when ye opened the hut door ye had tae be out and in in a flash. On the night shift like ye had tae be very, very careful wi' the blackout. They were black curtains that they closed at nights and then durin' the day they were opened. Oh, they were very, very strict about that. In fact, ah remember air raid wardens used tae phone the factory from Roslin because they could see a chink o' light. They would say, 'There's a chink o' light up there', and they would come round the buildins and check. Ah'm tryin' tae think – any air raids, where did we go ? There must have been something for the people tae go tae if there wis a warning.

There wis no soldiers on guard at the bomb factory, not tae ma knowledge, ah never seen any. The only thing that ah understood wis guarded at some point wis the main water pipe. That's down at the bottom o' the powder mill brae. And that's the only thing that ah have ever heard o' bein' guarded wis that water, in case maybe gettin' any plans tae blow it up or anything. For that wis water supply tae Edinburgh. And ah can't think o' seein' a barbed wire fence round the bomb factory. Oh, it wis open. Anybody that wis determined could quite easily got in there. They could have got in the main gate, ye know.

Ah don't remember the day a tank came in to visit the factory, I'd be on a different shift, ye see. But ah remember the day that Italy gave in, when the war wis finished with Italy.[52] Ah wis on the back shift that day and we got away early, they let us away early. And we all went up tae the Royal Hotel in Roslin for a celebration. And we had a sing-song and ah remember a girl from Rosewell, Betsy McGarey or McGarry wis her name, and she sang *Ave Maria*. And, ye know, ah know it's no' right, but she wisnae the type o' person that ye associated wi' havin' a voice. She wis terrific, a great voice. Ah think we were a' amazed at her really. She sang *Ave Maria* that night.

I honestly couldn't tell ye if we got paid holidays at the bomb factory. Ah don't remember if we got paid for holidays. But, oh, there must have been holidays, because ah remember goin' away by train wi' about another three girls down tae Morecambe for a week's holiday.

Ah can remember a night we had at Roslin Castle. Well, it wis two sisters that were the caretakers and a brother. And this time durin' the war they invited the men from the Overseas Club in Princes Street in Edinburgh tae come out tae a dance, and they invited so many o' us from the bomb factory tae come tae this dance. And I was at that dance. And it wis a' Canadians, Australians, all nationalities were there, and we had a great night there. And when it came tae midnight they spoke about the White Lady, the ghost, ye know, in the Castle. There is supposed tae have always been a White Lady in Roslin Castle. And ah remember Betty Ferguson, she worked in the Castle maybe at the week-ends when she wis off from the bomb factory, because at that time a lot o' visitors came out tae Roslin. The Castle had a tea room. And they got Betty tae go down in the dungeons and put a white sheet over her. And they got these servicemen, ye know, 'Oh, ah think this is the time the White Lady'll be walkin'.' There they a' were, down in the dungeons, and Betty goin' out and in the dungeons wi' the white sheet on her. And by luck it came on snow that night. And somebody – they must ha' been outside – they come in, 'It's snowing !' And some o' these men rushed out. They'd never seen snow. They thought this wis wonderful tae see the snow ! Oh, a really good night we had that night.

Durin' the war when ye worked in the bomb factory your hobby wis the dancing. We went up tae Roslin, the Miners' Institute. And then maybe there'd be a night we'd go tae Rosewell, tae the Miners' Institute in Rosewell. The Miners' Institutes, that's where the dances were held. Ye know, it wis jist a case o' working and out Friday and Saturday night at the dancing. And then at the bomb factory ye got in wi' these girls, ye know, became friendly wi' these girls. A nice bunch o' girls, ah must say. A lot o' them were about ma age – we'd been called up at nineteen. But then there wis others there that were there from the beginning o' the war, had started before me. But ye were a' nineteen, twenty-one, ye know. And then ye jist a' met, went tae the dancin' together, and different things. That wis your life during the war.

Ah can't remember what the wages in the bomb factory were, ah can't remember. And I don't know if we were in a union. Ah don't remember that at all.

Oh, there wis quite a lot of workers employed at the bomb factory. There wis quite a lot on each shift, over fifty anyway, maybe sixty, seventy. And then there wis the foremen and then the canteen workers. They had ladies on the canteen and they were three shifts, ye know, on the night shift, too. The canteen went the whole time. Ye had a meal in the middle o' the night. It wis very good food. You paid for that and you got a selection, ye know, there wis a choice. Oh, a good canteen.

Ah remember we were sittin' in the canteen and it wis mince that day. And, oh, gosh, ah took a terrible pain in ma right side, and ah went through and ah wis sick. Now they had a first aid room there, and they had a first aid person. And ah remember having tae go tae that first aid room and bein' put on the bed. And it wis jist this awfy pain, and they sent for the doctor. Ah think Mrs Bamber, the first aid person, thought, 'Is this appendicitis ?' However, Dr Gunn – he wis Loanhead, he wis the doctor for the bomb factory – he came and examined me. 'No, no,' he says, 'ah think,' he says, 'it's been a stone. It's passed through,' he says. Because ah wis as right as rain after that.

But Mrs Bamber that wis her job, first aid person. She must have been a trained nurse. But she wis there. Oh, they had all these facilities. And they also had a bath there, which wis there if there was an accident, for people tae be put intae the bath – maybe burns or things, ye see. It would be burns. But they did have a bath kept for that reason. But there was never need tae use it, not to ma knowledge.

Ah remember (ah don't know if ah should be tellin' this), but ah remember – of course, there were so many women, ye had all types of women comin' in there – and somebody must have had the nits in the hair and somebody must have reported it. So we were all called in in rows intae this first aid room tae have wir heads checked, because they didn't want the nits tae spread. Then there wis another time. There wis an outbreak o' smallpox in the country. Ah don't remember what time o' the war that wis. But there was an outbreak o' smallpox, and we had all tae be lined up and be vaccinated. The doctor came, and ah remember that happenin' in the first aid room. Oh, there wis no case o' smallpox in the bomb factory, nothing up there, no, jist a prevention. Mind, it had tae be done, and ah jist happened to be on one o' the shifts when it wis done.[53]

Ah wis in the bomb factory until the war finished. We were still there until the war finished. Ah wis there four years roughly.

When ah come out the bomb factory ah got a job with T. & J. Smith's chemical works out at Gorgie in Edinburgh, because ah had relatives worked there. Ma father worked there at one time before the First War, before he went tae Canada. Ah wanted tae work, ah wanted something tae do after being in the bomb factory. And ah got a job in the drugs department. Ah wis workin' wi' the morphine and a' the drugs. We were locked in that room. And ah worked two or three month, travelled out and in, eight till about five – a long day wi' the travellin' frae Roslin – in that until ah took bronchitis with the fumes off the powders. So ah didn't stick that job at T. & J. Smith's.

Then ah got a job in the carpet factory at Roslin. Ah got a job as a scale maker. That wis for the people in the colour shop, the people that put the colours on tae the yarn. Ah can see it: it wis on a big wheel. They wound it on a big wheel. And ah had tae have this chart wi' the colours, all numbered. Ah used tae write all the numbers out in tiny wee squares, ye know, on sheets o' paper. Ah had tae make a wooden board and glue this on to the wooden board, and they put that beside them on what they called their drum. Well, this wis the number o' the colour that they put along on this wheel. And then that wis carried off that drum – heavy work, it depended on the size o' the carpets. That wis taken away intae a steam place, where it wis all steamed before it went through tae the weaving shop, where the weavers put it on tae their frames for weaving.

The carpet factory wisnae well paid, it wasn't really. No, we didnae get much pay there. Well, ah done that for a couple of years until ah got married in 1947.

We were lucky. We got a house in Roslin Glen. We got a room and kitchen at No.12 – a house that used tae be Mrs Jack's sweetie shop when ah wis young. And we got married and we were in there. Wir first daughter wis born there in 1948, Freda. Nothing had changed in the houses in Roslin Glen, oh, nothing, oh, not a thing – no running water, no baths, dry toilets. When we got married we had the Tilly lamp still in that house, No.12. One time, oh, Freda she would only be a year and a half, we had terrible rain, terrible. The North Esk wis right up tae the top. In fact, it wis over the banking at the bridge end. And we packed the pram, we had everything packed in it, because we thought we would have tae go up there tae Roslin, where ma husband's aunt lived. Well, luckily the river sort o' went down a bit. But we were really waitin on it comin' over the top and intae the houses. That wis one time it wis really bad. Oh, the houses were never flooded. But at that time there wis whole trees went down the river, whole trees were washed down, coming down through the Glen.

Well, looking back tae those four years in the bomb factory, I jist feel, well, they were good days, they were happy days. Ah enjoyed them wi' the company. Oh, we had some good company, nice girls, ye know, and all the rest of it. The best years o' your life. You were dancing at night and you were working, you were sleeping. Ye know, that wis your life. That wis the war. Ye were doing your bit, ye were doing your bit for the war, that's right. But ye jist think: what did ye do ? Ah know we were doing something. But at the same time you say, 'What did we do a' these years ?' They were good days, they were happy days. But at the same time ah think what wasted years.

NOTES

1. The population of the electoral and county district of East Calder in 1921 was 996. *Census of Scotland, 1921*, 1249.
2. Shipley Gordon Stuart Erskine, 14th Earl of Buchan (1850–1934).
3. A gunpowder cartridge factory was established by West Calder Co-operative Society in 1878 at Camilty but closed about the later 1920s or early 1930s.
4. Conflicting evidence suggests that Roslin gunpowder mills were established in either 1801 or 1803, but the mills were certainly there by 1805, when an explosion in the corning house on 1 October that year killed two of the workers and destroyed part of the buildings. The mills at Roslin were the second to be built in Scotland, the first having been opened five miles further east in or about 1794 as Stobs Mills, Gorebridge. Quarrels among the partners at Stobs Mills led two of them, John Merricks and John Hay, to break away and build their own mills at Roslin which by the 1840s had become the largest gunpowder mills in Scotland, employing sixty workers. John Shaw, *Water Power in Scotland, 1550–1870* (Edinburgh, 1984), 469; *Edinburgh Evening Courant*, 3 October 1805; *Report to the Secretary of State for the Home Department on an explosion of gunpowder at Roslin gunpowder factory, on 22nd January 1890* (London, 1890), 3.
5. Originally the mills were owned by Messrs Hay, Merricks & Co. (which became a limited company in 1877), then from 1898 by Curtis & Harvey Ltd, which in 1918 became part of Explosive Trades Ltd. In 1920 the latter became Nobel Industries Ltd, and then in 1926 the mills became part of Imperial Chemical Industries Ltd (Nobel's Explosives Co. Ltd). Geoffrey Boothroyd, 'The Roslin Gunpowder Factory', in *Shooting Magazine* (Romford, 1984), July 1984, 15; *Report to the Secretary of State for the Home Department, 1890*, op.cit., 3.
6. James Paris was away on army service during the Second World War when a fatal accident took place at the Roslin mills that

193

resulted in the death of David Malcolm see above, pp. 50 and 128. From within two or three years of the opening of the mills at the beginning of the nineteenth century until their closure 150 years later, there were recurrent explosions that cost the lives of at least twenty-five workers or caused injuries of varying degrees of seriousness and damaged or destroyed parts of the mills. The first such explosion took place on 1 October 1805. A letter that day from a reader in Penicuik to the *Edinburgh Evening Courant* gives this harrowing account: 'As I was this day, about half an hour after four o'clock in the afternoon, walking quietly in the neighbourhood of Auchendinny, I was alarmed by a loud report just, as I thought, on the other side of the hedge. When, however, I ascended a small eminence, I was struck with the appearance of an astonishingly thick cloud of white smoke, rising in slow gyration from the vicinity of Roslin, more than a mile distant, which in a few minutes covered a large portion of the hemisphere. The first person I met with said on conjecture that the powder mills near the village must have blown up; and I followed a number of people attracted by the explosion. On arriving at the spot the effects of the sad disaster were fearfully displayed. All around lay the burning and blackened fragments of the utensils, machinery, and building of what is called the Corning House where, it was said, upwards of forty barrels of gunpowder had been in a state of preparation. The materials of the roof, the rafters, the immense water wheels, in fine, the thick stone and lime walls of a building forty feet in length had been broken into pieces, projected into the air, and scattered over the fields to a distance of several hundred yards; and the . . . scattered beams in all directions, standing upright, and deeply fixed in the earth, told the great height from which they had fallen . . . We soon, however, perceived from the lamentations and ill-concealed tears of a number of convulsed females, and from the mournful and solemn looks of the men, that something more terrible had happened. We learned with horror that two of the work people had perished. One man was thrown across the river Esk; the other to the top of a precipice overhanging the water – their mangled appearance was uniform, no remnant of their cloaths covered them, their skulls were torn from their heads, the one black and deformed trunk could be distinguished from the other only by the original size of the miserable sufferers. We saw them enveloped in cartridge paper like mummies, and carried off by their melancholy fellow labourers . . . Both of the unfortunate dead have left helpless widows behind them, one of

Notes

whom is now the unhappy mother of seven young and fatherless children.'

In early July 1811 an explosion at the mills cost the lives of three carpenters, and a year later on 7 July 1812 one of the corning houses blew up, killing one man outright and very seriously injuring another. *Scots Magazine,* 1811; *Edinburgh Evening Courant,* 9 and 11 July 1812.

Further research is needed to establish whether (or, more likely, how many) explosions occurred at the mills between 1812 and 1869. One was reported in the *Dalkeith Advertiser* on 15 December in the latter year that fortunately cost no lives or serious injuries. Further explosions occurred in 1872 and 1885, in which three workers were killed. In October 1889 there was another explosion that fortunately cost no lives. But on 22 January 1890, in the worst recorded explosion at the mills, that was clearly heard four or five miles away to the north and south in Dalkeith and Penicuik, six workers were killed. *Dalkeith Advertiser,* 23 January 1890; *Report to the Secretary of State for the Home Department, 1890,* op. cit., 5, 6. Almost exactly nine months later, on 22 October 1890, another explosion cost the lives of two men. *Report to the Secretary of State for the Home Department on an explosion . . . at . . . Roslin, on 22nd October 1890* (London, 1890), 5. In 1892 there were two further explosions at the mills: one on 12 January that fortunately cost no lives, though two men had very narrow escapes; the other on 17 September killed one man and severely burned two others. *Midlothian Journal,* 15 January and 23 September 1892; *Report to the Secretary of State for the Home Department on . . . an explosion . . . at Roslin, 17th September 1892* (London, 1892), 3, 5. Two workers had narrow escapes when on 13 September 1895 an explosion took place in one of the incorporating mills. *Dalkeith Advertiser,* 14 September 1895. Explosions occurred at the mills also on 25 March 1907 and in October 1911, but again fortunately without loss of life. *Midlothian Journal,* 29 March 1907; *Edinburgh Evening News,* 16 October 1911. But on 26 March 1908, Archibald Horsburgh, 'one of the oldest and most faithful servants of the company', was killed, along with his horse, by the explosion of a load of gelignite that he was taking on his cart to one of the magazines at the mills. *Midlothian Journal* and *Edinburgh Evening News,* 27 March 1908. An explosion on 16 November 1914 in the grinding mills fortunately caused no deaths or injuries. *Midlothian Journal,* 20 November 1914. But Margaret M. Gargan died on 16

March 1916 as the result of an accident at the mills some days earlier that was evidently not reported in the press because of wartime conditions of secrecy, and she was buried in Roslin churchyard. Two men, Alexander Robertson and Alexander Manson, both residents of Roslin, were killed in explosions at the press house and glazing house at the mills on 19 May 1924. Robertson, aged 21, was killed instantly. Manson, who had been a piper in the Gordon Highlanders, had settled in Roslin after the 1914–18 War and was a married man with two children under school age, died of his injuries within minutes of his admission to Edinburgh Royal Infirmary. *Midlothian Journal*, 23 May 1924; *People's Journal*, 24 May 1924. On 17 June 1925 two young Roslin women – Jemima (Pim) Arnott, aged 26, of Wright's Buildings, and Margaret (Peg) Lauder, aged 28, of Glenside Cottages – were killed, and a third young woman, Bessie Glass, Gourlaw Cross Roads, Rosewell, was severely injured in an explosion at the mills. Jemima Arnott was killed instantly, Margaret Lauder died a few hours later in Edinburgh Royal Infirmary, where also Bessie Glass was taken in a serious condition. The *Dalkeith Advertiser* of 25 June, reported that: 'The explosion, which occurred about 11.30 a.m., was of considerable violence, and was plainly heard in the village, where it caused consternation among the inhabitants. A large and anxious crowd soon assembled at the scene of the accident, one of the first to arrive being Mr Arnott, who collapsed on being informed of his daughter's fate . . . The explosion is understood to have occurred in a compress house, in which the three girls were at work. Miss Arnott, who was the eldest of a family of eleven, and a girl of bright and lovable disposition, had been employed in the mill for the past ten years. She was engaged and was to have been married before the end of the year. Miss Lauder, who was also much esteemed in the district, had worked in the mill for three or four years.'

7. The gunpowder mill closed in May 1954 because of subsidence caused by coal-mining in strata below it, and of the intention of the National Coal Board to continue mining there for years ahead. A statement issued by the Nobel Division of Imperial Chemical Industries said that floating the mill buildings on concrete rafts had been considered as a means of reducing the effects of subsidence. 'In view, however, of the magnitude of the subsidence involved, it is considered the requisite degree of safety cannot be sustained.' *Scotsman*, 6 April 1954. Roslin Country Park was created by Midlothian District Council from the later 1970s.

Notes

8. Esk Mills had been in 1778 the first cotton mill in Scotland and the *Old Statistical Account* in 1794 said the mill then employed about 500 workers. Sold to the government in 1810 the mill was briefly used to hold French and other prisoners-of-war in the Napoleonic Wars, after which it became a paper mill and remained in production until the 1960s.

9. Valleyfield had been a paper mill since 1709, apart from the latter years of the Napoleonic Wars when, like Esk Mills, it was bought by the government and used to hold French and other prisoners-of-war. In 1820 it was bought back by its former owners, the Cowan family, and continued to produce paper until its closure in the 1970s.

10. The Roslin Glen carpet factory began production in 1860 and ceased in 1960, though it continued to be used until 1968 as a carpet store.

11. The building, which is now a private house, stands at the entry to what were Valleyfield mills, and was a chapel and a school built about 1830. Colin McWilliam, *Lothian* (Harmondsworth, 1980), 382–3.

12. See above, Note 6.

13. Four workers were killed in a series of explosions in the corning house at Nobel's explosives factory at Ardeer in Ayrshire on 16 June 1937. The sound of the explosion was heard 25 miles away, and seven men working in a 30 foot deep pit a mile away from Ardeer at Garnock sewage scheme had a narrow escape when the sides of the pit caved in as a result of the explosion. The Ardeer works, largest of their kind in the world, had suffered, like Roslin gunpowder mills, successive explosions and losses of life since the first in 1882 when ten young women workers had been killed there. In explosions in 1902, 1907, 1913, 1914, and twice during the First World War, a total of twenty-four workers lost their lives and others were injured. *Scotsman,* 17 June and 20 August 1937.

14. Beeslack House at Penicuik is now a private nursing home.

15. The R101 flew over Scotland on Sunday, 17 November 1929, passing over Edinburgh and the East Lothian coast about 6.30 p.m., 'thousands of people obtaining a magnificent view of her progress at a comparatively low altitude . . . She seemed like a vision from a fantastic dream.' *Scotsman,* 6 October 1930. But what Elizabeth McCorry may have seen, particularly if she was actually in Glencorse School or its playground at the time, was the German airship *Graf Zeppelin*, which flew over Edinburgh and East Lothian

then out to the North Sea on Friday, 1 July 1930. 'The visit, which followed the Zeppelin's Scandinavian tour, was quite unexpected, and caused enormous delight to sightseers all down the east coast, and particularly in Edinburgh, where the *Graf* circled impressively round the centre of the city before continuing southwards . . . Everyone at first thought of [the British airships] R101 and R100, but as the airship passed along one could clearly see the red letters of its name along the starboard side of the nose.' *Scotsman*, 2 July 1930.

16. Dalmore paper mill was established at Auchendinny in 1835 and under successive owners has continued production there to the present.

17. Woodhouselee, an eighteenth century house a mile and a half south of Roslin, had a wing added to it in the mid-nineteenth century by George Meikle Kemp, architect of the Scott Monument in Edinburgh. All except the stables was demolished in 1965. The Dundases of Arniston have been among leading landowners in Midlothian for several centuries. The most eminent member of the family was Henry Dundas, 1st Viscount Melville (1742–1811), right-hand man of William Pitt the Younger and nicknamed because of his great political power, not least in Scotland, King Harry the Ninth. Arniston House, near Gorebridge, was designed by William Adam in 1726 for Henry Dundas's father, who was Lord President of the Court of Session, 1748–53. Captain Archibald H. Maule Ramsay (?-1955), Unionist M.P. for Peebles and South Midlothian, 1931–45, detained in Brixton Prison, London, from 23 May 1940 until September 1944 under Regulation 18B. Captain Ramsay, who believed that 'a conspiracy of Bolsheviks, Jews and Freemasons was threatening to dominate the world', founded the Right Club in the 1930s and one of its posters put up in London after the war broke out in 1939 declared: 'This is a Jews' war.' P. and L. Gillman, '*Collar the Lot !*' *How Britain Interned and Expelled its Wartime Refugees* (London, 1980), 116, 117, 124–5; Colin McWilliam, op.cit.79, 474.

18. I.e., the Silver Jubilee of King George V in 1935.

19. Charles McCorry (1918–1993), later a distinguished journalist on the *Glasgow Herald* and *Daily Mail*.

20. The Home Guard (the so-called 'Dad's Army'), originally titled Local Defence Volunteers (L.D.V.) until July 1940, were recruited from May that year up to age 65 as anti-invasion part-time soldiers, then compulsion was applied from early 1942. By summer 1943

there were one and three-quarter million men enrolled in the Home Guard. W.A.A.F. – Women's Auxiliary Air Force. Angus Calder, *The People's War* (London, 1969), 121–8, 341, 342.

21. See above, Note 6.

22. Knockshinnoch Castle Colliery at New Cumnock in Ayrshire was the scene of a disaster on 7 September 1950 when a big inrush of moss or peat from the surface trapped 129 miners underground. Thirteen of them died in the pit, the other 116 were all rescued about two days later. *Ministry of Fuel and Power, Report by Sir Andrew Bryan on Accident at Knockshinnoch Castle Colliery, Ayrshire* (London, 1951) (Cmd 8180), 3.

23. S.M.T. – Scottish Motor Traction Co. Ltd.

24. Salle – the French word used for the large room in the sorting department in a paper-mill. The plain salle was where uncoated paper was dealt with, the enamel salle coated paper.

25. Within three months of the outbreak of war 43,000 women volunteers had joined the women's sections of the armed forces. Conscription of women was first introduced in Britain in December 1941, initially for unmarried women aged between twenty and thirty, then early in 1942 those aged nineteen were included. All women conscripts were to be given a choice between the women's sections of the Forces and work in industry. Even before the introduction of conscription various government measures had affected the employment of women as well as of men. These included Order 1305 of June 1940, which made strikes and lockouts illegal where collective bargaining existed between unions and employers and provided for binding settlements by compulsory arbitration in unresolved industrial disputes; the Registration of Employment Order of March 1941 which, beginning with the registration of women aged 20 and 21 and men over 41 (and extended by the end of that year as far women aged 30 and men aged 46), enabled the government to direct people to essential work; and the Essential Work Order, also of March 1941, which debarred employers from dismissing any worker, and workers from leaving their jobs, without the permission of the Ministry of Labour. It was when such measures nonetheless failed to secure the enormous numbers needed for the armed forces and for civilian war work that the government went on to impose conscription for the first time on women in December 1941. Calder, op.cit., 54, 115, 235–6, 267–8.

26. E.N.S.A. – Entertainments National Service Association. Founded

shortly before the war with government support, by 1946 E.N.S.A. had given over two and a half million concerts to H.M. Forces and to industry, and had employed more than four-fifths of the entertainments industry at one time or another. 'Every factory on an approved list of over a thousand . . . had one or two E.N.S.A parties every week, generally performing in the canteen during lunch breaks . . . In general the complaint from troops and workers alike was not so much that E.N.S.A. . . .was synonymous with smut, as that the smut was far from funny.' Angus Calder, op. cit., 371–2.

27. I.e., to the Shotts Iron Co. Ltd. The National Coal Board was not established until the Coal Industry Nationalisation Act, 1946, created it to manage coal as a nationalised industry from 1 January 1947.

28. See above, Note 6.

29. Roslin Chapel, built in 1450 by William Sinclair, 3rd Earl of Orkney, and famous for its decorative stone carving that covers almost every part of the building. The Chapel is also graced by the famous Apprentice Pillar. McWilliam, op.cit., 409, 411, 414.

30. The disaster at West Silvertown on Friday, 19 January 1917 was not in a flour mill but in Brunner Mond's chemical works, when about fifty tons of T.N.T. exploded in a fire there. There were some 450 casualties, of whom 69 were killed (44 men, 11 women and 14 children) and 72 (34 women, 19 men and 19 children) were seriously injured. Some two and a half million pounds' worth of damage was wrought by the explosion, which devastated a large part of West Silvertown. 'The shock of the explosion was felt all over London. Many people were injured by falling masonry. In south-east London the explosion knocked over large numbers of people in the streets, and lifted tramcars and other vehicles from the ground.' The chemical works, which was engaged in refining explosives, was completely demolished by the explosion. About half the 43 men and women workers in the factory at the time of the explosion were killed. *Scotsman*, 22 and 24 January 1917; Ben Weinreb and Christopher Hibbert (eds), *The London Encyclopedia* (London, 1983), 786.

31. James Hamilton (1860–1929), general manager of Whitehill (Rosewell) and Polton collieries and brickworks, a director of the Lothian Coal Co. Ltd. For some other recollections of Hamilton's autocratic regime at Rosewell see I. MacDougall, *Mungo Mackay and the Green Table* (East Linton, 1995), 136–9.

Notes

32. For veteran miners' recollections of Mungo Mackay (1867–1939), agent and general manager of the Lothian Coal Co. Ltd, and of his son George, see MacDougall, op.cit., passim.

33. 'Rosewell was called Little Ireland because there were that many Irish Catholics in it.' (Pat Flynn, miner and son of a Rosewell miner, in MacDougall, op. cit., 143).

34. The Northover Projector was a primitive, barely portable by two men (the Projector and its mounting together weighed 134 lbs), smooth bore, breech-loading, two-and-a-half inch calibre, grenade-, mortar-, and petrol- or self-igniting phosophorus-bomb anti-tank weapon mounted on a tripod, that was widely distributed to Home Guard units after the massive loss of military equipment suffered during the British army's evacuation from Dunkirk in May-June 1940. Information provided by The Scots at War Trust, the Scottish United Services Museum, and the Imperial War Museum; see also Angus Calder, op. cit., 341.

35. W.R.N.S. – Women's Royal Naval Service.

36. See above, Note 6.

37. The Shops Act, 1934, (24 & 25 Geo. 5, Ch. 42), which came into effect on 30 December that year, regulated the hours of work of young people employed in retail and wholesale shops and warehouses occupied by retail and wholesale traders, or in street trading, and also provided 'improved arrangements for the health and comfort of shop workers generally.' Until then working hours of young people in retail shops had been limited to a maximum of 74 a week (including meal times). The Act of 1934 limited hours of the young people concerned under age 18 to a maximum of 52 per week (excluding meal times) for a period of two years until 27 December 1936, after which the maximum was to be 48 hours a week. The Act allowed young people aged 16 to 18 to work 'a strictly limited amount of overtime' (records of which must be kept by employers) 'on occasions of seasonal or exceptional pressure of work.' The Act also extended to the great majority of young people to whom it applied, 'the benefits of the weekly half-holiday and prescribed meal intervals hitherto confined to retail shop assistants', and prevented employment of young persons at night. The provisions of the Act that concerned health and comfort of all shop workers 'include requirements as to sanitary accommodation, ventilation, temperature, lighting, washing facilities, and facilities for taking meals.' *Scotsman*, 24 December 1934. Mrs Peebles also recalls, however, the prohibition by management at Woolworth's, where

she was employed for several years after the passing of this Act, of the use of seats by their counter assistants.

38. A.T.S. – Auxiliary Territorial Service, or women's army service.

39. See above, Note 25.

40. Mrs Neil's father may have worked first in the paper mills at Chirnside, originally founded there in 1786, which from 1887 were owned and managed by Young Trotter & Sons. After the mills ceased production for a few years they were re-opened by an American firm in 1971–3. *Third Statistical Account of Scotland: The County of Berwick* (Edinburgh, 1992), Vol.XXIII, 59, 72–3.

41. Bombs were dropped by German planes around Penicuik in early November 1940, and again on 29 November that year when 150 incendiary bombs were dropped. Andrew Jeffrey, *This Present Emergency. Edinburgh, the river Forth and south-east Scotland and the Second World War* (Edinburgh, 1992), 78, 80. A photograph of an army bomb disposal squad searching for an unexploded German bomb dropped on Auchencorth Moss near Penicuik, is included in Ian Nimmo, *Scotland at War* (Edinburgh, 1989) (pages unnumbered).

42. Vera Lynn (1917–), popular singer and 'Forces' Sweetheart' of the 1939–45 War, whose signature song was *We'll meet again*.

43. Alexander Wood Inglis (1845–1929), son of John Inglis, Lord Glencorse, Lord President of the Court of Session, who transformed into Loganbank House in the mid-nineteenth century a thatched cottage built in 1810 by his father Rev. John Inglis of Greyfriars Church, Edinburgh. McWilliam., op. cit., 316.

44. *Edinburgh and Leith Post Office Directory, 1937–8*, 634, gives: Andrew Whyte & Son Ltd, wholesale stationers, paper rulers, and stationery bookbinders, Bothwell Works, Bothwell Street and 14 Clyde Street, Edinburgh.

45. Rev. Donald M. Begbie, minister of Glencorse from 1928 until his death in 1954. The imposition of conscription for military service of six months for all men between their 20th and 21st birthday had been announced by the government on 26 April 1939, and was approved by the House of Commons by 376 votes to 145 – Labour and Liberal M.P.s voting against. Almost 25,000 young men registered accordingly in Scotland on 3 June under the new Military Training Act, and the first groups of conscripts arrived on 15 July at Glencorse and other barracks. *Scotsman*, 27 and 28 April, 5 June, and 17 July 1939 (which last includes a photograph of young conscripts at Glencorse being fitted out with army uniform).

Notes

46. Jenny Porteous and Elizabeth Dugan were the maiden names respectively of Janet Peebles (above, pp. 133–43) and Elizabeth McCorry (above, pp. 54–75).

47. German forces in north-western Germany surrendered unconditionally to Field Marshal Montgomery on 4 May 1945, and the Germans surrendered unconditionally on all fronts early in the morning of Monday, 7 May. Victory in Europe (V.E.) Day was celebrated as a national holiday throughout Britain on Tuesday, 8 May. A.J.P.Taylor, *English History 1914–45* (Oxford, 1965), 593–4.

48. V.A.D. – Voluntary Aid Detachment.

49. The Empire Exhibition, 'the greatest enterprise of its kind ever undertaken in Scotland', was opened in Glasgow by King George VI on 3 May 1938 and attracted 12,593,232 visitors by the time it ended on 29 October that year. Lord Elgin, President of the Exhibition, said a fortnight before it opened that it was 'something practical for peace as well as commerce. It would help people to think about something else besides the forging of armaments and the waging of war.' *Glasgow Herald*, 13 April, 4 May, and 31 October 1938.

50. Ella Mason was the maiden name of Ella Graham, above, pp. 108–32.

51. Clothes rationing was introduced by the government as a wartime measure of economy on 1 June 1941, with 66 coupons a year allowed everyone for clothing, footwear, cloth, and knitting wool. This ration was cut in spring 1942 to 48 coupons a year. Specified numbers of coupons had to be handed over by the consumer for any rationed article, irrespective of its price. Thus, for example, a woman's dress, irrespective of its price, took seven coupons. Hats and infants' clothing were exempt from the rationing scheme. Children's clothes and footwear needed fewer coupons than adults', and Mrs MacPherson's recollection about boys' shoes is correct as these needed only three coupons, compared with seven for a pair of adults' shoes. *Scotsman*, 2 June 1941; Calder, op. cit., 239–40, 279–80.

52. The Italians signed an armistice with the western Allies on 7 September 1943, which was publicly announced next day.

53. There were two outbreaks of smallpox in Scotland in 1942. In the first of these the outbreak began with the arrival in the Clyde on 29 May of a ship from Bombay one member of the crew of which was found to be suffering from the disease. Despite the detention of the

crew and vaccination of everyone on board the ship, 33 other cases of smallpox 'of the most virulent and infectious type' occurred during that summer in Scotland, ten of them traceable to contacts with the ship. There were four deaths. The second outbreak began in Edinburgh on 1 November, and in the following two months 36 people – including three in Midlothian and 21 in Edinburgh – were stricken and eight of them died. In Edinburgh alone about 274,000 people (64 per cent of the civilian population) were vaccinated during, or in the few months before, the outbreak. *Scotsman*, 4 and 9 July 1942, and 4 January 1943.

INDEX

accidents and injuries: acid, 132, at
Ardeer, 52, 197, to canon, 115, at
gunpowder mill and bomb
factory, 5, 6, 36, 48, 50, 51, 68,
70, 80, 104, 108, 110, 122, 123,
128, 166, 179, 180, 184, 190, 193,
194–6, in mines, 37, 55, 74, 133,
134, 199, road, 103, at Silvertown,
109, 200; *see also* explosions
Adam, William, 198
Addiewell, 14, 20, 30,
airships – *see* arms and armaments
Almondale: country park, 16, estate,
16, 26, House, 15, 17
ambitions – *see* youth
America, United States of, 32; *see
also* Pittsburgh
Anderson, Davie, 59
animals, birds and insects: dogs and
hounds, 16, 17, 29, 56, hens, 54,
130, horses, ix, 5, 16, 19, 23, 25,
51, 67, 69, 70, 103, 133, 173, 195,
lice, 154, ponies, 17, 81, rats, 61
Ardeer explosives works, 20, 21, 23,
24, 28, 29, 32, 52, 197
armed forces, 199; aerdrome, 63;
army, 1, 19, 20, 27, 65, 108, 109,
127, 168, 187, 188, 196, Gordon
Highlanders, 196, military police,
124, Reconnaissance Corps, 151,
Royal Army Medical Corps, 36,
Royal Artillery, 109, Royal
Electrical and Mechanical
Engineers, 27, Royal Engineers,
81, 92, Scots Guards, 168,
Seaforth Highlanders, 37, 170,
A.T.S., 138, 144, 151, 154, 167,

168, 179, 202; conscription to, 27,
92, 93, 129, 144, 151, 163, 167,
202; demobilisation from, 27, 28,
31, 158; E.N.S.A. concerts for,
200; Home Guard, 67, 164, 198,
199, 201; leave from, 74, 81, 126,
129, 130, 158; Local Defence
Volunteers, 198; Military Training
Act, 202; R.A.F., 20, 46, 63, 67,
127, 151; Royal Navy, 20, 46, 79,
123, 127, 139, 151, 165, 180;
W.A.A.F.s, 67, 138, 179, 199;
women and, 45, 81, 144, 189, 199;
W.R.N.S., 127, 133, 138, 201; *see
also* arms and armaments; British
Legion; Edinburgh, places in:
Overseas Club; Glencorse
Barracks and north camp; war
arms and armaments: airships, 55,
197, 198; bombs, 123, 139,
incendiary, 93, 94, 104, 151, 166,
202, unexploded, 202; Empire
Exhibition and, 203; flares, ix, 18,
151; hand grenades, ix, 139;
Northover projectors, 123, 126,
164, 180, 182, 183, 201;
parachutes, 138; pellets, 19, 20,
180; smoke bombs, flares and
floats, ix, 18, 20, 46, 79, 104, 139,
165, 180; tanks, 27, 123, 126, 180,
188; Verey lights and pistols, ix,
20, 46, 139, 180; *see also* armed
forces; gunpowder mill and bomb
factory; war
Arniston House, 60, 198
Arnott, Jemima (Pim), 6, 24, 70, 108,
122, 128, 180, 196; father of, 196

Index

Index

chauffeur at, 18, 25; clock at, 71; closure of, 1, 22, 32, 127, 196; corning house at, 21, 23, 24, 25, 30, 193, 194, 195; craftsmen's shops at, 30, 48; customers of, 20; dances and socials at, 26, 31, 81; demolished, 1, 32, 71; demonstration at, 93, 94; discipline at, 22, 126; dismissals at, 69, 152; doctor at, 189, 190; E.N.S.A concerts at, x, 4, 81, 126, 141, 156, 187, 199, 200; Essential Worker Order and, 143; film show at, 126; first-aid room at, 71, 189, 190; flexibility at, 139, 180; foremen at, 19, 22, 30, 31, 54, 55, 67, 68, 103, 104, 106, 124, 125, 130, 140, 152, 155, 156, 183, 189; gatehouse at, 5, 30, 32, 48, 49, 50, 71, 94, 105, 141, 181, 184; gatemen at, 22, 24, 25, 66, 69; history of, 1, 5, 21, 193–6; horses and horse transport at, 5, 19, 23, 25, 51, 67, 69, 70, 103; huts at, ix, 5, 18, 22, 30, 48, 49, 71, 80, 104, 125, 140, 152, 164, 181, 185, 186; inspections and inspectors at, 5, 80, 127, 129, 183; intensive work at, 165, 186; internal railway at, 23, 24, 48, 51, 69, 70, 81, 195; laboratory at, 21, 30, 31; long service awards at, 32; magazines and keepers at, 19, 21, 24, 25, 28–9, 30, 71, 195; making of gunpowder, bombs, smoke screens, Northover projectors, Verey lights, etc., at, 19, 20, 21, 26, 27, 46, 49, 68, 93, 94, 103, 104, 122, 123, 124, 139, 140, 151, 164, 165, 180; management and managers at, 4, 18, 22, 24, 31, 51, 74, 181, 183; meal breaks at, 73, 80, 123, 124, 142, 152, 156; medical examination for, 68; meetings at, 21, 129, 181; men workers at, 80, 81, 95, 165, 181; metal objects and, x, 5, 49, 68, 125, 151, 183; and mines and quarries, x, 20, 159, 181; minimum age for, 67; number of workers at, 4, 19, 72, 81, 105, 128, 140, 156, 164, 165, 189, 193; office and office workers at, 27, 31, 52, 71, 72, 181; owners of, 21, 22, 140, 193; Peeblesshire huts for, 127; proportion of men and women workers at, 4, 19, 47, 52, 72, 81, 129, 140, 156, 165; regulations, x, 49; retrospective views of, 35, 53, 107, 129, 143, 158, 169, 191, 192; safety precautions at, 5, 19, 22–5, 28, 29, 49, 50, 51, 68, 69, 70, 71, 72, 73, 74, 80, 94, 104, 106, 125, 129, 139, 141, 142, 151, 152, 165, 166, 183, 185, 186, 187; school leavers in, 114; secrecy at, 46, 79, 104, 105, 106, 139, 196; separateness of mill and factory, 47, 120, 129, 140, 181; showers and washing at, 23, 68, 71, 73, 125, 186; sisters kept separate at, 125, 139; and smell of powder, 106; smoking and, xi, 5, 22, 24, 49, 69, 71, 94, 95, 104, 105, 125, 141, 151, 166, 184, 186, 187; social mix of workers at, 129; special clothing at, 5, 19, 22, 23, 24, 28, 49, 50, 68, 69, 73, 80, 94, 104, 124, 125, 127, 141, 142, 151, 165, 166, 180, 184, 185, 187; starting work at, 18, 45, 46, 54, 67, 68, 79, 93, 103, 108, 122, 133, 139, 144, 151, 164, 170, 178, 179; storeman at, 19, 28, 68; store room at, 48, 51; suggestion box at, 181; Sunday walks round, 48; superannuation at, 160; supervisors at, 5, 129, 183; tank visits, 126, 188; theft of money at, 152; thunder and lightning and, 142; time off at, 152, 158; travel to and from work at, 4, 31, 32, 35, 47, 70, 71, 73, 80, 142, 153; tunnels at, 51; unguarded, 187, 188; vans, lorries and drivers at, 19, 20, 21, 28, 31, 71, 72; visitors

Index

mill, 57, 90, 91, 148, 161, 162, 165; in domestic service, 2, 115, 116, 118, 119, 120, 123; at Esk Mills, 33; in farm work, 88; forester's, 16; at gunpowder mill and bomb factory, 23, 26, 47, 48, 72, 94, 105, 182, five day week, 123, long, 94, 152, 156, shifts at, 4, 22, 26, 47, 72, 73, 81, 139, 151, 156, 157, 165, 169, 184, 185, 186, 189, night shifts at, 4, 48, 94, 105, 124, 152, 156, 157, 165, 166, 167, 182, 189, three shifts worked at, 47, 52, 79, 95, 123, 129, 140, 152, 165, 182, 189, two shifts worked at, 47, 73, 79, 105, 123, 124, 140, six day week at, 123, sleeping on night shift at, 182, 186, shortened for day, 188, vote concerning, 123; at laundry, Auchendinny, 57; miners', 86; part-time, 75, 131, 132; at rubber mills, 102; in shops, 2, 134, 135, 201; at Valleyfield mills, 78; in Woolworth's, 136, 137

housing, 2, 7; alterations in, 60, 61; aluminium, 131; back kitchen in, 61; baths or showers and, 2, 3, 14, 38, 40, 85, 86, 97, 98, 111, 131, 160, 173, 186, 191; bungalow, 40; but and ben, 159; capacious, 115; cleaning in, 86; cooking in, 61, 85, 86, 97, 98, 110, 174; council, 2, 28, 54; demolished, 32, 174; electricity and, 14, 40, 61, 86, 110, 116, 160; flats, 107, 109; flittings, 98; flooding of threatened, 191; front and back door in, 39, 60; gardens and back greens, 2, 85, 86, 131, 160, 174; gas in, 40, 61, 84, 98, 110; heating in, 3, 38, 85, 116; larder in, 61; lighting in, 2, 14, 40, 61, 84, 86, 97, 98, 110, 117, 160, 174, 191; lodgers in, 3, 4, 18, 47, 52, 71, 85, 86; miners' rows, 97, 98; neighbourliness and, 145; number of rooms in, 14, 38, 40, 61, 62, 85, 86; open fire in, 61,

97, 98, 110, 174; outside stair in, 60, 61; overcrowding in, 62, 128; owner occupied, 40; prefab, 131; private landlords', 28, 60, 84, 160; rents, 28, 61; room and kitchen, 2, 37, 97, 98, 110, 173, 174, 176, 191; schoolhouse, 99; scullery in, 110; shortage of, 52, 130, 131; single end, 2, 109, 110, 173, 174; single storey, 174; sinks in, 61, 110; sleeping arrangements, 14, 37, 38, 61, 62, 85, 87, 117, 160, 173, 174, 176; sloping floor in, 61; small, 109; stone built, 98; terraced, 110; thatched, 202; three-apartment, 160; three storey, 60; tied, 2, 34, 38, 40, 60, 77, 86, 108, 110, 121, 144, 145, 159, 172–5; toilets, 2, 14, 38, 60, 61, 85, 86, 110, 160, 173, 191; two-bedroomed, 3; two-roomed, 128, 131; two storey, 174; unchanged, 191; visitors and, 87; washing of clothes and, 111, 173, 174, 182; water supply to, 2, 3, 60, 61, 85, 97, 98, 110, 160, 173, 174, 191; *see also* individual towns and villages

Hughes, Betty, 113
Hughes, Mrs, 70

Imperial Chemical Industries Ltd, 140, 193, 196
Imperial War Museum, 8, 201
Inglis, Alexander, 160, 202
Inglis, John, 202
Inglis of Glencorse, 64
Inglis, Rev. John, 202
Inverness, 27
Italy, 130, 188

Jack, Mrs, 191
Jenkinson, Nan, 79
Jews – *see* war, 1939–45
John o'Groats, 171
Johnston, Rev. Mr, 111

Kaimes quarry, 30
Katmandu, 132

213

Index

Malcolm (or Manson), Mrs Barbara, 50, 51, 70, 80, 128

Manson, Alex, 50, 51, 80, 128, 196

Martin, Jimmy, 33

Martin, Mr, 88

Martyr's Cross, 166

Mason, Ella – see Graham, Ella

Mason family (Amisfield), 109, 110

Mason, Polly, 110, 111, 117, 118, 119, 122, 124

Maybank, 56

Maybole, 170

Melville, Viscount – see Dundas, Henry

Merricks, John, 193

Mid and East Lothian Miners' Association, 7

Mid Calder, 10, 13, 14, 17

Middle East, 27

Midlothian, ix, 1, 10–11, 198, 204; District Council, 196

Miller, Andrew, 103, 106, 183

Miller, Pipsy, 15

Milne, Mr, 183

Milton Bridge, 2, 10, 65, 66, 149, 150, 159, 160, 161, 162, 163, 165, 166; places at: the Tryst, 65, 66, 91, 92, 150, 160, 163

Milton Cottages, 64, 65, 71, 153, 156, 157, 159, 167

miners, 3, 30, 36, 55, 76, 77, 83, 84, 91, 92, 120, 121, 133, 135, 175, 201; institutes for, 91, 92, 133, 189; shale, 13, 30, 97; see also accidents and injuries; hours of labour; housing; Mid and East Lothian Miners' Association; trade unions and trade unionism; wages

mines and mining, 3, 20, 29, 30, 38, 74, 85, 87, 121, 134, 196, 200; Bilston Glen, 54, Fauldhouse, 36, 38, Knockshinnoch, 74, 199, Lady Victoria, 134, Moat, (Roslin), ix, 3, 36, 37, 38, 40, 51, 76, 77, 83, 85, 87, 92, 109, 121, Polton, 200, Ramsay, 74, 133, Stoneyburn, 55, Whitehill (Rosewell), 97, 121, 200; shale, 14, 20, 30, 97; see also

Lothian Coal Co. Ltd; National Coal Board; Shotts Iron Co. Ltd

Minister's Brig, 157

Ministry of Agriculture and Fisheries, 130

Ministry of Labour – see Labour, Ministry of

Mitchell, Willie, 18, 25, 103, 106, 124, 125, 183

Moat, the, – see mines and mining

Montgomery, Field Marshal Bernard, 203

Morecambe, 188

Mount Kilimanjaro, 132

Munro, Annie, 160, 161, 162

Murray, Mary, 4, 97–107 passim; brother of, 98; father of, 97, 99; grandparents of, 97; husband of, 107; mother of, 97, 98, 99

Murdoch, Miss, 55

music and song, 5, 31, 55, 61, 63, 121, 129, 156, 176, 188, 202; see also schools and education

Myles, Fiona, 8

National Coal Board, 196, 200

nationalities, 188, 189; American, 118, 119, 122; Australians, 188; Canadians, 188; French, 197; Germans, 25, 55, 127, 154, 155, 166, 168, 187, 197, 202, 203; Irish, 121, 201; Italians, 203; Norwegian, 115

National Museums of Scotland, 8

Neil, Jimmy, 29

Neil, Joe, 22

Neil, Lydia, ix, 4, 5, 46, 47, 144–58 passim; father of, 144, 145, 148, 202; husband of, 144, 150, 151, 158; mother of, 144, 145, 148, 149; sisters and brother of, 144

New Cumnock, 199

newspapers and periodicals, 6, 132, 150, 194, 195, 196, 198

Newton (Caithness), 171

Newtongrange, 11, 134

Nicol, Mr, 71

Nimmo, Willie, 71

215

Index